D1233572

DIRIGIBLE DREAMS

FORE
EDGE

C. MICHAEL HIAM

DREAMS

The Age of the Airship

ForeEdge ⇌ An imprint of University Press of New England ⇌ www.upne.com

Manufactured in the United States of America
Designed by Eric M. Brooks ⇌ Typeset in Arnhem by Passumpsic Publishing

Library of Congress Cataloging-in-Publication Data
Hardcover ISBN: 978-1-61168-560-2
Ebook ISBN: 978-1-61168-697-5
Library of Congress Control Number: 2014938707

5 4 3 2 1

CONTENTS

DIRIGIBLE DREAMS

INTRODUCTION

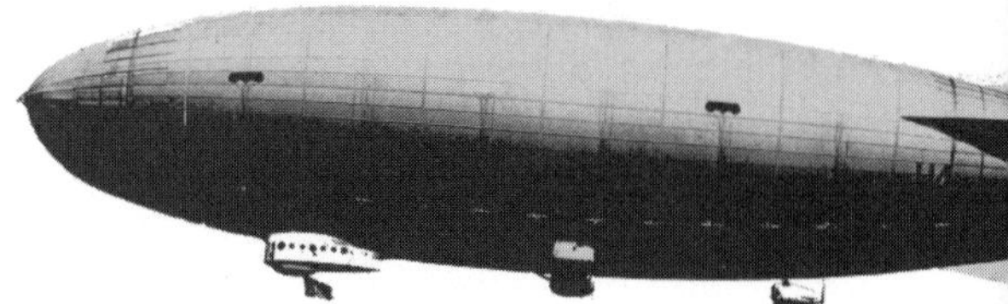

With plenty of *Hindenburg* tickets still available, Margaret G. Mather, an American in Europe wanting to return home, thought of buying one for New York. Although an experienced air traveler, she recalled her "strange reluctance" to make the purchase, but then she considered the alternative, which was "to cross the Atlantic in increasingly luxurious steamers, whose lavish comfort and entertainment meant little to a sea-sick wretch" like herself. She would fly. At a Frankfurt hotel she had her ticket and passport inspected, "and then the luggage examination began," she said. "It was courteous but very thorough; every inch of my bags was searched, every box opened. I had to pay for fifteen kilos overweight, and tried to argue that point, as I weigh twenty kilos less than the average man, but I was told 'it is the rule.'"[1]

Mather and thirty-five other passengers, half the *Hindenburg*'s usual complement, took a bus from the hotel to the airport, and when she saw the great silver airship tethered to the ground, a wave of joy swept over her and, she remembered, "Gone were all my doubts and reluctance; I felt all the elation and pleasure that had failed me until now." Retractable steps led her aboard, where on the lower deck she located her cabin, finding it "very tiny but complete, with washstand and cupboards and a sloping window." The room also had a narrow but comfortable bed furnished with soft, light blankets and sheets of fine linen, the same material that lined the pearl-gray walls. Having explored her lodgings, she went upstairs to join the other passengers leaning over the lounge windows to watch the ascent. The ground crew had just released the ropes and, this being Germany in 1937, a brass band thumped out martial music while little boy Nazis scurried after the rising airship. "It was an indescribable feeling of lightness and buoyancy," she recalled, "a lift and pull upward, quite unlike an airplane."

The *Hindenburg* might have been the sturdiest airship ever built, but like all airships it bruised easily when earthbound, and so departures came at either sunrise or sunset, when winds were lightest. For this reason lift-off had taken place at sundown, May 3, and through the growing dusk the passengers strained to catch a glimpse of the Rhine somewhere below. Flashing beacons guided the dirigible from hill to hill as it passed over hamlets and villages "gleaming jewel-like in the darkness," Mather said, before coming to Cologne and "a spreading mass of lights" that silhouetted the city's famous cathedral. At 10 p.m. she and her fellow travelers sat down for a late supper of cold meats and salads.

Unattached passengers ate together at a long table and Mather, as the lone single woman aboard, found herself placed at Captain Max Pruss's right elbow. She thought the captain both professional and genial, and the following day, May 4, he confided in her that because of the weather this was one of the worst trips he had ever made. Conditions outside may have been appalling, yet inside the airship Mather observed that "one felt no motion, though the wind beat like waves against the sides of the ship. It was almost uncanny." Enjoying the chance to rest, she spent most of that day looking "through my sloping window at the angry waves, whitening the sea so far below."

Living with others in close quarters allowed Mather to make acquaintances, acquaintances that at the end of any other airship voyage would likely have resulted in years of mutual correspondence, and perhaps hopes for a happy reunion. Among those she got to know included a red-faced man who drank and a gentle elderly couple from Hamburg who loved the *Hindenburg* and held tickets for a return flight. There was also a family aboard with a well-behaved girl and two boys that Mather liked to watch, the children obviously enjoying the trip so much. Among the other travelers heading to the United States were young American men happy to be going home, where, one of them told her, "you could drink plain water and there's no bother about passports." Mather also befriended a Long Island couple returning from a brief business trip but whom, to protect their privacy in death, she subsequently named only as "Mr. and Mrs. ——."

On the afternoon of May 5, the second full day of flight, Newfoundland came abeam and the winds lessened. The airship flew low, as low as six or seven hundred feet, over gray waters speckled with white icebergs. A double rainbow completely encircled the ship. That night, Mather slept like a child. At dawn, with no more land in sight, bad weather returned, and in Germany, where every day of every flight of the *Hindenburg* made news, the Berlin papers reported the airship being twelve hours behind schedule. Whether Mather knew of this she did not say, but it's unlikely she would have complained about additional time aloft. Indeed, when Boston suddenly appeared below on the morning of May 6, she turned to a fellow traveler and said of herself, "It is ridiculous to feel so happy."

The vessels in the harbor saluted the flying leviathan with horns and whistles, and in the suburbs cars pulled to the curb and their occupants leapt out to look heavenward. Resembling bees buzzing a bear, diminutive airplanes flew close to the giant dirigible as it headed toward Providence, Rhode Island. Then, over Long Island Sound, an excited "Yalie" searched the landscape to the north for a glimpse of his alma mater, and to the south Mr. and Mrs. —— showed Mather the bay where they lived and explained that their son would drive to Lakehurst, New Jersey, to meet them at the air station. Next, the *Hindenburg* reached Manhattan, and like a tourist taking in the sights, passed over Fifth Avenue and Central Park before heading west. Lakehurst was only fifty miles distant, and the airship arrived within the hour. Mather, however, noted a line of black clouds and bright lightning in the near distance, and saw that no attempt was being made to land.

As if patiently awaiting its appointment with fate, the *Hindenburg* left Lakehurst and marked time by flying over the beaches and forests of New Jersey or making short sorties out to sea. Mather was also in no rush, and remembered that "I was feeling foolish with happiness and didn't really care how long this cruising lasted." The stewards served an early tea, followed at 6:30 p.m. by sandwiches because, the passengers learned, the atmospherics remained unsettled and the ship might have to linger in the air for an hour or so longer. Apparently a decision to land had then been made by Pruss in the control car, and all at once they were over Lakehurst again. In rapid succession the airship circled the mooring mast, speed and altitude were reduced, ropes were thrown down, and as she leaned out an open window in the dining salon, Mather said she "heard the dull muffled sound of an explosion."

"Almost instantly the ship lurched and I was hurled a distance of fifteen or twenty feet against an end wall," she said. "Then the flames blew in, long tongues of flame, bright red and very beautiful." Amid the flames the passengers were thrown about by the continued lurching, cutting themselves against the sharp metal edges of the Bauhaus furniture. "They were streaming with blood," she said of those around her, "I saw a number of men leap from the windows, but I sat just where I had fallen, holding the lapels of my coat over my face, feeling the flames light on my back, my hat, my hair, trying to beat them out, watching the horrified faces of my companions as they leaped up and down." Mather was waiting for the inevitable crash but, as far as she could tell, there was none. She heard a loud voice in her direction: "Come out lady!" it said. She looked and saw that the zeppelin was on the ground and that two or three men were outside. "Aren't you coming?" asked one of them. Accepting his suggestion, she left the airship and ran across earth scattered with burning framework. She had survived but her hands were singed.

Mather was among the first to be driven to the first aid station. She was in great pain yet her condition was hardly as dire as others. "A terribly injured man was seated on a table next to me—most of his clothes and his hair had been burned off," she said, "someone told me he was Captain Lehmann." A commander of many *Hindenburg* flights, this time Lehmann had been aboard as a training officer, and she could see it was him. "During his infrequent appearances among the passengers he had worn a leather coat with fur lining, upturned collar, which partly hid his face," she remembered. "He always looked alert but genial, with keen blue eyes. Now his face was grave and calm, and not a groan escaped him as he sat there, wetting his burns." The two shared some ointment, he murmuring "danke schöne" every time she passed the bottle. "It was a strange, quiet interlude," she said, "almost as though we were having tea together. I was impressed by his stoic calm, but only when I learned of his death the next day did I realize his heroism."

"Terribly wounded people flowed in from all sides," Mather continued of her ordeal, "and I could not bear the sights and sounds. I went outside and saw an ambulance draw up. I waited to see if any of my acquaintances were in it." To her horror, when the doors were opened she saw a pile of bodies. "Two or three were lifted out, one remained. All I could see of him were his legs, burned and stiff like charred pieces of wood." She felt sick and went outside where the *Hindenburg* was still burning. "I watched it with anguish. Even in the midst of human

AUTHOR'S COLLECTION

Lakehurst, New Jersey, May 6, 1937.

suffering and death I could not but regret the destruction of so beautiful a thing. I thought of the happiness it had given to me and to many others; of the icebergs and rainbows we had flown over; I thought of how gently it had landed."

Few catastrophes have been so perfectly captured on film as was the fiery destruction of the *Hindenburg*. As horrific as the images were, however, the fact remains that two-thirds of those aboard survived, including, of course, Margaret Mather. Equally remarkable: up until then not a single fatality or serious injury had ever been attributed to an airship while in revenue service—something that could hardly be said of the airplane, which by 1937 had killed too many passengers to count. And even when operating safely, no aircraft of the day could possibly have flown nonstop from southern Germany to North and South America as the *Hindenburg* had done with regularity, let alone with a full load of seventy-two passengers, forty crew members, tons of mail, and on occasion an automobile, a private plane, or an antelope on board. Additionally, it would not be until the late 1950s that passenger planes could be expected to reliably fly the Atlantic in one hop, something the *Hindenburg* had done with ease some two score years earlier. And should, by a miracle of forbearance, Captain Pruss have opted not to land at Lakehurst that terrible night, he would still have had food and fuel to reach his alternative landing site in Akron, Ohio; the airship mast at Dearborn, Michigan; or, in a stretch, possibly the dirigible base in Sunnyvale, California.

With the promise of airship travel still salient, therefore, no one thought immediately after the nightmare at Lakehurst that the airship was dead. To the contrary, the United States moved to guarantee delivery of the nonflammable gas helium to Germany for the *Hindenburg*'s sister ship, the second *Graf Zeppelin*, thus making a similar conflagration impossible. And yet, after the tragedy of May 6, 1937, not a single customer was taken up in an airship ever again, and by the start of World War II just two years later, the airship had become entirely extinct. Yes, puny "blimps" of the Goodyear Tire variety, holding at best six people, can occasionally be sighted bobbing in the skies above, but these balloons with motors are but quaint reminders of the beginning of man's dirigible dreams, and not of their ultimate realization in gargantuan craft capable of fantastic feats of discovery, warfare, and commerce. Regrettably, the dirigible age came and went far too quickly—so quickly, in fact, that an infant at its advent would have been just a middle-aged man or woman at its conclusion—and arguably the dirigible remains one of the shortest-lived modes of transportation ever conceived. The brief epoch of the airship, however, was charged with incredible potential, it consumed nations and imaginations, and for an exciting period in aviation history it represented the future of human flight.

ONE

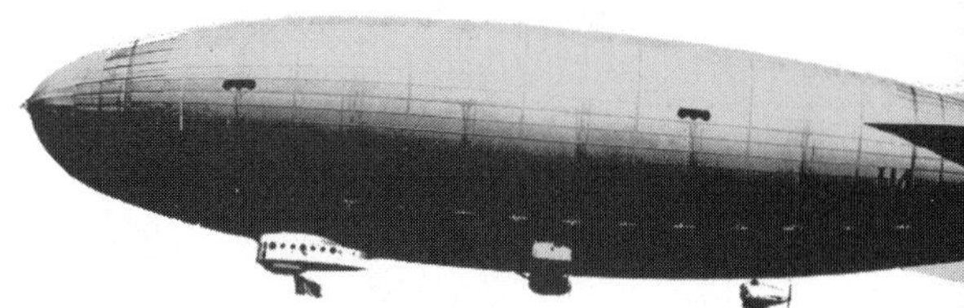

As enthusiastic supporters of the aeronaut's experiments, Parisians welcomed his newest creation, "Santos-Dumont Number 5," and early one quiet Saturday morning, July 13, 1901, No. 5 started off from the Parc d'Aérostation at Saint Cloud in the direction of the Eiffel Tower. At the controls stood the airship's designer and sole occupant, Alberto Santos-Dumont, while the Scientific Commission of the Aéro Club watched from the ground. Santos-Dumont reached the tower, about three and a half miles distant, in ten minutes, and, cautiously circumventing the structure, set a course back to Saint Cloud. Having made good speed thus far and cruising safely over the chimney pots and steeples of Paris, he had minutes to spare, but then, in the homestretch, No. 5 faced stubborn headwinds that proved too much for its sixteen-horsepower motor. Knowing he would not be awarded the Deutsch Prize that day, a frustrated Santos-Dumont passed over the upturned heads of the Scientific Commission at an altitude of 660 feet, the thirty-minute time limit allotted for the sortie having long since elapsed.

"Just at this moment," Santos-Dumont recalled of what happened next, "my capricious motor stopped, and the airship, bereft of its power, drifted until it fell on the tallest chestnut tree in the park of M. Edmond de Rothschild."[2] Inhabitants and servants ran out of the villa toward the stricken No. 5, and there they saw Santos-Dumont marooned on high.

Nearby lived the Princess Isabel, Comtesse d'Eu, exiled heir to the Brazilian throne, and she sent a champagne lunch up to her compatriot with an invitation to, after he got down, come tell her of his trip. "When my story was over," he recalled, "she said to me: 'Your evolutions in the air made me think of the flight of our great birds of Brazil. I hope that you will succeed for the glory of our common country.'"[3]

The Scientific Commission reassembled less than a month later, this time at 6:30 a.m., and its members again watched as Santos-Dumont flew toward the Eiffel Tower in his quest for the Deutsch Prize, named for the petroleum magnate and aviation enthusiast, Henri Deutsch de la Meurthe, who promised 100,000 francs to the first person to fly from Saint Cloud to the Eiffel Tower and back. The Brazilian aeronaut reached his goal in nine minutes—sixty seconds faster than his previous attempt, although along the way No. 5 had begun a slow descent because hydrogen had started to leak out from somewhere in the ellipsoidal-shaped gasbag. Ordinarily, Santos-Dumont would have come to earth immediately, but to do so would have meant abandoning the prize, and therefore he took the risk of going on. Again he successfully rounded the tower, although now his gasbag had shrunk visibly and, with the fortifications of Paris near La Muette beneath him, the suspension wires holding the keel of the craft to the gasbag had begun to sag. Some of the wires caught the propeller. "I saw the propeller cutting and tearing at the wires," he said. "I stopped the motor instantly. Then, as a consequence, the airship was at once driven back toward the Tower by the wind, which was strong."

Santos-Dumont always dreaded the prospect of being dashed against the Eiffel Tower in one of his airships and falling, he fretted, "to the ground like a stone," and so he frantically searched for a place to land. However, with No. 5 fast losing hydrogen, chances to do so appeared slim. "The half-empty balloon," he said of the gasbag above him, "fluttering its empty end as an elephant waves his trunk, caused the airship's stem to point upward at an alarming angle. What I most feared, therefore, was that the unequal strain on the suspension wires would break them one by one and so precipitate me to the ground."

He thought he could fly clear of the building immediately in front of him, the Trocadéro Hotel, and settle his craft on the Seine embankment just beyond, but instead he descended to about a hundred feet and hit the hotel roof, rupturing the bag. "This was the 'terrific explosion,'" he said, "described in the newspapers of the day." Santos-Dumont and his No. 5 tumbled into a deep courtyard, but before hitting the ground the keel of the craft, a sixty-feet-long framework of curved pine scantlings and aluminum joints, fortuitously wedged itself at a forty-five-degree angle between a side wall and scaffolding beneath. The Brazilian aeronaut, perched fifty feet from the ground and balancing precariously on his overturned basket, managed to climb onto an adjacent windowsill where, once again, he found himself marooned on high. "After what seemed like tedious waiting," he said, "I saw a rope being lowered to me from the roof above. I held to it and was hauled up, when I perceived my rescuers to be the brave firemen of Paris. From their station at Passy they had been watching the flight of the airship. They had seen my fall and immediately hastened to the spot." It had been a close call, and Santos-Dumont admitted as much. "The remembrance of it," he said, "sometimes haunts me in my dreams."

Before he began experimenting with dirigibles, Santos-Dumont had designed a balloon of the free-floating, rotund type and called it *Brazil*, after his native country. Compared to the other balloons then flying over Paris, *Brazil* was a speck of a thing, a scant twenty feet in diameter and, even when deflated, as light as a feather. Santos-Dumont, himself diminutive at five feet, five inches and—he claimed—110 pounds, used very thin but very strong Japanese silk to hold the balloon's 4,104 cubic

LIBRARY OF CONGRESS

Alberto Santos-Dumont.

feet of hydrogen. He also did everything else he could to keep the *Brazil* extremely light. The varnished silk envelope weighed only thirty-one pounds, the balloon's basket just thirteen pounds, the guide rope seventeen and a half pounds (yet was a hundred yards long), and the grappling iron a mere six and a half pounds. Despite the misgivings of experts, Santos-Dumont's little balloon proved successful. "The 'Brazil' was very handy in the air, easy to control," he said of his aerial runabout. "It was easy to pack also, on descending; and the story that I carried it in a valise is true."

To reinflate the *Brazil* he would need hydrogen, a gas relatively simple to make and praised by aeronauts because of its natural buoyancy. Fifteen times lighter than air, when hydrogen is trapped inside a balloon it can lift impressive loads. The gas expands and contracts with changes in atmospheric pressure and air temperature, but at sea level and at sixty degrees Fahrenheit a cubic foot of hydrogen will lift a little

AUTHOR'S COLLECTION

Santos-Dumont and his No. 5 rounding the Eiffel Tower, July 13, 1901.

more than an ounce. Under these conditions, therefore, to loft Santos-Dumont's 110 pounds required 1,760 cubic feet of hydrogen, meaning that his *Brazil*, with a capacity of 4,104 cubic feet, was more than adequate for the job. Hydrogen, of course, did have and still has one very severe drawback: its enormous explosive potential when mixed with oxygen. Many an unlucky aeronaut in Santos-Dumont's day met a ghastly end—often luridly depicted in the illustrated newspapers—through

AUTHOR'S COLLECTION

No. 5 with its keel wedged in the courtyard and its gas bag in shreds.

hydrogen explosions. Although acutely aware of this danger, he, like all aeronauts, stuck with hydrogen because there was no better substitute, hot air having far less lifting force and requiring that a flame be kept on board, while the nonflammable helium was still decades away.

Prior to his first flight in the *Brazil*, Santos-Dumont had made, by his estimate, about thirty ascents in other balloons, and the most memorable flights at night. "One is alone in the black void," he rhapsodized of his nocturnal jaunts, "in a murky limbo where one seems to float without weight, without a surrounding world, a soul freed from the weight of matter! There is a flash upward and a faint roar. It is a railway train, the locomotive's fires, maybe, illuminating for a moment its smoke as it rises. Then, for safety, we throw out more ballast and rise through the black solitudes of the clouds into a soul-lifting burst of splendid starlight. There, alone in the constellations, we await the dawn!"

The aerial explorer admitted that balloons were his obsession, and that he had the money to indulge in them. (The family plantation back in São Paulo had four million coffee trees and 9,000 laborers, not to mention factories, docks, ships, and 146 miles of private railroad line.) "Some of these spherical balloons I rented," Santos-Dumont explained of his hobby. "Others I had constructed for me. Of such I have owned at least six or eight."[4] Still, even with his great wealth, it took Santos-Dumont a long time before he could overcome his aversion to the costly "honorarium"[5] demanded by Parisian aeronauts for even the shortest of ascents.

It was in a Rio bookshop one day in 1897, while he was buying things to read for his second sea voyage to France, that Santos-Dumont, aged twenty-five, came across an account of Andrée and the giant polar balloon. Intrigued, when he arrived in Paris the young man sought out the balloon's builder, Henri Lachambre, and asked how much it would cost to be taken up. Lachambre, perhaps moved by the youthful Brazilian's enthusiasm, quoted a reasonable price. At the appointed day and hour

Lachambre's colleague, Alexis Machuron (just returned from the Arctic after inflating the Swedish aeronaut Andrée's balloon) gave the order "Let go all!" and instantly Machuron and his passenger were airborne.

"Villages and woods," said Santos-Dumont describing his first ascent, "meadows and châteaux, pass across the moving scene, out of which the whistling of locomotives throws sharp notes. These faint, piercing sounds, together with the yelping and barking of dogs, being the only noises that reach one through the depths of the upper air. The human voice cannot mount up into these boundless solitudes. Human beings look like ants along the white lines that are highways, and the rows of houses look like children's playthings." From down below a peal of bells sounded, the noonday Angelus ringing from an unknown village belfry. "I had brought up with us a substantial lunch of hard-boiled eggs, cold roast beef and chicken, cheese, ice cream, fruits and cakes, Champagne, coffee and Chartreuse," Santos-Dumont said. "Nothing is more delicious than lunching like this above the clouds in a spherical balloon. No dining room can be so marvelous in its decoration. The sun sets the clouds in ebullition, making them throw up rainbow jets of frozen vapor like great sheaves of fireworks all around the table."

The balloonists entered a fog. "The netting holding us to the balloon is visible only up to a certain height," Santos-Dumont said. "The balloon itself had completely disappeared, so that we had for the moment the delightful impression of hanging in the void without support—of having lost the last ounce of our weight."[6] After nearly two hours in the air, including fifteen minutes spent snagged on a tree while wind gusts "kept us shaking like a salad-basket,"[7] Machuron and his enraptured passenger came to rest on the grounds of the Château de La Ferrière, sixty miles from Paris.

By 1901, however, those days of free ballooning were over for Santos-Dumont, now in the midst of his dirigible obsession. Although the determined aeronaut had nearly come a cropper after his encounter with the Trocadéro Hotel, that very evening he laid out specifications for No. 6. The new airship was twenty-two days in the making, and test flights, with the exception of a mishap or two, proved highly successful. No. 6 was larger and, thanks to an air-cooled engine, more powerful than its predecessors. However, like them, it was elegant, even artistic, in appearance and spare in design, especially compared to the frumpy gasbags and the jumble of thick rigging that distinguished the other airships of the era. "I have always been charmed by simplicity," Santos-Dumont confessed, "while complications, be they ever so ingenious, repel me."

It was Santos-Dumont's earlier modification of a simple, two-cylinder, automobile tricycle motor—weighing just sixty-six pounds, yet producing three and a half horsepower—that allowed him to lay claim to having flown the world's first airship with true dirigibility. Others may have tried (most notably Henri Giffard's 1852 attempt with a steam-powered engine), but none were truly successful before Santos-Dumont.

"Dirigibility," as any nineteenth-century aeronaut would have known, meant the ability to navigate through the air by motive power. This is in contrast to being held captive to the wind, as balloonists had been for over a century, and indeed it did take that long before, on September 20, 1898, Santos-Dumont was able to demonstrate dirigibility with his first dirigible airship, No. 1, to great applause on the beautiful grounds of the new Zoological Garden west of Paris. "Under the combined action of the propeller impulse," he explained, "of the steering rudder, of the displacement of the guide rope, and of the two sacks of ballast sliding backward and forward as I willed, I had the satisfaction of making my evolutions in every direction—to right and left, and up and down."

Encouraged by the ease in which he could steer No. 1 through the air, Santos-Dumont allowed his craft to rise to 1,300 feet. Whether he estimated or measured this he did not say, but an altimeter, an instrument sensitive to changes in air pressure (which increases and decreases with altitude), would have told him how high he was flying. "At this height I commanded a view of all the monuments of Paris," he recounted, "and I continued my evolutions in the direction of the Longchamps race-course."[8] As long as Santos-Dumont retained this altitude, the expanding hydrogen kept the gasbag as tight as a drum, but when it came time to descend, the hydrogen contracted and the bag began to fold up like a jackknife. It had been a mistake to have gone so high, a lesson the novice airship navigator had just learned the hard way. "The descent became a fall," Santos-Dumont said. "Luckily, I was falling in the neighborhood of the grassy turf of Bagatelle, where some big boys were flying kites." The Brazilian, who spoke perfect French, cried out to the boys to grab the end of his guide rope and run as fast as they could against the wind. "They were bright young fellows, and they grasped the idea and the rope at the same lucky instant," he said. "The effect of this help *in extremis* was immediate and as such as I had hoped. By the maneuver we lessened the velocity of the fall, and so avoided what would otherwise have been a bad shaking up, to say the least." The small aeronaut thanked the big boys and then packed the deflated No. 1 into his wicker basket. "I finally," he said, "secured a cab and took the relics back to Paris."

When Santos-Dumont made his third attempt for the Deutsch Prize a month later, the ballooning season had nearly ended and so he had to make this last chance count. No. 6 was ready and, despite wind speeds on top of the Eiffel Tower measuring fourteen miles per hour, telegrams had been sent out to members of the Scientific Commission requesting their presence at Saint Cloud on October 19 at 2 p.m.

The official start came forty-two minutes later and, with a southwest wind striking his craft sideways, Santos-Dumont held an ascending course straight toward his dangerous goal. He reached the tower in record time, but it would not be smooth sailing from then on. "The return trip," he complained, "was almost directly in the teeth of the wind."[9] After battling the elements for one-third of a mile homeward, his engine threatened to quit, providing "a moment of great uncertainty." He realized that he had to make a quick decision, and to make it fast. "It was to abandon the steering wheel for a moment, at the risk of drifting from my course, in order to devote my attention to the carbureting lever and the lever controlling the electric spark."

At the sound of a spluttering engine coming from somewhere above, crowds at the Auteuil racetrack, where the Prix Fin-Picard had just finished, averted their eyes from the horses on the ground. When the cause of the noise was located it provided a splendid sight: that of Santos-Dumont passing perhaps two to three hundred feet overhead with the nose of No. 6 pointing diagonally upward. Although the applauding throng did not know it, the aeronaut was desperately fighting for altitude when, suddenly, his engine came back to life. Spitting thunder, No. 6 shot upward to shouts of alarm below, but Santos-Dumont knew what he was doing and remained composed. "In the air I have no time to fear," he said, "I have always kept a cool head. Alone in the airship, I was always very busy."[10] The airship commander maintained a firm grip on the rudder while letting his craft climb on its own accord before coaxing it back down to a horizontal position. Then, at an altitude of almost 500 feet and with the propeller spinning madly, No. 6 soared above Longchamps, crossed the Seine, and continued over the members of the Commission gathered at the Aéro Club grounds.

The triumphant journey ended with thirty-one seconds to spare, and of the prize money awarded, Santos-Dumont gave more than half to the Prefect of Police of Paris to be used for the deserving poor. The rest he distributed among the loyal employees who built and maintained his

AUTHOR'S COLLECTION

Santos-Dumont (standing center above everyone else), his No. 6, and assembled admirers.

airships. Then, unanticipated, from the government of Brazil came a gift to their native son in the sum of money equal in value to that of the Deutsch Prize. Also from his country came a large and beautiful gold medal struck especially in his honor, and on it was an adaptation of the opening line of Camoens' epic poem *Lusiad*. In Portuguese it read, "Through heavens heretofore unsailed!"

With winter approaching, and with Parisian insurance companies refusing to quote him a rate for aerial liability, Santos-Dumont took his flying operations south. "From my friend, the Duc de Dino," he said, "and his charming American wife, I had received an invitation to their Monte Carlo villa; while from the Prince of Monaco assurances were sent me that the Prince, himself, would be pleased to build me a balloon-house directly on the beach of the Condamine."[11]

When Santos-Dumont arrived in Monte Carlo in late January, he saw that the Prince had kept his word and that a new building stood next to the bay. "It was an immense empty shell of wood and canvas over an iron skeleton," wrote the journalist Sterling Heilig, a confidant of Santos-Dumont, of the building. "It is 182 feet long, 33 feet wide, and 50 feet high. It had to be solidly constructed so as not to risk the fate of the all-wood Aërodrome of Toulon, which was twice all but carried away by tempests."[12] The hallmark of the solid structure was its two huge doors weighing 9,680 pounds each, and on the morning of January 29, 1902, those doors rolled open and Santos-Dumont, like a jockey taking a thoroughbred out for its daily run, rode his champion No. 6 into the sunshine and across the Boulevard de la Condamine. There, with the help of assistants and supernumeraries, rider and mount clambered over a seawall and, from a landing platform on the beach, took to the air to sprint circles around the Bay of Monaco.

"Here in the azure solitudes," Santos-Dumont said, "there were no chimney pots of Paris, no cruel, threatening roof corners, no treetops of the Bois de Boulogne. My propeller was showing its power and I was free to let it go." Santos-Dumont treated his sojourn by the sea as an opportunity to add to his education as an airship captain, and so he ventured from the sheltered bay and out into the windy Mediterranean. Flying over the ocean may have had its hazards, but it was arguably safer than racing around the Eiffel Tower, and certainly far more relaxing. "Fresh from the troubling time limit of the Deutsch Prize competition, I amused myself, frankly, with my airship," Santos-Dumont said, "making observations of great value to myself, but not seeking to prove anything to anyone."

Mainly, the aeronaut concentrated on speed and maneuverability, all the while tethered to the ocean by a thick guide rope that he let drop so that about ten feet of its even thicker end dragged in the water. "Guide roping," as Santos-Dumont termed it, slowed his forward motion to around twenty miles per hour, but had the advantage of keeping his airship at a steady altitude of 165 feet and allowing him to concentrate on other things. "I had plenty of leisure to look about," he said of his first expedition. "Presently I met two sailing yachts scudding towards me down the coast. I noticed that their sails were full-bellied. As I flew on, I heard a faint cheer, and a graceful female figure on the foremost yacht waved a red foulard. As I turned to answer the politeness, I perceived with some astonishment that we were far apart already."

The aeronaut ventured up and down the coast, trailed by prominent people in their yachts below who wished to assist him with his experiments, or ready in case of accident. "From Beaulieu, where his steam yacht *Lysistrata* was at anchor," Santos-Dumont said, "came Mr. James Gordon Bennett, and Mr. Eugene Higgins had already brought the *Varuna* up from Nice on more than one occasion. The beautiful little steam yacht of Monsieur Eiffel also held itself in readiness." On February 12, 1902, Santos-Dumont embarked upon his longest flight yet, traveling east toward Italy. Acting as guardians stationed along the way were seven vessels: the yacht *Princess Alice*, with His Serene Highness and also the Governor-General of Monaco on board; a steam chaloupe piloted by the Prince; two petroleum launches; and, finally, three well-manned rowboats. Meanwhile, keeping an eye on Santos-Dumont from shore were Clarence Grey Dinsmore in his forty-horsepower Mors automobile and M. Isadore Kahenstein behind the wheel of her thirty-horsepower Panhard.

Facing a headwind that bent the white sails of yachts below, Santos-Dumont held his rudder firm and put on all speed. "I could see the ragged outlines of the coast flit past me on the left," he remembered, while "along the winding road the two racing automobiles kept abreast with me, being driven at high speed." The ocean headwind increased, a situation that made Santos-Dumont uncomfortable, and so opposite the Villa Camille Blanc, not far from Cap Martin, he brought the rudder hard over and headed homeward. Pushed swiftly by the same wind that a minute ago had been his adversary, his speed reached upward, he estimated, of thirty-five miles per hour. The aeronaut delighted in the power and maneuverability of his dirigible, and his arrival back at the bay would be a memorable one. Along the shore a thousand handkerchiefs fluttered, and "to those watching my return from the terraces of Monte Carlo and Monaco town," he said, "the airship increased in size at every instant, like a veritable eagle bearing down upon them." Approaching the inner harbor as a heavy rain began to fall, the aerial navigator shut off his engine and coasted toward the landing platform. Wishing to be of help, the Prince in his steam chaloupe attempted to grab the heavy guide rope, but instead was struck by it in the right arm and knocked to the bottom of his little vessel, sustaining severe contusions.

Only a fortnight since they had begun, and after only five flights had been taken, Santos-Dumont's maritime experiments ended eventfully on the afternoon of February 14, 1902, when the gasbag of No. 6, having been improperly filled with hydrogen, began to fold up shortly after takeoff. Panicked, he immediately descended to the water's surface and the next day No. 6 had to be fished from the bottom of the bay and sent to Paris for repairs. Newspapers around the globe knew that the Brazilian's aerial exploits made for good copy, and the Monaco Bay plunge joined his previous mishaps in picturesque places in becoming international news. Chagrined, Santos-Dumont pointed out that the public thought no less of its automobiles when they had minor problems, "Yet let the airship have the same trifling accident," he protested, "and all the world is likely to hear of the fact!"

Back in the birthplace of aviation, his beloved Paris, Santos-Dumont was a celebrity. His apartments were on the Champs-Élysées and his guests might be a Rothschild or two, plus such other luminaries of the era as the jeweler Louis Cartier, the Brazilian Princess Isabel, or the designer Gustave Eiffel, whose tower had caused him so much bother.[13] Host and guests would dine aloft, seated around an elevated table reached only by the help of servants and a stepladder, and when not holding an aerial dinner party in his bachelor quarters, Santos-Dumont ate alone at Maxim's or could be seen driving around the city in his electric buggy, which he preferred to a regular automobile for its quiet and odorless engine. On the ground or in the air, the dapper little aeronaut dressed the same way, in trimly cut suits and oversized collars that were dandyish even by Parisian standards. His persona was mysterious and his appearance fodder for the press.

"He is not a handsome man," a reporter remarked, "His teeth are, though, beautifully white and regular, and his smile is charming. It spreads all over his face, beginning with his eyes, and as it steals over his features its softens and lightens them delightfully . . . It is his voice, too, which is low and strangely gentle, which somehow conveys the idea of effeminacy which one cannot help but feel no matter how often one is reminded of his daring feats of courage. This effect is added to by a gold bracelet which Santos wears on his wrist, although his sleeve hides it, except occasionally, when some gesture of the arm shows it for a moment. This is rare, however, for Santos thinks much more than he talks, and talks much more than he gestures."[14]

Finding the Aéro Club grounds at Saint Cloud too confining, Santos-Dumont built the world's first airship station, located on a plot of land he had purchased on the Rue de Longchamp at Neuilly Saint James. There, on that narrow suburban street, and perhaps to the chagrin of his neighbors, he constructed an enormous tent-like structure capable of holding not only No. 6 but his newer airships as well. These amounted to the speedy No. 7, with its forty-five-horsepower engine driving two propellers; the omnibus No. 10, designed to carry ten people; and his favorite of all, the little No. 9.

Much as his mini-balloon *Brazil* had been, No. 9 was a small and practical aerial runabout, and on calm summer days Santos-Dumont, the "bird man"[15] of Paris, would guide-rope the little craft along the city's streets and well below the roof lines of surrounding buildings. He might circle the Arc de Triomphe ("to the right," he explained, "as the law directs"), fly up the Avenue du Bois de Boulogne, or guide-rope down the Avenue des Champs-Élysées to his front door on the corner of Rue Washington. There his servants would rush out to serve him a demitasse of coffee. Alternatively, Santos-Dumont might cruise leisurely to Les Cascades and his favorite café. But returning home late and dragging his line, he had to contend with high obstacles hidden in the diminished light. "It is evening. I am walking under the trees," reported André Fagel in *L'Illustration*. "Suddenly I stumble against a rope. It is by no means a gossamer thread. I hear the noise of crumpling leaves above me, and an angry voice shouts, 'I can't see a thing! I shall split my skull!'"[16]

The private airship station at Neuilly Saint James became a social hub as the well-connected flocked to see Santos-Dumont and his latest inventions, and a great Cuban beauty named Aida de Acosta, aged nineteen and well known to New York society, expressed interest in flying one of his airships. The aerial experimenter gave De Acosta a few instructions, put her in the basket of No. 9, and then, on June 29, 1903, after a successful solo flight, she became the world's first woman airship pilot.

Although the most gentle of men, as concerned about causing harm to anyone on the ground as his own welfare up in the air, Santos-Dumont made no secret of his belief that the airship would one day realize its greatest potential as an instrument of war. "The farseeing Henri Rochefort," he said of an acquaintance in Monte Carlo, "who was in the habit of coming to the aerodrome from his hotel at La Turbie, wrote a most significant editorial in this sense after I had laid before him the speed calculations of my 'No. 7,' then in course of building." According to Santos-Dumont, Rochefort predicted in his editorial that "The day when it shall be established that a man can make his airship travel in a given direction and maneuver it at will during the four hours which the young Santos demands to go from Monaco to Calvi, there will remain little more for the nations to do than to throw down their arms." Indeed, Santos-Dumont envisioned a future where naval airships, speeding in the air at twice of the rate of submarines submerged below, would signal to friendly warships where the prey lay, or even better, destroy the submarines themselves with arrows filled with dynamite.

With the exception of this prediction, and also of piloting No. 9 over a gathering of French army troops in the presence of the president of the Republic, Santos-Dumont, being a peaceable fellow, dropped his interest in aerial warfare in order to tackle the problem of heavier-than-air flight. He was not alone in trying to get off the ground by means of wings and mechanical propulsion, as this had become an area of intense study by others in recent years, but his were the first efforts to appear successful. On November 12, 1906, while piloting his box-shaped machine No. 14-*bis*—with its roaring engine and spinning propeller merely inches from his back—Santos-Dumont demonstrated winged flight in front of the Aéro Club Observation Committee and a crowd of hundreds at Bagatelle. Within twelve months of this very public and well-documented flight, thought by everyone to be the first of its kind, it emerged that the Wright brothers, Wilbur and Orville, had been flying airplanes in secret in the United States since November 1903, thus beating Santos-Dumont by nearly three years. Disappointed but unbowed,

Santos-Dumont went on to make and fly other airplanes, like his sportive *Demoiselle*, but then one day in 1910, offering no explanation, he quit aviation work forever. Over the next two decades, while ailing both mentally and physically (one theory, never confirmed, held that he had suffered from multiple sclerosis), the famous aerial pioneer led a wandering life until his death in 1932. Remembered with great affection, Parisians mourned his passing, and today in Brazil every schoolchild rightfully knows Alberto Santos-Dumont as the "Father of Aviation."

Before his conversion to aircraft, of course, Santos-Dumont had been a dirigible dreamer, and he hoped that in the near future civilization would witness the development of highly organized airship stations, ones that would be a far cry from his simple affair on the Rue de Longchamp. These large stations would have, he foresaw, elevated and spacious landing platforms for safety and convenience, trolley tracks to lead the airships efficiently by their guide ropes to and from their hangars, and observation towers equipped with wireless telegraphs to communicate with dirigibles in flight. The airship stations would also have, he envisioned, gas-generating plants, workshops and repair shops, and sleeping quarters for those who wished to rise at the crack of dawn, when flying weather was best.

He additionally guessed that, just as "I guide roped up the Avenue of the Bois, so someday will explorers guide rope to the North Pole from their ice-locked steamship after it has reached its farthest possible point north. Guide roping over the pack ice, they will make the very few hundreds of miles to the Pole at the rate of from sixty to eighty kilometers per hour. Even at the rate of fifty kilometers, the trip to the Pole and back to the ship could be taken between breakfast and supper time. I do not say that they will land the first time at the Pole, but they will circle round about the spot, take observations, and return—for supper!"

Santos-Dumont envisioned this fanciful polar flight in 1904, well aware, as was everyone, of Salomon August Andrée's actual attempt seven years earlier.

Andrée, a prominent Swedish engineer, had publicly announced his plans to reach the top of the world by air on February 15, 1895. He had done so during a lecture hosted by the Swedish Anthropological and Geographic Society, and in his talk he pointed out to the members of the Society that no ocean-going vessel could penetrate the ice-filled Polar Sea; and, while crossing the ice pack by sledge remained feasible, so far all attempts to do so had met with failure. "Has not the time come to revise this question from the very beginning and to see if we do not possibly possess any other means than the sledge for crossing these tracks?"[17] Andrée asked. Then he answered his own query: "The means is the air balloon; not the dreamed-of, perfectly dirigible air balloon, so devoutly longed for, since we have not yet seen it, but the air balloon which we already possess and which is regarded so unfavorably merely because attention is focused on its weak point. Such an air balloon is, however, capable of carrying the explorer to the Pole and home again in safety; with such a balloon the journey across the waste of ice *can* be carried out."

Andrée outlined four conditions necessary for successful polar flight. First, the balloon must have sufficient carrying capacity for a four-month journey, meaning the ability to hold three persons as well as observation instruments, sledges, survival gear, ballast, provisions, and other things necessary both for the journey and any eventuality, for a total weight of 6,600 pounds. Second, the balloon must be so gas-tight that it could remain in the air for at least thirty days. Third, the filling of the balloon with gas must take place in the polar tracts. And fourth, and perhaps most importantly for a journey such as this, "The balloon must, to some degree, be dirigible." Of this last point, the issue of dirigibility, Andrée explained that the balloon "shall be provided with a system of sails and with several drag—or guide—ropes, all which must be made of impregnated coco-nut fiber, so that they can float on water; then the balloon will retain the same height above the water as it will over ice or land. In addition it must be provided with a large number of freely hanging, heavy ropes—ballast lines—which shall serve partly as ordinary ballast and partly as automatic life-saving apparatus in the event of an unexpected descent to a very low height."

The importance of guide ropes and ballast lines to a polar flight came to Andrée by accident on October 19, 1893, while riding his first balloon, the 37,230-cubic-foot *Svea*. The balloon had ascended from the barracks of the Royal Engineers in Stockholm for a trip over Sweden when, unexpectedly, strong winds instead hurtled it across the Baltic Sea. Ten hours later Andrée landed on a lonely island in a Finnish archipelago 170 miles away, with such force that his watch stopped, his instruments lay ruined, and many of his photographs lost. After enduring "an extremely unpleasant night," the Swedish aeronaut was rescued, but the misadventure over the Baltic had not been for naught, because earlier in his journey, as the mainland fast dropped away and the *Svea* headed out to sea, he had let his guide rope float along the waves for control; and for even more control, he had lowered the anchor and two ballast lines into the water. This arrangement worked, leading him to two discoveries.

One of these, Andrée said, was it showed that "a guide-roping balloon of a suitable form can be supported by the same wind that drives it onwards"; the other was that it demonstrated "that a guide-roping balloon, with the same use of ballast, can traverse greater distances than a free balloon of equal dimensions. I scarcely need point out of what extreme importance this is for the possibility of making long balloon flights for geographical purposes."

Trials with the *Svea* continued, and Andrée kept a detailed diary of each, making hundreds of observations at different heights of such

AUTHOR'S COLLECTION

Salomon August Andrée.

things as temperature, humidity, clouds, and optical phenomena, as well his own thirst, facial color, and respiration. Although Andrée once reached 14,250 feet, on his fourth ascent, on July 14, 1894, he only rose to 10,700 feet before landing some twenty-one miles from the city of Jönköping. After making sure that the balloon lay safely at rest, he walked to a nearby building where, he recalled, "I met a women and a boy who had locked themselves in, and they did not dare to come out before they were quite assured that I was an ordinary man." After that flight, Andrée intended to more systematically test the guide-roping and ballast-line effect that he had witnessed over the Baltic the summer before, only now with the addition of a "steering-sail" to better, he believed, control the craft. Although it's highly dubious whether Andrée could actually steer his balloon, he at least thought he could, and stated that from now on "the traveler will not be entirely dependent on the wind but will, to a considerable degree, be able to follow the route he wishes."

On the strength of his lecture to the Swedish Anthropological and Geographic Society, Andrée began to raise the considerable funds required for a journey that would take him from Spitsbergen in the Svalbard archipelago, halfway between Norway and the North Pole, over the Pole and, depending upon the winds, to either Siberia or Alaska on the other side.

It would be a 2,200-mile journey across the top of world, the first ever, and made entirely by air. The scheme may have been audacious, but Andrée argued that the trip would take no more than six days. "And who," he had asked the Society, "are better qualified to make such an attempt than we Swedes? As a highly civilized nation, characterized for ages by the most dauntless courage, dwelling in the neighborhood of the polar regions, familiar with its climatic peculiarities, and by Nature herself trained to endure them, we can hardly altogether help feeling that we have a certain obligation in this matter."

The polar project enjoyed wide public support and, as importantly, Andrée had the unconditional approval of renowned Arctic explorer Baron A. E. Nordenskiöld. The project's leader also had the financial backing of, among others, the inventor of dynamite, Alfred Nobel, and additionally the sovereign of Sweden and Norway, King Oscar II. Because of these and other friends, Andrée secured the money he needed, and on December 24, 1895 he signed a contract with Henri Lachambre of Paris for the construction of a gigantic balloon.

Andrée was a product of the Royal Institute of Technology in Stockholm, and after graduation became chief engineer of the Swedish Patent Office. The founder of the Society of Swedish Inventors, he embodied the modern, technical man of his age. In a 1930 retrospective, the Swedish Society for Anthropology and Geography remarked that "Andrée with his sober intellectualism, his systematic turn of mind, and his unbounded belief in the power of applied science, was in a high degree a child of his time—the eighties of the last century, with their practical ideas and their fierce zeal for reform. He possessed the most optimistic belief in the power of technology and industry to make the human race happier, by creating for the masses better conditions of existence and more leisure, with its attendant opportunities for mental development and bodily culture." Andrée had an appreciation for nature, but in his rational and methodical mind there was no place for much else (something that, the Society observed, "must be considered a defect in his character"). When it came to marriage, for example, Andrée had no personal use for it, reasoning that "One has to deal with factors which cannot be arranged according to a plan."

Polar projects, however, could be planned, and he took pains to make sure his was planned to perfection. Accordingly, the freighter *Virgo* arrived in the Spitsbergen area in early June 1896, carrying Andrée and his fellow balloonists, meteorologist and astronomer Dr. Nils Ekholm and physicist Nils Strindberg. The ship also bore a supporting cast comprising the balloon builder from Paris, Henri Lachambre, as well as specialists in chemistry, zoology, hydrography, and geology, plus the *Virgo*'s captain and his thirty-man crew. After scouting various islands, Andrée selected a spot (soon named Virgo Harbor) on the north side of Danes Island to be the expedition's base. The unloading of the hydrogen gas apparatus, the balloon, and the balloon's little "car," a tarpaulin-covered gondola that would be the cramped home for the three explorers during their planned journey, took almost a month, as did the construction of an immense six-story shed for the balloon. An unmanned trial balloon, the *Sverige* (Sweden), rose high in the air amid cheers from the ground, and by the first days of August the actual polar flight was ready to depart. However, an accommodating southerly wind to usher Andrée and his two companions to the Pole and beyond never materialized, and on August 17, the short Arctic summer having ended and the *Virgo*'s insurance policy expiring, the balloon was bled of its gas and packed aboard the ship.

The Swedish gunboat *Svenksund* accompanied the *Virgo* back to the base on Danes Island, both ships arriving there on May 30, 1897. Remarkably, the enormous shed survived the Arctic winter mostly intact, and by June 14 the balloon had been placed inside and, three days later, with the help of Lachambre's assistant from Paris, Alexis Machuron, inflated by means of pouring sulfuric acid over iron shavings to produce hydrogen. There followed a delay of many days while workers varnished the humongous balloon and tested it for leaks, and then another delay occurred when a violent storm blew through the base. Finally, at 1:46 p.m. on July 11, 1897, Andrée cried "Cut away everywhere!" and, with the ground ropes severed, the balloon, christened *Örnen* (Eagle), ascended from the shore and headed out over Virgo Harbor in a northeasterly direction, two to three hundred feet above the waves.

On the *Örnen* was Andrée, the "old man" of the expedition at the age of forty-three, and his two young and fit colleagues: Nils Strindberg, aged twenty-five and a veteran of the past year's aborted mission, and Knut Frænkel, aged twenty-seven and a replacement for Dr. Ekholm, who had lost his nerve. Seconds after lift-off, the three aeronauts unfurled steering sails to take advantage of the wind, while the ballast ropes carved the surface of the harbor water, marking the first minutes of the expedition's progress. All seemed routine until the *Örnen* reached the middle of the harbor where, caught in a sudden downdraft, the car dipped into the waves. To Machuron watching on shore, it looked as if Andrée and his crew might have to be rescued, but the fright passed and the *Örnen* quickly rebounded high into the air. The balloon rotated completely around its vertical axis and Frænkel could be seen climbing into

AUTHOR'S COLLECTION

At the base on Dane Island: testing the balloon for leaks.

the bearing ring under the hydrogen bag to remove the sails. Ten minutes later the ground crew observed the balloon flying over Holländer Naze and eighteen minutes after that, the middle of Vogelsang Island at a height of about 2,000 feet. It then swung off to the east where it entered a cloud and could be seen no more. "Look!" a sailor cried back at the base, "The drag-lines are lying here on the shore!" That the drag-lines had somehow fallen off the *Örnen* meant there was little chance for dirigibility, putting the flight to the Pole in great doubt.

Of the many communications sent out by the balloon during its four-day polar odyssey, only three were subsequently recovered. The first, ironically, was the last one found, stuffed inside a cork buoy and discovered on the coast of Finmark, Norway, three years later. "July 11, 10 p.m.," the note read. "Our journey has so far gone well . . . We are now in

AUTHOR'S COLLECTION

The Örnen *takes flight over Virgo Harbor, July 11, 1897.*

over the ice which is much broken up in all directions. Weather magnificent. In best of humors."

The second communication sent by the lost explorers was the next one found—in Kollafjord, on the coast of Iceland, two years later: "This buoy was thrown out from Andrée's balloon at 10.55 G.M.T. on July 11, 1897, in about 82° latitude and 25° long."

The third communication in the series was the first one received, at a time when Andrée, Strindberg, and Frænkel would have still been alive. Their winged messenger had landed on the masthead of the Norwegian sealer *Alken* on July 15, only to be shot. It was a needless death because the poor little carrier pigeon, hungry and exhausted from a day and a half of continuous flying, and sitting on its perch with its head tucked under its wing, could simply have been had for the grabbing. When the bird's body (now stuffed and in a museum) was plucked from the sea and the letter-cylinder opened, a brief note was found inside. "July 13.

12.30 midday," the dispatch read, making no mention of the dire straits that the expedition was in. "All well on board. This is the third pigeon-post. Andrée."

The troubling events that occurred shortly after ascent and caused such alarm on shore—the loss of the draglines and the dunking in the harbor—concerned Andrée, Strindberg, and Frænkel not in the least, and certainly never made the three think once of aborting their mission. Immediately they set about fashioning a dragline to replace the one left behind. Similarly, the loss of sand ballast that had to be hastily discharged during the dip into Virgo Harbor caused no worries since 300 pounds still remained.

High above Vogelsang Island shortly after the exciting events of initial ascent, the temperature registered thirty-four degrees Fahrenheit and the balloon's speed was estimated to be a respectable twenty miles per hour. Strindberg remembered a note he had written to his fiancée and placed it in a tin before tossing it down onto the island (where, over a century later, it still remains for the finding). Then, over the next forty-five minutes, the three Swedes flew in and out of clouds, causing the *Örnen* to alternately rise and descend with the changes in temperature. At 1,625 feet, some 117 cubic feet of hydrogen escaped, an insignificant amount considering the cavernous size of the balloon's 170,000-cubic-foot gasbag. Off a cape at Wijde Bay, Andrée took bearings, and at the north point of Vogelsang he and his two companions, who had all the while been busy with myriad tasks, took a break and made a meal out of several bottles of ale.

The altimeter read 1,600 feet, they reckoned the wind to be south-southwest, and they could see drifting ice ahead to the north. Standing on the roof of the car and relieving themselves into the forty-two-degree air, Andrée, Strindberg, and Frænkel had a magnificent view of Wijde Bay. A seagull kept them company while Spitsbergen dropped out of sight, and then they found themselves over a sea of finely divided ice and flying at a good rate of speed in a north-northeasterly direction. Entering a light mist, they slowly descended in a winding curve to 780 feet, where four of the expedition's thirty-six carrier pigeons were released. The first "pigeon-post," however, disappeared into thin air. At 6 p.m. the three polar explorers ate sandwiches and warm broth and macaroni, the shrieks of birds and the crackling of the ice below providing musical accompaniment to their heavenly repast. Their compass showed that a southerly wind was taking them in the desired direction: north.

Seeing that all was going smoothly, Andrée left the roof and squeezed himself into the car's tiny compartment beneath. He slept several hours, leaving Strindberg in charge while the endless Arctic sunshine broke through the mist and the *Örnen* rose to 1,950 and then 2,270 feet. Hydrogen warmed by the sun could be heard whistling out of the safety valve, and this agreeable state of affairs lasted a few hours until the balloon passed under higher clouds. In the cooling conditions the balloon lost altitude, and at 9:43 p.m. Strindberg dropped eighteen pounds of sand ballast to maintain altitude. Shortly thereafter he sent the first buoy overboard, the one found three years later. "We are still moving at a height of 800 feet," the message read. Eight minutes after this Strindberg, still fighting for altitude, dumped another eighteen pounds of sand, plus eleven rungs of the rope ladder. The second message buoy went overboard, and now the news was "We are floating at a height of 600 meters."

With Andrée still asleep, Strindberg drew his attention toward an altocumulus cloud throwing a dark shadow over the ice. At eleven minutes past midnight, July 12, the *Örnen* entered the shadow at an altitude of 1,500 feet, and in just four minutes lost so much height that its dangling guidelines touched the ice less than 400 feet below. "The sun has gone," wrote Strindberg nonchalantly, "but we keep a very level course."

Fifty minutes later more sand, twenty-six pounds this time, lay scattered on the ice below. Ominously, a bird, black and distant, appeared on the horizon. Then the wind died completely and the expedition found itself becalmed. A third message buoy (never found and its contents unknown) went overboard. The balloon sat bathed in fog, with visibility reduced to around one mile.

"Ugh!" the famous Arctic explorer Dr. Fridtjof Nansen, a contemporary and a rival of Andrée's, once said. "This infinitely tenacious Polar Sea fog! When it covers you with its mantle and hides from your eyes the blue above you and the blue around you and turns everything to a grey, wet mist, day in and day out, then there is required all the buoyancy of soul one possesses in order not to be depressed by its close embrace. There is fog and fog and nothing but fog wherever we turn our eyes. It rests on the rigging, and every patch of the deck is soaked by its dripping. It rests on one's clothes and at last wets them through. It lies on one's soul, it lies on one's senses, and everything becomes a greyness within a greyness."

Andrée was called up to the roof of the car at around 2 a.m., and Strindberg and Frænkel took his place below to get some sleep. If Andrée had been worried about the loss of altitude and ballast during his absence, he did not mention it. "No land in sight," he observed. "The horizon is not clear however. It is indeed a wonderful journey through the night. I am cold but will not wake the two sleepers. They need their rest." The next few hours afforded no break from the monotony except when Andrée sighted a bearded seal fifty or sixty feet below. Soon Strindberg and Frænkel awoke, however, and Strindberg took care of some personal business ("I pooped for 1st time"). The three aeronauts then prepared breakfast by lowering a remotely controlled stove, the ingenious invention of Andrée's friend, Ernst Göransson, twenty-six feet beneath the car. There it hung at a safe distance from the potentially explosive hydrogen bag, and soon coffee was ready. The three men dispatched a second pigeon post but, like the first, it too vanished. By midday the aeronauts, airborne now for nearly twenty-four hours, passed a vast ice field more than a thousand yards wide and covered with pools of fresh water. That afternoon, Strindberg saw, through the mist and drizzle, "Blood-red ice, perhaps a relic of a bear's meal." At 3:06 p.m., first mention was made that the balloon car "stamped" the ice.

Instantly, the startled balloonists scrambled to climb to a higher, sunnier, altitude. They tossed out everything not urgently needed, including heavy knives, fifty-five pounds of sand, ropes, anchors, pulleys, and ballast lines. Even the "Pole-buoy," with its spring-loaded Swedish flag, intended to mark the North Pole, had to go.[18] But these sacrifices made no difference and the balloon, oppressed by fog and drizzle, hovered so low over the ice that the car hit the surface forcibly several more times. Over the next six hours Andrée kept a meticulous record of the torture—noting, for example, that at "5:14 p.m." there had been "8 'touches' in 30 minutes." An hour later, according to Andrée, the car touched down once "every five minutes" and then "once every 500 feet" until finally at "10.53 the balloon stopped." Everything outside and inside of the *Örnen* dripped with cold moisture, and the miserable explorers, their balloon stalled and its car hovering only a few feet above the ice, had no option but to wait the fog out.

"Is it not a little strange to be floating here above the Polar Sea?" Andrée wrote philosophically after telling Strindberg and Frænkel to go to bed. "To be the first that have floated here in a balloon? How soon, I wonder, shall we have successors? Shall we be thought mad or will our example be followed? I cannot deny that all three of us are dominated by a feeling of pride. We think we can well face death, having done what we have done. Isn't it all, perhaps, the expression of an extremely strong sense of individuality which cannot bear the thought of living and dying like a man in the ranks, forgotten by coming generations? Is this," he wondered, "ambition?"

Keeping vigil that night, Andrée observed that "The rattling of the guide-lines in the snow and the flapping of the sails are the only sounds heard." The temperature stayed at thirty-two degrees and the balloon, trying to free itself from the ice where one of its guidelines had become stuck, swayed, twisted, rose, and sank incessantly. Strindberg took over the watch and, somehow, Frænkel slept until awoken at 9:30 the next morning, July 13, when the fog began to lift. An hour and a half later, and after spending half a day on the ice, the *Örnen* resumed flight. They lowered the Göransson apparatus and, according to the menu, "Dîner du 13 Juillet," consisting of "Potage Hotch Potch, Chateaubriand, The King's Special Ale, Chocolate with biscuits, Biscuits with raspberry sauce and H_2O," was served at noon.

Encouraging words were sent out to the world via the third pigeon post, and this time one of the pigeons got through (the one that reached the *Alken* only to be killed). Shortly thereafter, though, the car resumed its horrible "stampings" along the ice and, desperately seeking relief from the "heavy shocks," Strindberg took refuge up in the balloon's bearing ring, where he found it "confoundedly pleasant. One feels so safe there and so at home."

The early-morning hours brought more fog and more drizzle, and also a new danger in the form of heavy hoarfrost forming on the balloon ropes. The "touches, touches" came in ever-quicker succession as the water-soaked balloon dragged its three suffering occupants over the ice hummocks. In an unsuccessful attempt to become airborne again, they tossed a buoy and a box of medicine over the side. Mockingly, one of the carrier pigeons returned to circle the *Örnen* before flying off, and for the three humans trapped in their dying balloon the situation must have been hell. During the thumping along the ice Andrée received a hard blow to the head, something in the car caught fire, and Strindberg, nauseous, vomited; he escaped to the bearing ring again, followed this time by Frænkel. At eight that night, the three desperate adventurers decided that they must gain altitude at any cost, and within minutes 440 pounds of buoys, winches, sand, barrels, and provisions lay scattered over the ice. The drastic action worked and the *Örnen* took to the air, its sails unfurled and its journey renewed. "The balloon goes extremely beautifully," exalted Andrée. "Altogether it is quite stately!"

The respite in the air afforded the trio a chance to rest, take bearings from the sun to determine position, write personal letters, and be thankful that a passing polar bear, as Andrée said, ignored the guide ropes and "Did not try to climb up to us." At ten-thirty, however, the fog became dense and the car began to strike the ice violently. The interminable stamping and dragging continued throughout the early hours of July 14, and not surprisingly the expedition's notes were brief and indecipherable during this nightmarish period, but they did indicate that at the very end the *Örnen* attempted one final dash to the heavens: "6:20," the log read, "the balloon rose to a great height, but we opened both valves and were down again at 6:29."

Sixty-five hours and thirty-three minutes since their ascension from Danes Island, the three balloonists had traveled hundreds of meandering miles, and with their partially deflated balloon resting nearby like a beached whale, Andrée, Strindberg, and Frænkel stepped out onto the soft summer ice. Now the stranded aeronauts faced the daunting task of marching south, where they hoped to reach the Svalbard archipelago's easternmost islands, 200 miles away. Meticulous as always, Andrée took his time packing and organizing three sledges and a canvas boat, finally departing the landing site eight days later with an inordinate amount of provisions and gear. His sledge alone weighed about 600 pounds and contained such items of dubious necessity as a sounding cable 179

AUTHOR'S COLLECTION

On the ice, July 14, 1897.

fathoms long. Hauling so much weight became absurd, and after several days of travel, and only several miles of progress, they decided to lighten their load by, among other things, eating as much food from the sledges as they could. Discovering a bottle of champagne among the provisions, they downed that too. With careful rationing, however, the ice-bound aeronauts had provisions to last several weeks, and by hunting polar bears—Andrée bagged his first on July 17—prospects of unlimited food.

Ice hummocks and an uneven surface hampered the journey, and frequently the sledges somersaulted and spilled everything onto the ice. On occasions the three men managed barely a mile a day. Through it all, however, they maintained a high degree of camaraderie, and on Strindberg's birthday, September 4, Andrée presented him with a surprise cache of letters—stored earlier aboard the *Örnen*—from his sweetheart and family back home. Sometimes the men marched day and night in

AUTHOR'S COLLECTION

Frænkel (left) and Strindberg with a welcome supply of meat.

the Arctic sunshine; other times they got lucky and could sail in the canvas boat for miles in open water; but diarrhea, sore feet, accidents, and illness took their toll. Eventually the sledges wore out and, the trek having come to a halt, they decided to ride an ice floe as it drifted south. The strategy worked, and on September 15 they sighted uninhabited White Island, and three days later celebrated the 25th anniversary of King Oscar II's ascension to the throne with a meal of seal steak fried in blubber accompanied by an 1834 bottle of port. For the next two weeks White Island lay tantalizingly close, but Andrée, now building an ice hut, made no effort to reach it. Then, on October 2, catastrophe struck. Exactly what happened remains a mystery, but apparently the ice floe broke up, forcing its three inhabitants to make for the island, a task that apparently took several days. Practically nothing is known of what happened next, except that Strindberg wrote cryptically on October 17, 1897, "Home 7:05 a.m."—and then wrote no more.

Thirty-three years later, in August 1930, sealers from the vessel *Bratvaag*, led by Dr. Gunnar Horn of the Norwegian Svalbard and Polar Sea Research Institution, came ashore on White Island, and there they found a body. "It was frozen and the legs lay in a perfectly natural position," Horn said. "On the feet were Lapp boots, and these lay partly beneath the snow. Higher up, the bones stuck out from among the clothes.

Various articles of clothing lay scattered about, and, as there was not much left of the upper part of the body and the head was missing, it was clear that bears had been there destroying and consuming what they could. We opened the jacket carefully and saw that inside, on the back of the garment, there was sewn a large monogram A., from which we drew the conclusion that it was Andrée's remains we had before us."

Andrée's companions were found nearby, and from the position of the bodies it was theorized that Andrée and Frænkel had died together in their tent, and that Strindberg, whose body was buried under a pile of stones, had succumbed some time earlier. It is also thought that cold and exhaustion were the most likely cause of all three deaths, because on the sledges would have been hundreds of pounds of food and drink taken from the car, as well as enough guns and ammunition with which to hunt the abundant Arctic wildlife far into the foreseeable future. Also found at the death site were the expedition's diaries, letters, almanacs, undeveloped film, and logbooks detailing the brief flight and the long months spent traversing the ice.

The *Svenksund*, the same Swedish gunboat that had accompanied Andrée's expedition north to Danes Island three decades earlier, arrived in Stockholm on October 5, 1930. Oscar II had died long since, but at the dock three coffins were laid at the foot of his son, King Gustaf V, who stood at attention as guns fired a salute and every bell in the city rang. Then, amid a pelting rain, tens of thousands of people jammed the processional march to the city's cathedral, the Church of St. Nicholas.

At the state funeral, Archbishop Nathan Söderblom went to the pulpit. "Welcome home!" he thundered. "Welcome, Strindberg! Welcome, Frænkel! Welcome, Andrée! You have been many years away. And what we now receive," the Archbishop said of the contents of the coffins before him, "are merely the ruins of magnificent, well-tempered instruments fitted for indomitable longing and clear-sighted achievement."

TWO

Walter Wellman, an American newspaperman, visited Norway in 1893 and talked to Norwegian skippers with knowledge of the Spitsbergen waters. Encouraged by what he learned, back home in the United States he raised money for an assault on the North Pole, and in April of the following year returned to Norway with fellow Americans Charles R. Dodge, O. B. French, and Dr. Mohun in tow. Wellman chartered the old ice vessel *Ragnvald Jar* and loaded it, he said, with "Norwegian scientific men, athletes, and sailors."[19] His cargo also included three lightweight aluminum boats and working dogs of a breed he had seen in Holland and Belgium. With these and other additions, the expedition was ready to depart.

Wellman was a hero of his own making. He was a tireless self-promoter, had boundless energy and confidence, never wanted to hear a discouraging word, and had a way with the locals, "my Norwegians" as he fondly called them. Although totally inexperienced in the ways of the Arctic, the American possessed total faith in his untested ideas and beliefs, and dove headlong into his quest for the Pole.

Against all advice, Wellman set sail for Spitsbergen unusually early in the season, reaching Danes Island (and future home of Andrée's expedition) on May 11, 1894. A born raconteur, Wellman described the surroundings not as they were then, barren and desolate, but what they must have been like "In the palmy days of the whale fisheries." That was when, he said, "Hundreds of whaling ships made this port their rendezvous. Houses were built and thatched with Dutch tiles. Cafes, dance halls, and worse places to get money out of sailors existed. At times the population rose to three or four thousand souls, all men save a hundred or two women of a certain class. There was much drinking and fighting, the country being then as now without laws or police authority or supervision. But this reeking city of blubber existed only in the summer. In the autumn all went home to Holland, to come out and try their luck the next year."

Wellman established a supply depot on the shore, and before sailing north left a Norwegian scientist behind who was discovered by a passing party of English sportsmen some months later. "As a result of this incident," Wellman complained of the notoriety it earned him, "I got my first taste of newspaper sensationalism and misrepresentation." This was despite the fact, Wellman argued, that far from being cruelly abandoned, the scientist "was perfectly safe" and "had a good house, tons of provisions, a gun and a dog, and was not likely to be lonesome."

The *Ragnvald Jar* soon reached Walden Island at the most northerly part of Spitsbergen and there, sledges, dogs, and, especially, the three aluminum boats that were such an integral, if unproven, part of Wellman's Arctic strategy, were unloaded. The caravan with Wellman in the lead then headed for the Pole while the *Ragnvald Jar* and its crew, under the command of Captain Bottolfsen, awaited its triumphant return. Bottolfsen anchored the vessel behind a projecting shard of heavy ice where he thought it would be safe. However a few days later, Wellman said, a "storm came down from the northwest, bringing the great ocean pack with it." Under enormous pressure, the shard gave way. "The ship was caught in the jaw," he explained, and "great masses of ice went right through her hull as you stick the tines of a fork through an egg shell,

LIBRARY OF CONGRESS

Walter Wellman.

and the *Ragnvald Jar* was no more." The caravan had, fortunately, only made it a few miles northeast by this point and so the expedition leader was summoned back by Bottolfsen. Wellman, who was from the American Midwest, advised the Norwegian mariner to abandon the rest of his crew and take a hand-picked party and one of the three boats south in search of help. "We decided to go on with our trip," Wellman said of his own itinerary, "though forced in prudence to modify the plan in important particulars, because our ship had been destroyed behind us, and there was no certainty of finding another."

The same great mass of ice which had crushed the *Ragnvald Jar* had also acted as a veritable Great Wall of China along the shore, preventing the caravan from getting out and onto the polar ice pack. After several days of arduous travel east in an attempt to find an opening, Wellman decided to shoot the dogs and take to the water in the remaining two boats. A lover of dogs, he would have preferred to see them live, but on this, his first trip to the Arctic, he had taken a gamble and instead of using sledge dogs had brought with him the Dutch and Flemish imports. Out of their element in the frozen north, the animals became confused and useless, and "Worst of all," Wellman said, "suffered frightfully in their feet. The snow and ice worked in between their toes, drew the blood, and our trail for days was marked with streaks of red which hurt me perhaps more than it hurt the poor beasts."

The expedition never could get to the ice-pack proper, and hauling the aluminum boats behind them, Wellman and his men suffered a series of misadventures. "One of our best and bravest Norwegians, Herr Alme," he said, "broke a bone in his foot one day, leaping from one ice floe to another." The foot was attended to by Dr. Mohun and that night Wellman found Alme crying bitterly because he would not be able to walk for a month.

"That means I can't help pull the boat," Alme sobbed, perhaps mindful of what had become of the dogs.

"Don't worry about that," Wellman replied.

"But, *but* you won't leave me on the ice, will you?"

This amused Wellman no end: "He had actually feared we would abandon him to perish out there in the wilderness of ice!"

When the explorers made it back to Walden Island, Bottolfsen, gone now several weeks, had yet to return. With winter approaching, Wellman organized his men and the remaining sailors into one group and they all trudged south together. "Storms came on, the ice was drifting violently to and fro, and we had many close calls from being crushed and wrecked," he said of the passage. "Once in the nick of time we managed to pull the boats upon an iceberg, while masses of ice were crashing together all about us." Finally, a sealing sloop, sent out to look, appeared and took the men back to Danes Island.

While pulling and pushing the boats over the heavy Arctic ice, it had occurred to Wellman that there must be an easier way. In Paris afterwards he spent several weeks consulting with the aeronautical firm of Godard & Surcouf, and came to the conclusion that the Pole could be conquered from the air in a monster balloon, costing as much as

$100,000. After giving it serious thought, however, Wellman abandoned the idea. "There seemed to be little prospect of success with a motorless balloon, a mere toy of the winds, without propulsive power or ability to steer to the right or left," he said. As there were presently no non-motorless balloons (Santos-Dumont's No. 1, for instance, had yet to fly), Wellman decided that the traditional ways of traversing the ice would suffice.

Within a few years, Wellman was ready for his second Arctic venture, having raised a good sum of money from, among others, U.S. President William McKinley and Vice President Garret Hobart, as well as millionaires J. Pierpont Morgan and William K. Vanderbilt. The ice-steamer *Frithjof* was chartered for the summer of 1898 and Wellman gathered together a group of Americans and Norwegians, some being bona fide Arctic experts, and loaded them aboard. This time, he brought along a pack of real sledge dogs from Siberia, and also left the aluminum boats at home. His destination was Franz Josef Land, an archipelago to the east of Spitsbergen, and along the way he kept a keen look-out for Andrée and his two companions who after twelve months might, it was hoped, still be alive; but he found no trace of them. The stores, equipment, and dogs were unloaded at Cape Tegetthoff (where the Austrian ship *Tegetthoff* had floundered in 1874) and then, with Wellman and the men of his expedition watching from shore, the *Frithjof* embarked for Norway.

On August 4, 1898, two days after the *Frithjof* departed, expedition member E. B. Baldwin of the U.S. Weather Bureau set out from Cape Tegetthoff. With Baldwin were four Norwegian scouts, and their mission was to establish an outpost farther north, which, after many trials and tribulations, they succeeded in doing. Baldwin patriotically named the place Fort McKinley, and in October he returned to the expedition's main base having left two of the Norwegians, Paul Bjoervig and Bernt Bentzen, behind. Speaking of Bjoervig and Bentzen, Wellman said,

"They were delighted. Neighbors and comrades at home, adventurous spirits both, this chance of spending an Arctic winter together in a snug little hut, with plenty to eat and smoke, was to them the realization of a dream."

While Baldwin was still at Fort McKinley, Wellman and two other Americans on the expedition, the physician Edward Hofma of Michigan and Quirof Harlan from the Coast and Geodetic Survey, assisted by "our Norwegians," had erected a collapsible house. The house had been tested by earlier Artic explorers who deemed it not fit for human habitation, but Wellman had his own ideas and he weather-proofed the structure by wrapping it in oiled canvas, wooden planks, and an old sail. Then he added double-doors and a vestibule before burying the whole thing in a blanket of snow, five feet thick. This was "Harmsworth House," and to conserve coal the temperature inside never went much above freezing, but even then the rule was "no bathing indoors." "In order to inure myself to cold," Wellman boasted, "I always washed face and hands in snow before breakfast, no matter how great the cold, and have often washed my feet in the same way, out-doors, in low temperatures. It is refreshing, but in amusing himself this way one must look sharp or he may get frost-nip, our pampered feet are so sensitive to cold."

The dark Arctic winter months passed pleasantly enough in the little house on Cape Tegetthoff, and often during the sunless days the men and the dogs were outside, busying themselves with preparations for the dash north, scheduled for early spring. Equipment was tested, there were outings filled with adventure, and there was also a lot of polar bear hunting.

"I think we had more fun out of polar bears," Wellman admitted, "than anything else." A memorable but "pathetic" occasion was when, Wellman recalled, "Mother and cub came ambling along the plateau side by side, and of course the dogs soon had the pair surrounded. When we arrived upon the scene, after a sharp run of a mile, the battle was in full course, with the dogs getting decidedly the best of it. The poor dam had been harried almost into a state of exhaustion. Still, she kept up the desperate struggle, and never once permitted her young hopeful to get five feet from her side. After each lunge at the nearest dog, she quickly returned to her baby, and this fat graceful little fellow did his best, you may be sure, to keep close under mama's protecting paws. It seemed impossible to shoot without hitting a dog, but I decided to risk it, and sent a bullet clean through her body. With the blood streaming from both sides, she continued to fight for her cub, and as more bullets crashed through her body and she felt her hour at hand, her last instinctive movement was to gather the little fellow to her breast with her fore-paws, that her tusks [*sic*] might give him protection to the last. Then," Wellman concluded, "she died."

With each sledge carrying 500 pounds of essentials, the expedition embarked for the Pole, stopping on February 18 at forward-base Fort McKinley nine days later; a journey of over a hundred miles. Paul Bjoervig, dressed in furs and his face blackened from months of burning driftwood and walrus blubber, met the travelers and led Wellman to a rock tunnel, pulling him down onto the ground. There, Wellman was greeted by a growling dog nursing her squeaky brood, and getting down on all fours, he followed Bjoervig through a small opening covered by a bear skin and into the "fort." Except for a smoldering blubber fire which offered no heat, it was dark and the ice encrusted roof was so low that Wellman bumped his head, and when he went to sit down he noticed that everything was white with frost.

"Poor Bentzen is dead," Bjoervig said, his black face streaked with tears, "I have not buried him, Sir. He lies in there."

As Bjoervig went about boiling some coffee, he explained that his dying comrade had begged his body be spared from the bears. "I shall never forget that moment," Wellman recalled of what Bjoervig had just told him. "At first the words did not appear to me to mean that very much, only that the dead man had not been buried. Gradually the full proportions of the tragedy dawned upon my consciousness. This man with the black face who was cutting up walrus meat and feeding the fire had been compelled to pass two months of the Arctic night in this cavern with no other companion than the body of his friend. I lit a little oil lamp, it was a bicycle oil lamp, and made my way into the dark end of the hut. On the floor at my feet lay a one-man sleeping bag, empty, with a blanket tumbled over it and showing signs of occupancy the night before. Just beyond within an arm's reach lay a similar bag. This one was occupied. The flap at the top had been pulled carefully over the face of the sleeper within. Bag and contents were frozen as hard as a rock. There, side by side, the quick and the dead had slept for eight weeks . . . I marveled that Paul Bjoervig was still sane."

After providing Bentzen with a proper Arctic internment complete with rock cairn, Wellman, the dogs, and the Norwegians continued their race north in minus forty degree weather. It was March 17, and on March 20 Wellman broke his right leg when it became lodged in a crack in the ice, the kind, he said, of "tiny little crack such as we had crossed everyday by the scores." It was a bad spot to have broken one's leg, as there were still 560 miles to go before reaching the Pole, followed by a further 700 miles of sledging back to Harmsworth House. With a broken leg, and probably even without a broken leg, it would have been suicidal for Wellman to continue, and there was nothing to do but admit defeat.

During the long trek south the expedition leader's suffering was intense, and he took out the handbook *Hints to Travelers* to see what could be done. "The patient should lie perfectly quiet," it recommended, and the injured leg "should be constantly bathed in hot water and be permitted to rest upon soft pillows." Having at last reached Harmsworth House, Dr. Hofma did what he could, but for almost four months Wellman lay in agony on the floor while Baldwin and the Norwegians made a survey of Franz Josef Land, thoughtfully naming the islands, capes, and straights after the expedition's financial backers. Then the steamer *Capella*, chartered by Arthur Wellman, Wellman's brother, arrived and Cape Tegetthoff was evacuated.

It took Wellman years to recover both physically and financially before he was ready for his third Arctic venture, and during this time he had come to the conclusion that lightweight motor sledges, weighing only 200 pounds, and which could easily be lifted over the ice hummocks and ridges by two stout men, was the solution. "I planned not only for the motor-sledge to pull loads . . . at an accelerated pace," he explained of his coming ice journey, "but a warmed hut for the men to sleep in." No sooner had Wellman struck upon the idea of motor sledges, though, than his attention was drawn to advances in dirigible flight.

Although Alberto Santos-Dumont's own dirigible days were behind him by this point, he freely gave advice to others. "Going to Paris the first of January, 1906," Wellman said, "I at once set on foot an exhaustive inquiry as to the practicability of motor-balloons in exploration. All the known experts and authorities were consulted." Among them was "Santos-Dumont, the young Brazilian who had done such valuable experimental work with motor balloons." The young Brazilian, he reported, "thought so well of our project that at one time he seriously considered joining me in the effort."

Wellman was evidently one of those people who make a great first impression, and in Paris he was invited to become a member of the Aéro Club of France, and also spoke before the French Academy of Sciences. And it was not only the French whom the handsome and gregarious American impressed, but also his own countrymen. The newspaperman's plans were taken so seriously in the United States that they were officially endorsed by none other than Alexander Graham Bell and the National Geographic Society. "The plans outlined by Mr. Walter Wellman for reaching the North Pole," the board of the Society resolved, "are carefully and thoroughly considered, and give good promise of success."[20] Just as importantly, the trip was backed, to the tune of over $250,000, by Victor F. Lawson, owner of the *Chicago Record-Herald*.

"Those early months of 1906 were days of feverish activity," Wellman recalled, "Perhaps it would have been better not to try to go on with the expedition that summer, but we Americans like to do things rapidly, and the rapidity of our operations astonished the slow-going people of Europe."

Preparations took on all the trappings of a military campaign. The trusty *Frithjof* was booked for the invasion of Spitsbergen, and to make hydrogen in that distant spot a hundred tons of sulfuric acid was to come from Hamburg and seventy tons of iron shavings from Norway. Also, mountains of processed ham were ordered from Armour & Company of Chicago, a shipload of timber and other building material was procured in Norway, clothing and instruments were obtained in London, steel boats were being constructed in Ohio, and boxes of malted milk were manufactured by the celebrated Horlick establishment of Racine, Wisconsin. Along with all this, pumping engines, a steam engine and boiler, lathes, drills, and tools for a machine shop came from England. Meanwhile Siberian Huskies, bought for seventy dollars apiece, were on their way from Russia. Wellman also did not give up on his motor sledges, and had prototypes built for him in Europe. Having been away at the time and unable to supervise construction, however, he discovered that the vehicles were much too heavy and would be worthless over ice.

The Wellman *Chicago Record-Herald* Polar Expedition, as it was officially called, was incorporated under the laws of the State of Maine, and Lawson became president, Frank B. Noyes, editor of the newspaper, treasurer, and Wellman general manager. In terms of the expedition itself, it would be comprised of Wellman as leader, Major Henry B. Hersey of the U.S. Weather Bureau as both meteorologist and airship navigator, and W. N. Fowler, M.D. of Bluffton, Indiana, as chief medical officer. Also recruited for the adventure was Felix Riesenberg, a young sailor from the U.S. Revenue Cutter Service. By way of foreigners, Wellman hired skilled machinists in Paris and about twenty-five mechanics and general workmen in Norway, among them Paul Bjoervig, formerly of Fort McKinley. Santos-Dumont in Paris was a technical advisor as were other famous Continental names in aeronautics, including Monsieur Goupil the well-known mathematician and, according to the *National Geographic Magazine*, "the greatest authority in France on aerial screws."

The contract to build the airship was awarded to Louis Godard of Godard & Surcouf, and Godard was assisted by a staff of engineers expert in every facet of airship design and construction. The craft was to be nothing like the puny specimens known to the United States. "Our polar dirigible is an entirely different sort of affair," Wellman stated, "Its great size enables it to lift not only the balloon, but the car of wood and steel, the three motors, comprising a total of eighty horsepower, two screws or propulseurs, a steel boat, five men, food for them for seventy-five days, instruments, tools, repair materials, lubricating oils, and 5,500 pounds of gasoline for the motors." To keep all this in the air, the airship's hydrogen bag would not be of varnished silk, as Santos-Dumont's and Andrée's had been, but instead made of layers of rubberized silk and cotton fabric pressed together for strength and impermeability. Every one of the thousands of seams was to be reinforced with overlapping material, and the stitching was to be covered with bands of cemented fabric, making the envelope rigid and virtually gas-tight.

The *Frithjof* arrived at Danes Island on July 8, 1906 and aboard was Wellman and the disassembled dirigible. Major Hersey and a construction crew had been deposited there by the ship a month earlier, but sailing into Virgo Harbor, Wellman was disappointed to see that "Camp Wellman" was still without the big balloon-house. With no time to spare, a location next to Andrée's former home for the *Örnen* was chosen, and the men got to blasting out ice and rock to prepare the site for foundation work. Busy enough, all summer long Wellman had to contend with hundreds of camera-bearing visitors, disgorged from tourist ships and seeking autographs and asking innumerable questions. Even the Prince of Monaco, aboard the *Princess Alice*, paid a visit.

While anxiously waiting for the balloon-house to be finished, Wellman decided to put his mechanical staff to work assembling the car of the airship and starting up the motors. He was in for an unpleasant surprise. "The motors could not be made to work right," Wellman explained, "the driving gear went to pieces, and the propellers could not stand even half of the strain which it was designed to put upon them." It was a problem that had no fix at Virgo Harbor, and the flight north was cancelled.

Having returned from his latest, lavishly funded Arctic venture empty-handed once again, Wellman faced increased criticism that he was nothing more than a beguiling huckster. He was, after all, the same man who in an 1891 exclusive for the *Chicago Record-Herald* claimed to have found the exact spot where Christopher Columbus first stepped ashore in the New World, a remarkable find that up to then had eluded scholars (and still eludes them today). Wellman, however, genuinely believed that his Arctic venture was for the betterment of civilization, and that if it "must be regarded as either foolishly reckless or deliberately dishonest," he said, then it should also be known that it had been "commended by many men of science, particularly by those familiar with the art of aeronautics." Back in Paris after a fruitless summer spent at Camp Wellman, he was determined to enlarge and improve his airship, and for this was fortunate to have been introduced to Melvin Vaniman, an American engineer and an experienced hand in aerial affairs.

Vaniman suggested that Wellman's craft be fitted with a brand-new V-shaped car, 115 feet long and 12 feet wide, made of steel tubing and with solid wire rigging. Wellman liked the proposal because the commodious structure, once enclosed in oiled silk, could accommodate a three-man crew, ten dogs, one sledge, a small boat, provisions, repair tools and materials, 250 pounds of lubricant, 300 pounds of fresh water, and about three tons (1,200 gallons) of gasoline, enough for a cruising radius of 960 miles (assuming an average Arctic headwind of ten miles per hour). He agreed to Vaniman's suggestions, and additionally ordered that the dirigible's gasbag be lengthened from 165 to 185 feet to hold 258,500 cubic feet of hydrogen for 19,000 pounds lifting capacity. Motive power this time would come from a single ninety-horsepower Lorraine-Dietrich engine driving two steel screw propellers, each eleven feet in diameter. With these substantial modifications the airship, named *America*, would be twice as big as anything the French had, and thirteen times larger than the *Baldwin* just purchased by the U.S. government. Only Germany's radical new zeppelins could best *America* in size, but the zeppelins were reputed to be woefully underpowered, and so could never survive the Arctic.

Wellman's plan for his fourth Arctic venture was not necessarily to reach the North Pole in the *America*, although that was his preference, but to get near enough that a sledge could cover the final miles. And should misfortune strike the airship at any point along its journey, there would be enough food and equipment to provide the crew, taking shelter under the dirigible's deflated hydrogen bag, with everything it needed for ten months' endurance; long enough to winter on the ice before sledging back to Spitsbergen in the spring. Survival provisions were to be carried in the airship's "equilibrator," a 1,200-pound contraption never before seen in the annals of aviation. "Our equilibrator," Wellman explained, "was the much talked of 'stuffed serpent' or 'sausage,' a long steel-scaled cylinder of leather, water-tight, [and] buoyant." The serpent, encased in a coat of armor, was intended to drag along the ice in the same manner as a guide rope, keeping the *America* at a steady height.

The *Frithjof* broke up enough ice to enter Virgo Harbor in June, 1907, and who should greet the ship but the faithful Paul Bjoervig, having wintered at Camp Wellman. To Wellman's relief the balloon-house was intact (he had cut some corners in its construction the previous summer to save time), but then a July 4 storm nearly wrecked the building. Reconstruction efforts delayed the first flight of the *America* and a series of gales delayed it further. Wellman was impatient to be off and, according to him, "The big ship also seemed eager to try her wings in the element for which she had been designed, as she constantly strained at her leashes and set up such violent swaying to and fro under the influence of the air currents which crept in the cracks of the building that at times we doubted our ability to hold her fast." To his extreme frustration, bad weather continued and soon enough the Arctic summer had ended, another year lost.

Last-minute guests, a group of German officers sent to study the airship, however, showed up in early September aboard the steamship *Express*. With the *America* in perfect flying condition it would, Wellman thought, be a shame to pack it up without first demonstrating its potential, so he hitched the craft to the *Express* and had the ship tow it out and around Smeerenburg point. Hovering over Virgo Harbor and off the stern of the *Express*, the dirigible made for an imposing sight. Although built by the French, the *America* certainly had an "all-American" look about it, with its fat, cigar-shaped gasbag above, its long car slung

AUTHOR'S COLLECTION

The airship America *at Spitsbergen.*

below, resembling an Indian war canoe, and its large powerful propellers jutting business-like from its sides.

The flight represented Wellman's first time aboard the dirigible or, for that matter, any dirigible. "The engine was started," Wellman recalled, "and the *America* leaped forward. With a thrill of joy we of the crew felt her moving through the air. Looking down from our lofty perch, we could see the equilibrator swimming along in the water, its head in the air, much like a great sea-serpent. We soon ran away from the steamer, and could hear the men upon her cheering us as we lost sight of her. Soon the wind freshened from the northwest, accompanied by snow. We were in danger of being driven upon the mountainous coast, which would mean the destruction of the ship and probably the loss of our lives as the steel car went tumbling down the cliffs into the sea."

Vaniman ran the engine, Reisenberg took the helm, and the three aerial explorers fought their way past jagged mountains, frequently averting catastrophe by mere inches. Yet the open Arctic Ocean beckoned, the Pole was within reach, and the desire for adventure irresistible. "Head her North!" Wellman cried as the *America* ran into a snow squall of increasing violence. "Just then we learned that our compass had been deranged by an accident," he explained, "The air was so thick with flying snow we could not see the mountains, and were lost in a snowstorm threatening to drive us to destruction upon the coast." Three times they came so near the snowy peaks that they thought it was all over, and each time Vaniman's skill with the engine and Reisenberg's adeptness with the wheel saved their lives.

The war with the snow squall was a bitterly fought affair which stretched out for thirty-five miles and lasted two hours before it was over. The snow squall won. "There was but one thing to do," Wellman concluded, "and that was to try to land the ship where she could be saved. In a momentary break in the thickness of the weather we saw before us a glacial mass of ice filling a valley between two mountains and decided to make an effort to bring the *America* down upon its smooth surface." The valve cord was pulled, the airship descended, and then a ripping knife—kept aboard for just such emergencies—was run into the sides of the huge envelope overhead. "The gas rushed out, with a sigh the *America* gave up her life-breath, and settled down," Wellman recalled. He looked below him and into the deep precipice that the car was astride of and, to his satisfaction, he could see the equilibrator, having been severely tested, hanging there perfectly.

When Wellman returned to the United States he faced renewed criticism that this, his fourth Arctic venture, had been nothing but a tawdry scheme to promote Lawson's *Record-Herald* and its advertisers, but if it had been such a scheme then apparently Lawson thought it an effectual one, and plans were made for a repeat performance the following year. In the meantime, Lawson put his intrepid journalist to work covering the 1908 presidential elections. Howard Taft grabbed the headlines with his landslide victory, but sometime also that fall, probably buried in the back pages, readers might have noticed a brief mention that the gallant *Frithjof* had gone down off the coast of Iceland, all hands lost save one.

Unfortunately, the motor schooner *Arctic* proved an unsuitable replacement for the *Frithjof*, and despite its name was stymied by the smallest amount of ice. The captain wanted to turn back but Wellman's brother Arthur said, "No, never. Walter ordered me to go to Camp Wellman, and to Camp Wellman we are going, if it takes all summer." It was the spring of 1909 and who should greet the *Arctic* at Virgo Harbor but Paul Bjoervig, alone with several dogs. "Again," explained Walter Wellman, "the fates had played him a cruel trick. He and his comrade were out hunting on the sea-ice one day during the winter, when an ice-cake turned turtle, the man fell into the icy seas, and was lost. Once more, Bjoervig was the sole survivor of an Arctic wintering party." Wellman, Vaniman, and the rest of the expedition arrived on the second voyage of the *Arctic* three weeks later. Thankfully, Lawson had generously loaned them all the old Wellman *Chicago Record-Herald* Polar Expedition property including the dirigible, and so Wellman and his men did not have to build this, his fifth Arctic venture, entirely from scratch.

The first order of business was to clear away the remnants of the balloon-house, victim of severe storms, and build a new one, and this was done in record time. The next order of business was to assemble and inflate the *America*, which, since its emergency landing astride the precipice two years earlier, had been rebuilt in Paris. The airship was larger now, and Vaniman had installed two engines, a main one augmented by a reserve motor. The dogs, sledges, boat, and enough provisions to spend the winter on the ice if necessary, were readied for flight just as they had been in 1907, although this time the aerial crew would comprise four men. Wellman remained as commander, but replacing Reisenberg as helmsman was a dashing young Russian named Nicholas Popov, and assisting Vaniman with the two engines was another new man, Vaniman's brother-in-law, Louis Loud. Aided by good weather, on a fine August day the *America* headed out across Virgo Harbor.

"One look back at our camp showed the men there waving their hats in excited glee and running for the hilltops," Wellman said, "the better to see the airship as she moved towards the northern horizon. It was with inexpressible joy we of the crew noted how strong and fast we were going north. The engine was running steadily. The ship was not pitching or rolling. The equilibrator seemed to be riding well. Helped a little by the breeze, we were making close to twenty-five knots per hour, northward, toward the Pole."

The four aeronauts rounded Smeerenburg point and the sizable *America* pushed through the clear air and up the Spitsbergen coast. Progress was rapid and quickly the inept *Arctic*, trying to follow, was out run, soon appearing as a mere a dot on the waters.

A confident Wellman handed the wheel over to Popov and climbed to the upper deck to consult the compass. He took a bearing and then looked down approvingly at Popov at the wheel in front and at Vaniman and Loud tending to their engines in back. It was a scene of tremendous satisfaction, and he knew that in only thirty hours, he and his able mates would be at the North Pole. Wellman then got back to work, writing up the log and preparing the data for the navigation of the ship. He glimpsed over the side of the car and checked the waters below. They were specked with ice. Then he saw something drop—could he believe his eyes? "Yes," he said, "it was the equilibrator."

The vast leather-and-steel serpent crashed into the sea, carrying with it all of the expedition's emergency rations, and suddenly 1,200 pounds lighter, the *America* shot up into the clouds. During the uncontrolled ascent the crew's ears rang as the atmospheric air pressure dropped precipitously, the temperature grew colder and, Wellman said, "The whole northern part of Spitsbergen spread out in one great frozen picture before our eyes, and I imagined that away in the east I could see Walden Island where the old *Ragnvald Jar* had been crushed in the ice in 1894. Would the Arctics [*sic*] never bring me anything but bad luck?" At its great altitude strong winds carried the airship far over the icepack while the Spitsbergen coast faded in the distance. Sixty or seventy miles the *America* roamed, when finally Vaniman, tugging on the valve line, was able to release sufficient hydrogen for the craft to begin a slow descent.

Having gained mastery over the situation, Wellman ordered that the "retarder" be lowered. The retarder was a leather tube weighing 400 pounds and covered with spikes that ended in a noose of steel cable. The device looked like a giant medieval weapon, but was really an emergency-brake designed to snag itself onto the ice; and this, Wellman learned, it did all too well. "We fought our way south, mile by mile and hour by hour," he said, "often delayed by the cable loop fouling anew in the ice below, but still making headway, the *America* giving a right good account of herself."

Popov went back to feed the frightened huskies, and his voice could be heard reassuring them in Russian when a ship was sighted. It was the *Fram*, now under the command of Captain Isachsen, and the famed vessel that, beginning in 1893, had spent the next three years deliberately locked in ice during Nansen's failed attempt to float across the top of the globe. The distance between sea ship and airship was considerable, and only after several hours of moving toward each other did the *Fram* and *America* meet and consummate a union of sorts. The airship lowered its line and the steamship caught it and began towing the airship homeward. The airship, however, did not tow well and ran up alongside the steamship, jerked back with a shock, and then swung to the other side with another jerk. When the wind strengthened, all of this jerking threatened to tear the steel car apart and, to prevent this, Wellman released gas until the *America* was just touching the surface of the water. For safety's sake, towing was temporarily halted so that dogs and instruments could be transferred to the *Fram*. When towing recommenced, Wellman, ignoring the gigantic gasbag overhead that still contained enough hydrogen to have blown all to oblivion, lit a cigar and contemplated his most recent failure.

Late that evening and after a 120-mile round trip to nowhere, the *America* arrived safe and secure at Virgo Harbor, but as the unmanned dirigible was maneuvered into the balloon-house a gust of wind hit it, tilting the car, spilling the engines to the ground, and tearing the gasbag free. The bag rose high in the air, ruptured, and, weighing two tons empty, plummeted back to earth. The catastrophe was only partial, however, because upon examination engines, gasbag, and other parts were deemed salvageable, and so before Camp Wellman broke for the season, its namesake ordered that the balloon-house be lengthened for use again in 1910.

Upon his return to Norway, however, Wellman was met with devastating news: the race to the top of the world had been won, and by sledge, back in early April by Robert E. Peary. "How much trouble," he lamented, "I could have saved myself if I had only known that Peary had reached the Pole before I sailed from America!" Wellman was convinced, and arguably so, "that if the airship had had one or two years more in which to be perfected and developed, the victory would have perched on its banner." Peary's claim to have reached the Pole in the time he claimed to have reached it, however, meant that he, his sleds, and his dogs would have had to maintain the fantastic pace of a hundred miles a day. Critics thought this an utter impossibility over treacherous Arctic ice, but

Wellman accepted defeat. The newspaper man had, though, other ambitions besides reaching the Pole, and one of them was to be the first to fly the Atlantic.

Interest in Wellman's latest venture was strong, and he raised $40,000 from the *New York Times*, the *Chicago Record-Herald*, and, on the other side of the ocean, the London *Daily Telegraph*. The rest of the needed funds came out of his and his crew's pockets. The airship *America* had again been loaned to him by Lawson, and preparatory for what would be, incredibly, only its third flight, the airship's gasbag was lengthened forty-one feet to hold 345,000 cubic feet of hydrogen for 23,650 pounds of lifting force. It took more than one hundred tons of sulfuric acid, sixty tons of iron shavings, and hundreds of tons of water to generate all the hydrogen needed to fill the vast bag, and the cost, including the labor of ten men working each shift, night and day for a week, was $5,000. Vaniman also fashioned a new car for the dirigible, 156 feet long and 8 feet wide, and attached it to the gasbag by 188 hemp cords. No dogs were allowed on board this time, just a cat, and celluloid windows were placed at intervals along the side of the car to give man and beast a view of the ocean during the journey.

As before, the *America* had dual power comprising a big eight-cylinder engine augmented by a smaller, four-cylinder one, although now the engines were driving not two, but four propellers. Wellman calculated that 200 hours of motoring time would be needed to reach Europe 3,500 miles away, requiring 9,000 pounds of gasoline and oil. The gas was stored in both of the airship's bunkers, which ran along the bottom of the car, and in its equilibrator, which had been refashioned into a flexible chain of thirty steel gas tanks connected to each other by means of a tube. Press interest in Wellman's newest gambit was intense, and to provide the outside world with reports of its progress, the dirigible was equipped with a 250-watt Marconi radio.

Predictably, Wellman had not test-flown his airship preparatory to its Atlantic flight, but even if he had wanted to, the time had now passed since he was already badly behind schedule. Therefore when the conditions were right (on Saturday, October 15, 1910, at 8 a.m.), he seized the moment and had the *America* towed from its new $12,000 wooden hangar at Atlantic City and a short distance out to sea. Despite a favorable weather forecast, however, the usually confident Wellman was not sure all would go well, but felt compelled to leave for Europe because the press and public had questioned his resolve.

"Mr. Wellman is still hardening himself for the journey at the Hotel Chalfonte," a reporter from a rival paper had mocked just the day before, explaining that "Since August 1 he has followed the Spartan regimen he set for himself without complaint. As usual through the hard and trying period of preparation, Mr. Wellman left his rough Louis XIV couch on the side of the Chalfonte that is entirely exposed to the uncouth and untamed ocean at 8 o'clock this morning. Continuing the usual course, he bathed in water heated to not more than 95 degrees . . . At the breakfast table Mr. Wellman ate the frugal but sustaining meal which wide experience at the wildest hotels along Broadway and other channels of travel has taught him is best for adventurers. He rarely has more than steak, eggs, buckwheat cakes, potatoes, fruit, biscuits, and coffee for breakfast. A pause in training might be expected here, but Mr. Wellman is made of sterner stuff. He returned to his room, got his strength together, and when a newspaperman called up and asked 'when the old gas-bag was going up,' Mr. Wellman told him to go where a gas-bag would explode."[21]

In addition to being the butt of jokes, before the flight Wellman also had to contend with interminable delays, some of them because the rebuilding of the airship, under Vaniman's supervision, was plagued by weight problems. The dirigible's lifeboat was supposed to weigh 1,000 pounds, for instance, yet tipped the scales at 1,800 pounds, and as a result of this and other overruns the *America* emerged from its shed that Saturday morning 4,000 pounds heavier than intended.

Fifteen minutes after being towed from Atlantic City and into a fog-shrouded ocean, the large eight-cylinder engine was fired up and then promptly shut down. Frantically working over the motor, Vaniman and his two assistants, Loud and a new addition, Fred Aubert, could not get the thing to work properly. As a result, the bloated and underpowered *America*, vibrating considerably, hugged the water and inched out into the Atlantic while dragging behind it, like an enormous ball-and-chain, the equilibrator loaded with 13,000 gallons of gasoline. The large engine worked weakly in fits and starts and the smaller engine put in an equally dismal performance. That first day the airship enjoyed the benefit of motive power for only four hours in total. What little progress the transoceanic adventurers made was almost entirely due to a quiet sea, and a gentle wind blowing in the right direction.

Besides Wellman, Vaniman, Aubert, and Loud, also on board was Murray Simon, the navigator, Jack Irwin, the Marconi operator, and a favorite with the press, the ship's mascot, Kiddo the cat. The start had been inauspicious and the situation worsened after nightfall. Unlike the Arctic where the summer sun shone constantly, off the eastern seaboard of North America the sun vanished at night and this cooled the airship's gasbag, contracting the hydrogen and causing a loss of lift. To avoid sinking into the ocean, therefore, Wellman was forced to open the bunkers and release gasoline, that precious fluid needed to run the engines if, he thought bitterly, the engines would run. Instead of trying to reach Europe, the challenge Wellman now faced was an easterly wind that threatened to blow him back to New Jersey and make him an international laughingstock.

Having given up on the large eight-cylinder engine entirely, Aubert and Simon finally got the smaller engine running so it wouldn't stop all the time, but the exhaust pipe, Wellman saw to his horror, grew bright red and spewed a thick shower of sparks. The gobs of fire flew aft along the varnished cotton enclosure of the steel car, still containing thousands of gallons of gasoline, brushed up against the vast hydrogen bag, hit the canvas rudder, and singed the American flag flying off the stern. "It seemed to me only a question of time," Wellman worried, "when one of these fiery, incandescent masses would lodge in some nook or cranny, set fire to the canvas, and bring our little world to an end." He cried to Vaniman to stop the engine. "It's been doing that all day," Vaniman assured, "it looks lots worse than it is."

The fog persisted and the fireworks emitting from the exhaust provided the only scenery around when, from out of the gloom, came the specter of a schooner dead ahead. Simon threw the wheel over, the *America* nearly scrapped the topmast, and sailors could be seen running around and shouting to each other on the deck a hundred feet below. But what they were saying was drowned out by the whir of the propellers and the clatter of the fire-spewing engine

All night long, Wellman and his crew waited for the moment that the engine would either stop for good or blow them to kingdom come, and in their anxiety no one slept. At 5 a.m. on Sunday, however, the engine was still running and the dirigible, all in one piece, was well out to sea and the humiliating prospect of crashing ashore had passed. It was decided therefore to give the engineers a rest and, instead of the motor, let the heavy gusts of wind from the southwest speed the airship along. While happy for the boost from the wind, the crew soon grew concerned that the equilibrator riding the waves below would be torn from the airship. To get the equilibrator partially out of the water the airship had to be lightened, so more weight in the form of a heavy cable, gallons of bunker gasoline, and various spare parts were tossed overboard. The wind took the sea-skimming dirigible 140 miles beyond Nantucket Island and into the busy transatlantic steamer lanes, and here the risk of collision with a speeding ocean liner was very real. To gain more altitude Wellman had his men disassemble and toss parts of the useless eight-cylinder overboard.

The *America*, however, continued to fly low and continued to be buffeted by heavy gusts, making the newest worry that the equilibrator, now bounding and leaping from wave to wave, would create so much strain on the wires holding it to the car that they would snap. Vaniman saw no reason to prolong the inevitable and urged that the lifeboat be lowered, but Wellman counseled patience and refused. Famished, the crew then had their first real meal since departure, sitting down to coffee, bacon, and fried eggs, as cooked by Aubert on a gasoline stove stored in the lifeboat slung under the car. It was now Sunday evening.

The airship was out of broadcast range but the Marconi wireless could still receive messages being beamed from stations on land and ships at sea up and down the Atlantic coast, asking each other if there had been any news of the *America*. Another anxious night passed and again the crew got no sleep. Two men at all times were assigned to keep watch on the equilibrator, and when too much of it became submerged a cry would go up to lighten the load again. Cans of lubricant, more gasoline, and more parts of the eight-cylinder engine were sent over the side. Periodically, Loud and Aubert were sent to investigate any unusual sounds for fear that might indicate that the airship was breaking apart. At midnight the wind shifted, blowing the dirigible away from Europe, and Wellman knew then that the end was at hand.

Throughout the early morning hours the dirigible was pushed toward the southeast coast of the United States by strong winds of between fifteen and eighteen knots per hour. Daybreak revealed clear skies and bright sunshine, expanding the hydrogen inside the heat-absorbing gasbag. The airship rose and the equilibrator emerged from the water to dangle straight down from the car like some obscene appendage. Vaniman, fearing a repeat of last year's high-altitude fiasco over the Arctic, reached for the nearest valve and opened it, but he reached for the wrong valve and instead of discharging hydrogen, discharged pressurized air, used to maintain the rigidity of the gas envelope. Because air is about twelve times heavier than hydrogen, its loss made the dirigible lighter and it rose still faster, until leveling off somewhere between 2,600 and 3,600 feet, causing the crew to experience a ringing pain in their ears. The view, though, was spectacular. "Overhead there are blue skies flecked with white flurries of passing clouds," Simon said, "We are all as happy as can be. I could do with a couple of months of this job."[22]

Vaniman managed to locate the correct valve and, losing hydrogen, the dirigible descended to two or three hundred feet above the ocean where, in an undignified manner, it spent some time rising and falling like a rubber ball, but it became evident that the deflated dirigible was mostly falling. Irwin told his mates to keep a look out for the steamer *Trent* which, he knew from experience, left Bermuda for New York on Mondays.

Neither the steamer nor any other vessels were sighted but fortunately the night was warm, which kept the remaining hydrogen from contracting, and then at 4:30 a.m. Wellman thought he saw the lights of a ship. To draw attention, Vaniman made a torch out of waste soaked with gasoline, lighted it, and suspended the blaze from a wire beneath the dirigible's car. Meanwhile, Irwin attempted to raise the ship, which was indeed the *Trent*, by radio but got no response. He then tried the electric blinker and this time the ship's officers answered, saying that they would standby for rescue. With every passenger, some weeping and praying, on deck to watch, the steamer tried to attach a line to the *America*, but it wasn't easy and for a panicked moment the dirigible's great

The end is near: America *as viewed from the* Trent, *October 18, 1910.*

gasbag became unbalanced and threatened to rise up and go end-over-end. A fast-acting Fred Aubert saved the day, however, by opening the correct valves and restoring the gasbag's equilibrium, and when that crisis passed Wellman decided not to wait around for another such to take its place. He swiftly ordered the lifeboat lowered. Soon Kiddo the cat and the four man crew were celebrities bound for New York.

"The last we saw of our good airship," Wellman said of the abandoned *America*, "she was floating about 800 feet high, 375 nautical miles east of Cape Hatteras. A day or two later, in all probability, she disappeared beneath the waves; the gas-valve was tied open when we left her, and the big steel gasoline reservoir, with a capacity of 1,600 gallons, had been cut open so the sea water could enter and sink it. With just a little

AUTHOR'S COLLECTION

Melvin Vaniman and Kiddo after their ordeal.

moistening of the eyes, Vaniman and I said goodbye to the big craft that had brought us so much trouble."

The curving course that the *America* took over the Atlantic with Wellman and his crew had shattered all records for human flight: over one thousand miles and seventeen and a half hours in the air. However, Walter Wellman considered it an abject failure, and although he lived until 1934 his feet would never again leave the ground. Vaniman, on the other hand, could not escape the grip of dirigibles so easily, and quickly made plans to set out from Atlantic City for Europe aboard an airship of his own design. He named the 400,000-cubic-feet giant airship *Akron* in honor of its sponsor and builder, the Goodyear Tire and Rubber Company of Akron, Ohio.

As could be expected of a Vaniman creation, the *Akron* had multiple innovations such as "orientable propellers" that could be used for both forward and downward thrust, a "hydrovelator" that sucked up sea water for ballast, engines that in an emergency could run on the gasbag's hydrogen, and a rail mechanism that shifted 600 pounds fore and aft to lower or raise the dirigible's nose. The *Akron*, though, was more balloon than airship, designed to drift with the wind with minimal engine use, thus sparing Vaniman the necessity of having to carry vast amounts of gasoline as Wellman had been forced to do in his infernal equilibrator. Vaniman never got to fly his promising concept across the ocean, however, because shortly after the cry "Let go all!" was given at Atlantic City on July 3, 1912, the *Akron*'s gasbag, for reasons unknown, ruptured at a height of 1,000 feet. As Vaniman's wife watched in horror from the front porch of their home nearby, the airship caught fire and plunged to earth, killing Vaniman and his four-man crew, among them his brother Calvin. With Wellman no longer interested in airships, and now with Vaniman's death, there was no one left to pilot the United States into the dirigible age. For the next decade Americans could only dream dreams while the Germans took the lead.

THREE

The Zepelins were an ancient family from the village of Zepelin in Mecklenburg, North Germany. By the year 1286 they were spelling their name with two p's, and in the 1700s a Zeppelin by the name of Ferdinand Ludwig went to South Germany by invitation of the King of Württemberg. A diplomat, Ludwig ably served the king and was made a hereditary count, but his son, Count Friedrich, had little interest in Württemberg officialdom and did not follow his father into affairs of state. In contrast, he preferred a quiet existence on the family estate close to the border with Switzerland and near the shores of the Bodensee (known in English as Lake Constance). His son, Count Ferdinand von Zeppelin, was born in 1838 and would have a lifelong affinity for the lake, launching his airships from above its waters.

Young Ferdinand spent his childhood years in the manor house with his parents and siblings. He received his early education from first his mother Amélie, an invalid and daughter of French émigrés, and then tutors of a modern, progressive bent. Although Ferdinand was of German aristocracy this was never impressed upon him as a child. Likewise, he and his brother and sister were spared the harsh Prussian discipline visited upon other children of their caste. Life in the Zeppelin household was ideal: wealthy, peaceful, isolated, harmonious, simple, and democratic.

If "little Ferdy" did have particularly notable attributes, they were his blue eyes and blond curly hair, which made him quite beautiful, as well as his strength and courage.[23] A strong swimmer even at an early age, one winter he accidentally broke through the frozen lake in the company of a playmate, who began to cry hysterically. Clinging to a piece of ice, Ferdinand sternly told his friend to calm down and crawl over the ice toward him and to grab hold of both of his hands. With those instructions, little Ferdy was able to save his own life. The German Revolution of 1848, when Ferdinand was ten, was to intrude upon his family's quiet existence when an uncle, Wilhelm, was wounded and was sent to Switzerland for treatment. Swiss guards sealed the border, and it became impossible to send Wilhelm a message. Chosen for a clandestine mission, Ferdinand hid a letter in his stockings and, riding a white pony and appearing quite harmless, was permitted to trot across the Swiss line.

The boy's mother became increasingly unwell and died when he was fourteen. By age nineteen, the gentle life by the lake long over, the young count was a lieutenant in the Eighth Württemberg Infantry Regiment. That Zeppelin, as a male aristocrat, would become anything other an officer was never in question, and his military career was nothing if not exemplary. Throughout his years in uniform the count was a loyal soldier, dedicated whole-heartedly to the mission at hand, and it was only after being forced from the army at age fifty-two that he turned his passion entirely to the construction of his first *luftschiff* (airship). But this would still be many years away.

Shortly into his army career, Zeppelin transferred to the Engineers Corps after completing one year of studies. Bored, in 1863 he received permission to cross the Atlantic to observe, from the Union side, the civil war then raging between the states. With a letter of introduction to President Abraham Lincoln, Zeppelin was granted an interview at the

White House. There he presented his credentials, careful to mention that he was from nobility. "Well," Lincoln assured, "that need not trouble you. That will not be in your way if you behave yourself."[24]

Zeppelin was granted an army pass to go and see whomever or whatever he pleased. He dined with Union generals and witnessed the Battle of Fredericksburg in Virginia, but as insurance in case he met up with the other side, in his pocket he kept a letter of introduction to General Robert E. Lee, given to him by Lee's niece in Philadelphia. Having seen enough of the war, Zeppelin joined a four-man expedition to trace the sources of the Mississippi. The men became lost, suffered from hunger and thirst, and almost died. They finally reached Saint Paul, Minnesota, and there the adventurer Zeppelin ascended several hundred feet in a balloon filled with poor-quality lamp gas. Whether he took this flight on a whim, or had long hoped for such an opportunity, is not known. Whether there was a relationship between this aerial ride and his subsequent fascination with air travel is also not known; it would be hard to believe, however, that there was not.

Württemberg entered the 1866 war between Prussia and Austria on the Austrian side, and Zeppelin became personal adjunct to the king. He took part in four battles and almost drowned when, in full cavalry regalia, he swam across the river Main to deliver an urgent communication to a headquarters on the other side. A modest man, he was embarrassed to receive the Military Cross for his actions. The war ended and by the time another war, this one between Prussia and France, broke out in 1870, Zeppelin was married and had a family. Württemberg joined its former adversary Prussia to fight the French, and Zeppelin volunteered for a dangerous mission deep into enemy territory. Leading a raiding party on horseback, he and his men reconnoitered the area while also cutting telegraph lines. The raiders were discovered during the second day, forcing them to disband. Zeppelin reached German territory and was the party's lone survivor. For this, and for subsequent acts of bravery, the count was again highly decorated.

The Franco-Prussian War provided the first use of balloons during wartime for purposes other than observation. The French had been overwhelmed by the superior Prussian forces and Paris quickly found itself besieged. Zeppelin was attached to the German General Staff Headquarters at Villiers on the outskirts of the city, and peering through field glasses he watched with interest as, from September 1870 to January 1871, Parisian aeronauts took to the air in their balloons. These one-way trips out of the city carried important persons, wounded soldiers, messages to the outside world, and carrier pigeons for return communications. Mostly, the dauntless aeronauts succeeded in their mission, but occasionally a change in wind direction resulted in capture. Parisians ultimately sent sixty-four balloons aloft, and the world's first airlift became one of the most colorful events in early aeronautical history. The airlift did nothing, however, to alter the outcome of the war (France lost), and based on his observations, Zeppelin concluded that a wind-borne balloon was of no military value. But this was not to say that air travel itself had no merit, and back in Württemberg, and in the peacetime army, the count became engrossed in Heinrich von Stephan's 1873 pamphlet, *World Post and Aeronautics.*

"Providence has surrounded the entire earth with navigable air," Stephan, who was the equivalent of Germany's postmaster general, wrote, "This vast air ocean . . . which, today, still lies waste and empty, is not yet used for human transportation."[25] Zeppelin became obsessed with the possibilities of aerial transportation, and without sharing his thoughts with anyone, for the next fifteen years read extensively on the relevant engineering, while also pondering the minutest of details as to how this could be achieved. Eventually, he arrived on the idea of the "rigid" dirigible.

Prior to the count's innovation, the only conceptualization of what "motor balloons"—if and when such things ever became feasible—should look like was that they must have a basket, suspended from a hydrogen bag above, to accommodate both aeronaut and engine. Yet Zeppelin took an entirely different approach. He initially thought of an air train with interconnected cars, but then settled on the prototype of what was to become the rigid dirigible. As he envisioned it, the rigid dirigible would be a ship of the sky capable of spanning immense distances. Its rigidity, giving it strength to withstand forward air pressure and the ability to support gondolas for crew, passengers, and engines below, would come from an elongated metal frame, covered by fabric. The hydrogen needed for lift would be kept inside the covered frame and divided into rubberized cotton cells, each cell free to expand or contract without affecting the oblong shape of the airship. And much like the water-tight bulkheads of an ocean liner, the multiplicity of hydrogen cells would assure airworthiness should one or more fail.

While engrossed in his secret passion, Zeppelin meanwhile rose in rank to become military attaché for Württemberg in Berlin, and he additionally held various political and diplomatic posts of great prestige. The count briefly broke his silence regarding airships in 1887 when he sent an unsolicited report to King Charles V of Württemberg on the desirability of obtaining such craft for "military purposes."[26] Charles may have been perplexed as to why his small principality needed such a thing, and nothing came of it. Zeppelin, meanwhile, continued on his upward career trajectory and was made Brigadier-General. Then for reasons not entirely clear, but which had to do with Württemberg–Prussian tension within a newly unified German army, Zeppelin was cashiered by Kaiser Wilhelm II. Suddenly retired at age fifty-two, Zeppelin was free to pursue his dream and, using his personal fortune, he hired an engineer to draw up plans for an airship. The reception his invention received at the Ministry of War in Berlin was cool but, on appeal to the kaiser, a special commission was convened to investigate its potential value. The initial finding was that Zeppelin's notion was "not impossible to execute," but then the final ruling, made on September 8, 1894, was that the rigid dirigible was "practically useless."[27] Zeppelin told the press, "I do not blame anyone for considering me a fool, but I am sure it is my duty to go on with my work steadfastly and to hold fast to my idea which I know is right."[28]

Two years elapsed as Zeppelin and his engineers worked on new plans, and then he prepared a memorandum to the Union of German Engineers, asking it to pass judgment. The Union complied and was so favorably disposed to his ideas that, in 1897, it appointed experts to help the count build his aerial colossus. Zeppelin formed a joint stock company "for the promotion of air navigation and dirigibles"[29] and, with half the money coming from his own pockets, raised a small fortune for those days, 800,000 marks. The money was put to use and on July 2, 1900, a fabric-covered aluminum craft was carefully towed (an earlier attempt ended in a costly repair bill) from its floating hangar on the Bodensee. The airship Luftschiff Zeppelin (LZ 1), was 420 feet long and 32 feet in diameter, had 400,000 cubic feet of hydrogen stored in seventeen cells (the gas arrived in 2,200 steel cylinders), two gondolas, and two 16-horsepower Daimler engines driving four propellers. Steering was by means of two small rudders, and pitch control came from a 550-pound weight that shuttled back and forth on a wire below.

With the count in command, the airship rose to over 1,300 feet and stayed airborne for about twenty minutes before landing three and a half miles away. To the tens of thousands of spectators who lined the shores of the lake, the flight was a triumph. However, any expert could plainly see it was exactly the opposite. During the abbreviated flight the little rudders got stuck, the feeble Daimlers were no match for the wind,

AUTHOR'S COLLECTION

With only the semblance of control, LZ 1 arises, July 2, 1900.

the 550-pound weight jammed on the wire, and the flying sausage, its frame visibly sagging in the middle, was ignominiously blown sideways at an awkward angle. The next day Zeppelin read in the newspapers that his aerial experiment had failed, which proved, according to one article, "conclusively that a dirigible balloon is practically unusable."[30] In October, two more flights of LZ 1 were undertaken with only marginally better results, but despite this the airship had caught the imagination of the German public, now swept up by "zeppelinism."[31] The government, engineers, and industrialists who had given money for the project, though, kept their emotions in check and, disappointed with the dirigible's negligible performance, pulled out of the scheme. Airship and hangar were taken apart, and it would be five long years before Count Zeppelin took to the air again.

The "crazy count," as he was called, lectured and spoke out forcibly in favor of another attempt, and Kaiser Wilhelm, who had earlier fired him from the army, was nominally impressed with the three flights over the lake and awarded him the Order of the Red Eagle, First Class.[32] The kaiser also promised a private audience, but then promptly forgot about it. The count was depressed but not despondent, and turned to his public.

He sent 65,000 fundraising letters, asking recipients "to sacrifice themselves for my undertaking and to support me in my persevering duty."[33] Only a few donations trickled in yet, buttressed by his call that a German dirigible be presented at the 1904 World's Fair in Saint Louis, Missouri, another fundraising campaign met with greater success, and enough money raised to build a second airship. Of equal significance, King William II of Württemberg became an ardent supporter, providing land, government funds, and revenue from a special state lottery so that Zeppelin could realize his dreams.

LZ 2 emerged from the floating hangar on the Bodensee, January 17, 1906. An improved version of LZ 1, its aluminum frame was lighter but stronger, and its two new Daimler engines weighed no more than the old ones had, yet produced five times the power. The propellers of LZ 2 were also much larger than before, and it had an advanced system of pitch control, employing internal ballast moved by pulleys.

The day soon came when, with the Daimlers running smoothly after having spent the past twenty-four hours in continuous operation, LZ 2 ascended from the lake in a bold bid to prove its worth. However, at 1,640 feet the thoroughly warmed-up engines faltered, the large propellers stopped, the advanced controls were overwhelmed, and the airship was carried along by a strong, southwest wind. The craft was last seen high over Friedrichshafen making good speed—but where to, no one knew. The count eventually brought the airship down near the town of Sommersried, twenty miles distant, late that afternoon, and had it securely tethered. By morning, strong overnight winds had wrecked the thing, and what could not be salvaged was chopped up for scrap. In terms of there ever being funding for an LZ 3, Zeppelin's wealth was by now exhausted (he had even mortgaged his wife's property), the Ministry of War in Berlin rejected his request that a special lottery be authorized, and the kaiser refused his plea for more money. The loyal King

William, however, agreed to a second Württemberg lottery, and barely ten months after the demise of Zeppelin's last airship, its replacement, LZ 3, was already flying.

The crazy count, the "old fool," was a German hero and no longer snubbed by authorities in Berlin.[34] A national lottery was created to assist him in the design and construction of more airships, funds for the same purpose were also included in the national budget, and the Ministry of War built the largest building Germany had ever seen. This was an enormous barn floating on the surface of the Bodensee. Supported by thirty-eight pontoons, it was 500 feet long, 82 feet wide, 75 feet high, and, perhaps unwisely, was made of iron. Before it sank during a December 1907 storm, the building had served as home to LZ 3 during the time that the airship was demonstrating its airworthiness in front of German royalty, military officers, government officials, and high society.

In Germany, all things Zeppelin became the fad and, taking advantage, the count asked that Berlin reimburse him 500,000 marks for his airship work over the years. He also insisted that government money be readied for LZ 4, and the authorities acceded to both demands, only requesting that this newest airship, to prove its military value, be able to stay aloft for twenty-four hours and, in that time, travel 450 miles.

Initial flights in the larger and more powerful dirigible were satisfactory, and on August 5, 1908, Zeppelin took twelve observers up for his second trial run over the Alps. Although engine problems required a brief landing, and the requirement of 450 miles in twenty-four hours was not met, LZ 4 did fly a total of 380 miles before it needed to settle down for engine repairs. The unmanned airship was held to the ground at Echterdingen near the Daimler factory by a company of soldiers before, unexpectedly, a squall caught the dirigible and heaved it into the air. Wisely, the soldiers let go, and their charge floated away at an altitude of 500 feet, descended, hit some trees, and exploded. By the time the count, who had retired to a hotel for food and a well-deserved rest, reached the scene, LZ 4 was nothing more than twisted and melted alloy. He, according to observers, had suddenly become a very old man.

Paradoxically, the LZ 4 disaster became an epiphany in the count's crusade, and came to be known as the "Miracle of Echterdingen."[35] Although ending in debacle, the epic flight had ignited the Teutonic imagination, and in a fit of patriotism for the Fatherland—and of hero worship for Count Zeppelin—men, women, and children donated over six million marks for LZ 5. And the good citizens of Germany got what they paid for. On Saturday, May 29, 1909 the nation's newest rigid dirigible, with the seventy-one-year-old Zeppelin at the helm, ascended from the shores of the Bodensee and remained aloft for thirty-eight hours, covering a distance of 690 miles. All of Germany basked in the count's glory, and the fact that LZ 5, upon landing at Göppingen, impaled itself on a pear tree was of no import.

As with its predecessor, LZ 4, LZ 5 was equipped with a narrow vertical shaft leading from a gondola forty feet up through the aluminum framework and hydrogen cells to an open-air platform on top. From that high vantage point astronomical studies could be conducted—or a machine gun placed. The count was a military man who had witnessed war, participated in battle, and had no fear of the fight, and German society in the early years of the twentieth century was marching in a martial direction. In accordance with the national mood, Berlin's response to the public's demand for airships was to order them for the army and navy, and Count Zeppelin, naturally, had no objection. "The German people's desire to send out airships built on my system to conquer the world," he said, "will give me the courage and strength to continue my undertaking."[36] LZ 3 was given to the German army to become Zeppelin I (Z I) early in 1909, to be followed by Z II and a further requisition for Z III. While the first two airships soon passed from the scene, and

AUTHOR'S COLLECTION

The pride of Germany, LZ *5 hovers near the floating hangar on the Bodensee.*

the third was never delivered, by mid-1914 the army had seven newer ones in service. To avoid inter-service rivalry, in 1912 the German navy received Luftschiff 1 (L 1), at the time the largest airship in the world, and soon after, L 2, which was smaller but, with its twin 180-horsepower engines, more powerful than those that came before. By early 1914 the navy had additionally ordered a third example, L 3.

Like Andrée and Wellman, Count Zeppelin was not immune from the pull of the Arctic, and in 1910 he led the German Arctic Zeppelin Expedition aboard the steamer *Fönix* to Virgo Harbor. There he ascended in the expedition's balloon and, with all of Spitsbergen laid out before him, was introduced to the wonders of polar flight. Upon landing, the count sledged for miles around to find the best spot for an airship base. While his plans for an air trip to the North Pole went no further than this, back home in Germany the expedition revived public interest. "People were again beginning to doubt the future possibilities of my airship; people did not seem to realize that my airships will be the safest means of transportation over distant seas. It was necessary," the count explained of the expedition, "to convince people with actions."[37]

At the recently enlarged Zeppelin works at Friedrichshafen on the shores of the Bodensee, military orders were slow in coming, and so the count formed the Deutsche Luftschiffahrts-Aktiengesellschaft (German Airship Travel Corporation), a cumbersome name shortened to "Delag." The Delag's business was to purchase and fly airships for passenger service, and local municipalities and businessmen, vying for the honor of hosting a "zeppelin" (the dirigible now being synonymous with its inventor) subsidized the venture. The first Delag ship, the aptly named *Deutschland*, was ordered in November 1909, and designed to carry twenty people willing to pay the hefty airfare of 200 marks apiece. LZ 6A, with room for only twelve customers, was the next one to be delivered, followed by the second *Deutschland*. After that came the popular *Schwaben*, capable of speeds up to forty-four miles per hour, and having the ability to host twenty-five guests in its nicely appointed compartment amidships, where all were served champagne and a cold luncheon. None of the Delag zeppelins were put into scheduled service, however, and they never flew in winter. As goodwill ambassadors of Count Zeppelin's organization, the Luftschiffbau Zeppelin (Zeppelin Airship Company), their task was instead to carry paying sightseers for short excursions and, as importantly, to impress dignitaries who rode for free. And to cement public support, the giants of the air visited all corners of the Fatherland, and literally gave every German the opportunity to see a zeppelin soaring in the skies above. For Count Zeppelin this was the best publicity money could buy, and in its five years of pre-war existence, the Delag conducted 1,600 flights, flew more than a 100,000 miles, and carried 30,000 passengers. The Delag, however, also lost the majority of its airships to accidents, and it was a miracle no one was ever killed.

Having commenced operations in 1910, by 1911 all three of the Delag's zeppelins had been destroyed. The first to go was the *Deutschland*, just delivered from the Zeppelin factory. It was on a demonstration run with twenty-three journalists on board when strong winds blew it backwards, one of its three Daimlers failed, and, in command, Captain Kahlenberg was unable to prevent the ship from rising to 3,600 feet. The journalists were then treated to a nine-hour (six hours longer than advertised) ride, while being buffeted throughout by high winds and heavy rains. Finally the zeppelin crashed into the Teutoburg Forest, coming to rest on pine trees, thirty feet from the ground. One person broke their leg climbing down and, after just one week in service, the *Deutschland* had to be written off. Kahlenberg was sacked. The next to go was LZ 6A, which had only been flying for three weeks, and yet to be named. It exploded by accident in its shed at Baden-Oos but fortunately no one was injured. The last to perish was the second *Deutschland*, successor to the one destroyed, and it met its end when, in the course of leaving its shed at Düsseldorf, it was caught by a gust of wind and damaged beyond repair. That airship had been in service but five weeks.

With its entire zeppelin fleet now eliminated, the Delag had to consider the wisdom of staying in business. After a brief debate, however, the decision was made to take a final gamble, and soon thereafter the *Schwaban* was delivered. Although the *Schwaban* eventually went the way of the second *Deutschland*—destroyed on the ground at Düsseldorf—before doing so it compiled an accident-free flying record of 480 hours, hence becoming the most reliable zeppelin built to date. Somewhat smaller than the two *Deutschland*s, the *Schwaban* had a modified tail plane of rudders and elevators for better flight control, and it also had the more powerful and reliable Maybach engines instead of the disappointing Daimlers. Having hit upon a winner, the Delag went on to order three more ships of the same class: the *Viktoria Luise*, *Hansa*, and *Sachsen*. All survived until civilian flight ceased in 1914, and all served as invaluable training platforms for Germany's wartime airships.

While the Delag may have been plagued by zeppelin accidents, these had resulted in neither serious injury nor death. In contrast, the German Navy had been having an altogether lethal time. The first naval zeppelin, L 1, had crashed off the German coast on September 9, 1913, killing the head of the Naval Airship Division and thirteen others. Shortly thereafter, October 17, the just-delivered L 2 exploded over Berlin, and all twenty-eight aboard, including one of the airship's chief designers, Felix Pietzker, perished. The twin tragedies represented the world's first two worst air disasters, and also the first fatalities associated with the count's invention. Then with the outbreak of European hostilities, August 1914, it was the army's turn to suffer. LZ 6 was shot down by ground fire on August 6, and LZ 7 and LZ 8 were similarly downed on August 23, and then on October 7, LZ 9 was bombed from the air in its shed at Düsseldorf.

The elderly count had been busy designing a metal-clad three-million-cubic-feet dirigible, capable of cruising to the United States, when war broke out. He donned his old uniform, barracked with his old regiment at the Front, but despite intense lobbying, was forbidden to fight. His offer to become an admiral of airships was equally unsuccessful, and to add insult to injury he was pushed out of the organization he had created, the Luftschiffbau Zeppelin. Now run by the government, the Luftschiffbau began work on the L 10–type zeppelin, of which twenty-eight would be produced.

Like all zeppelins, the L 10s were prohibitively expensive to build. Additionally, they consumed vast amounts of resources in terms of the

AUTHOR'S COLLECTION

One the eve of war: Count Ferdinand von Zeppelin (right) during the 1913 Imperial Maneuvers.

millions of man hours needed for their design and fabrication, and they required an inordinate amount of duralumin, a German-invented alloy of which the L 10's frames were constructed. The results of these sacrifices, though, were impressive. The hulls of the L 10s were 530 feet long and 60 feet wide, held a million cubic feet of hydrogen, and were more streamlined than anything seen before. The L 10s could cruise at 11,000 feet and carry two tons of explosives and incendiaries, while locomotion came from four Maybach C-X engines generating 840 horsepower and allowing for speeds of sixty miles per hour. Equipped with radio compasses for navigation and able to fly 2,700 miles without having to refuel, the type was ideal for long-range operations.

The German public fully expected that zeppelins would bring the war to a swift and satisfactory conclusion. Captain Peter Strasser, trained on the *Sachsen*, took over as Commander-in-Chief of the Naval Airship Division after the loss of L 1, and fully concurred with the public's expectations. Strasser was an aggressive proponent of air power, and like many Germans longed to strike at the enemy's financial heart, the Bank of England and the Stock Exchange, located in the center of London. Kaiser Wilhelm, though, had "very serious scruples" about doing so.[38] First, there was the matter of international law. Civilians would inevitably be killed, and bombing non-combatants was against the Hague Convention. Second, Germany had to consider the danger of a misplaced missile hitting St. Paul's Cathedral or other historic sites. And third, wayward ordinance might injure or kill his cousins George and Mary, the King and Queen of England. The German army, determined to keep the German navy in its place, which was out to sea, meanwhile put up a fierce fight to prevent the airship service from expanding its role beyond naval reconnaissance. It was not until August of 1915, exactly one year after war started, that the last of these obstacles was removed, and Strasser was able to launch an unrestricted zeppelin campaign against England. That campaign began in earnest on the evening of August 17.

In the darkness, bombs from L 10, captained by Friedrich Wenke, spread wanton death and destruction across a northern stretch of London, miles from any banks or stock exchanges. Records show that on Baker's Avenue four flats were demolished: six people injured. At Baker's Almshouses, twenty tenements were slightly damaged. The tramway on Lea Bridge Road was destroyed, windows shattered, and a small fire started. The Midland Railway Station was also hit, wrecking the booking office and a nearby billiard hall. Next, the house at 153 High Road was damaged, as were fifty-three houses nearby: four people killed, fourteen injured. The structure at 117 Claude Road was wrecked and windows in 175 surrounding houses broken: three people killed. The house at 78 Oakdale Road was badly damaged and others less so: two people killed. St. Augustine's Church was gutted by fire. On Southwell Grove Road, two houses were badly damaged and 132 others slightly damaged: one person killed. Finally, at Wanstead Flats the last of the blasts broke windows in seventy-three nearby houses. Then from somewhere in the night sky above the devastated neighborhood, the eerie whine of engines and soft clatter of propellers could be heard as Wenke steered home.[39]

Three weeks later, army airship LZ 74, captained by Friedrich George, passed directly over the Tower of London and let loose its wrath on the populace below, killing eighteen people and injuring twenty-eight. Two other army dirigibles accompanied LZ 74 that evening, but lost their bearings and bombed helter-skelter, killing, among others, a husband, wife, and their three children. The next night the navy's L 13, commanded by Heinrich Mathy, made for central London, and when its work was done, which included delivery of a 660-pound explosive, the lifeless bodies of twenty-two Londoners had to be pulled from the rubble. (A year later Mathy met his own terrible end when his zeppelin erupted in flames over England, and not wanting to be burnt alive, and not having a parachute, he leapt to his death.)

The next raid in the series was October 14. That night L 15, captained by Joachim Breithaupt, maintained a parallel course with the Thames as it flew over the city, bombing in a straight line as it went. Four other zeppelins in the same squadron, however, became disoriented and blasted the city and surrounding countryside willy-nilly. From the German perspective the raid was not the knock-out punch hoped for (Breithaupt flew over but failed to bomb the Bank of England), but on the ground damage was severe. Scores of buildings were destroyed, and seventy-one people killed, making this the deadliest zeppelin raid of the entire war. Frustratingly for the British, searchlights brilliantly lit one of the ships, L 15, as it flew over the chimneys of London, yet neither guns nor airplanes could shoot the enormous target down.

"Baby-killers" is what British postcards called the "zepps," and fear of the aerial monsters, a condition half-jokingly referred to as "zeppelinitis," gripped the English populace. In Germany, the public's attention was likewise gripped by the zeppelin raids, but for a different reason: revenge. Military authorities in Berlin embellished the effectiveness of the raids to the point of pure fiction, but for the average German, suffering severe privation on the home front because of an English sea blockade, the fiction was good news. For the German citizenry it was comfort enough to believe that the British public, once thought safe and sound on their island fortress, were being hammered from the air. The German army, however, did not believe Berlin's propaganda and, to stem its aerial losses, which by the end of 1915 had amounted to ten zeppelins, ceded the airship war against Britain to the navy. Undoubtedly to his joy, Strasser now had all England to himself and redoubled his efforts.

On January 31, 1916, Strasser unleashed his aerial dreadnoughts. Under cover of darkness, nine zeppelins wended their way across the Channel to the British coast where, once ashore, they groped through English fog and roamed blindly over the Midlands. Down below, the unsuspecting Brits had no idea what the zepps were up to as the unseen monsters dropped explosives hither-thither. Other raids followed, such as the massive one of September 2, 1916, in which 54,000 pounds worth of bombs and incendiaries were dumped on England. Then, twenty-one days later, the Naval Airship Division relieved itself of 37,000 pounds of similar devices by also dropping them on England.[40] This was followed by twenty-nine year old Lieutenant Kurt Frankenburg's September 25 attack on Lancashire. As was usually the case with a zeppelin raid, in

Lancashire it was the innocents who died, as a list of the fatalities at one location, Kirk Street, Bolton attests:

Males	
An ironworker	aged 43
An ironworker	aged 42
A warehouseman	aged 34
A packing case maker	aged 62
A laborer	aged 36
Females	
A mother of five children	aged 44
A baby (daughter of the above)	aged 2½
A married woman	aged 40
A mother of two children	aged 36
A daughter of the above	aged 5
A married woman	aged 32
A mother of three children	aged 42
A weaver (daughter of the above)	aged 17[41]

By war's end, 557 deaths, almost all of them civilian, in England were attributed to the German airship in combat, but by late 1916 significant advances in British air defense systems had begun to take their toll on Strasser's crews as well, necessitating zeppelins that could fly higher and faster. These new dirigibles were the six-engine, two-million-cubic-feet ships of the L 30 class. The "super zeppelins," as the English called them, were not only the most rigid and aerodynamic ones yet produced, capable of a cruising speed of one hundred kilometers an hour at heights of 13,000 feet, but were also able to loft 11,000 pounds worth of bombs. The first of their class was delivered from Friedrichshafen by air to the navy on May 30, 1916 and, like a proud parent, aboard that day was Count Zeppelin.

Captain Strasser's raids, comprising up to seventeen airships, and sometimes led by the fearless Strasser himself, originated in Germany from one of many Naval Airship stations. The most famous was Nordholz with its cavernous twin shed that rotated 360 degrees on an axis. Noontime before a raid, the shed's entrance doors were swung away from the wind to protect the first zeppelin as it was led out by hundreds of sailors of the ground crew, known as "acrobats," who then rushed over to ready the second ship for departure. The sprawling base at remote Nordholz had its own gasworks for hydrogen and also contained huge stationary sheds, and from these more zeppelins emerged for that night's raid. Similar scenes repeated themselves in Ahlhorn, Hage, Tondern, and other bases as Strasser's ships were released into the air to rendezvous from all points at Heligoland Bight on the German coast. There the vast, forty-ton dirigibles gathered at sunset to hover a few hundred feet above the North Sea like a school of floating leviathans. Forming a loose squadron, the zeppelins then ascended from the Bight and, to the accompanying roar of over a hundred Maybach engines gaining speed, moved west toward their targets.

"The course our raids pursued was always the same," recalled zeppelin captain Treusch von Buttlar-Brandenfels, who was formerly commander of L 6, L 11, and L 30, but now led L 54 with a crew of nineteen. "The scene at our departure, the scene when twilight began to fall, when the darkness of night spread over the sea, and the first lights of the English coast began to gleam in the distance—all this was always the same, even to the great island suddenly plunging itself into the deepest gloom the moment the news of our raid had been reported to the authorities. Then came the same gleaming white searchlights, exploring every corner of the heavens for airships, until one here and there suddenly shone out all milky white; the same white clouds of shrapnel smoke, thinning out into diaphanous veils; the same red lights from the gun-flashes below on the ground, the same fires kindled by our bombs, which poured out pools of burning red flame."[42]

On this raid the captain's ship was caught by a searchlight, immediately followed by more. "Two, three, four!" he counted. "We were flying through a cloud of glaring light. I could read the smallest print on the map before me." English gunners on the ground were shooting 3,000 feet short, "But they corrected their range damnably quickly," he said. "Now they were getting very close indeed. We could hear the shells bursting all round and the whine of the splinters as they hurtled through space—high explosive shells. Should we climb higher," the captain wondered, "exhaust our last reserve strength, and, for the sake of 300 feet, risk being brought down by a hit, in which case all would be lost?" But then, "Suddenly on our port bow we saw a brilliant light, but no searchlight beam. It was deep and broad, a regular bank of light. The searchlight was penetrating a cloud. 'All engines full throttle.' We were saved! Up we climbed into the cloud. The next salvo would certainly have hit the ship if we had not been able to hide. I felt like shouting aloud for joy."[43]

Buttlar-Brandenfels had much to be joyful about, as did any of Strasser's men who made it back, because so many did not. For the Naval Airship Division, "The cost in personnel was proportionately greater than that of any branch of the German Navy," the historian Douglas H. Robinson notes, "exceeding, according to some figures, the percentage of losses in the submarine service." The historian continued that, "Of the 50-odd flight crews trained during the war, about 40 per cent were killed—40 officers, 34 warrant officers, 264 petty officers, and 51 ratings. A few of these died in industrial-type accidents at the bases—like L 30's sail maker, Johannes Heesen, who on August 14, 1916, was asphyxiated by hydrogen gas while working between the cells of the ship in 'Norman' hangar at Nordholz. But the majority was killed in combat or in flight operations."[44]

Strasser began his command with just one zeppelin, L 3, but during the war acquired sixty more. Three of these became training ships but forty-five met violent ends. A German list of losses included:

L 17 Caught fire and burnt in Tondern, December 28th, 1916.
L 18 Suffered the same fate, November 17th, 1915.
L 19 Shot down by British anti-aircraft fire and sank in the North Sea, February 2nd, 1916.
L 20 Stranded on the Norwegian coast, May 3rd, 1916.
L 21 Shot down over England, November 18th, 1916.
L 22 Shot down over England, May 14th, 1917.
L 23 Shot down near Jutland, August 21st, 1917.
L 24 Took fire and burnt in Tondern, December 28th, 1916.[45]

While thirteen zeppelins survived the war, the majority did not, and for these the average service life was just six months, with the average number of flights just thirty-five. Twenty-two of Strasser's zeppelins lasted no more than seventeen flights, and nine lasted not even ten flights; two being lost on only their second flight. A detailed tally of Germany's losses indicates that fifteen navy zeppelins were forced down by gunfire over land or water, that another fourteen were lost to accidents, that thirteen were shot down in flames, and that three were bombed on the ground.[46]

There were, of course, as many stories of how the zeppelins crashed, burnt, or blew-up as there were zeppelins that did so. Hit during a raid on London, August 1915, the crew of L 12, for example, managed to fly several more hours with three gasbags deflated before settling down in the English Channel off the coast of Belgium. All aboard were safe, if a little wet. An unidentified torpedo boat approached to take the crew prisoner when, to the crew's astonishment, the German war flag was raised. Now in friendly hands, L 12, commanded by Werner Peterson, was successfully towed to Ostend, but then destroyed when lifted by a salvage crane. Peterson's luck held out for another year when, on his eleventh mission over England, his brand-new L 32 was attacked by the Royal Flying Corps (RFC) and became a ball of fire. Zeppelin crews eschewed the newfangled parachutes because of the extra weight, and there were none aboard L 32 that night. A body, believed to be Peterson's, was found indented in a field on Snail's Hall Farm, and later buried by the RFC with full military honors.

Another of the many times an entire zeppelin crew was wiped out occurred on a beautiful fall afternoon, September 1915, when L 10, captained by Lieutenant-Commander Hirsch, arrived for a routine landing at Nordholz. Finding his ship too light to land, Hirsch ascended to valve off hydrogen. At that moment, the lovely weather was interrupted by the appearance of a squall, which enveloped L 10 in a cloud. The cloud, thought later to be electrically charged, suddenly turned bright red and from out of it the flaming mass of what once was an airship fell to earth. Then there was the case of L 19, which also lost its entire crew. The zeppelin failed to make a showing back at base after a London raid, January 31, 1916, and the mystery deepened as time passed and there was still no word. Finally, numerous messages in bottles were retrieved from the ocean, and one of them revealed, poignantly, the zeppelin's fate:

> My Dear Ada and Mother,
>
> It is now eleven o'clock on the morning of the 2nd of February. We are all still alive, but we have nothing to eat. This morning an English steam-trawler came up to us, but refused to rescue us. It was the *King Stephen* from Grimsby. My courage is ebbing away, and the wind is growing fiercer. Your loving Hans, who will think of you in heaven.

At 12:30 p.m. we all prayed together and bade each other good-bye.

Your

HANS[47]

At six o'clock one quiet morning, July 19, 1918, three British pilots displayed remarkable derring-do and good sportsmanship when they arrived at the Tondern air base unannounced. Already flying in incredibly low, and going even lower when the German anti-aircraft batteries began to bark, the three Englishmen, each in a tiny Sopwith Camel airplane, made straight for the giant airship shed. In seconds the shed, with L 54 and L 60 parked inside, had become a raging funeral pyre. Then the invaders buzzed around the base merely feet off the ground as dazed German sailors, many still in their underwear, spilled out of their beds and desperately fired rifles at them. The Brits could justifiably have used their machine guns on the armed horde below, but instead waved cheerfully as they dove under the Tondern high-tension wires, and were gone as quickly as they came.

The "black day for zeppelins,"[48] as it came to be called by Strasser's men, was October 20, 1917, after an attempted raid on Manchester and other industrial centers. Eleven ships had set out from bases at Nordholz, Tondern, Ahlhorn, and Wittmundhaven. As was not uncommon, the weather reports given out at Ostend and Heligoland Bight were incorrect, and what was predicted to be a light wind over England turned out to be a strong northerly gale. Blown southward, the aerial armada became lost over England and, although it had set out to bomb Sheffield, L 45 instead bombed London. At their great altitude over England, to their south, across the Channel in France, the zeppelins could glimpse in the darkness the fiery gates of hell. These were the killing grounds of the Western Front, brilliantly illuminated, as they had been for years, by explosions, star-shells, and rockets. Alarmingly for the zeppelin crews, the wind began carrying them directly over the Front, where they could easily be shot down. Buttlar-Brandenfels in L 54 managed to escape and to struggle home to Tondern, but back at the airship bases there was no report regarding seven of the other ten raiders. That evening came bad news. While L 52 and L 55 succeeded in traversing the Front (although L 55 was damaged in landing beyond repair), the rest were done for: L 44 fell to an onslaught of enemy planes; L 45 was hit, landed in France, and was torched by its crew; L 49 came down at Bourbonne-les-Bains and was captured intact; and L 50 was forced down in southern France with the loss of four men. The unfortunate four had failed to tumble out of the airship quickly enough with the rest of their mates, and now suddenly much lighter, L 50 had shot up into the sky and vanished over the Mediterranean.

The debacle at Ahlhorn during another gale, January 5, 1918, represented a second black day for zeppelins. The large aerodrome served as Strasser's headquarters and boasted four sheds with two more under construction. At the time it was home to a quartet of zeppelins. In the late-afternoon winter darkness, the sentry in Shed I heard what sounded like the crack of a pistol. "Who's shooting there? Who's there?,"[49] he shouted. No one answered, but the sentry saw tongues of fire leaping off the shed floor as the petrol tanks of L 51 ignited, sending sparks onto its stable-mate, L 47. Shed I was now consumed by flames and, blown by strong winds, burning embers rained down all over the place, some landing on and igniting three other sheds in which L 46 and L 58 were stored. The fire lifted one of the shed roofs clear into the air and, carried by the gale, it crashed onto the sailors' huts, killing fifteen men and severely injuring another thirty. The cause of the fire, sabotage or not, was never known, but four zeppelins ruined in one day was a severe blow. Strasser, though, stoically transferred his headquarters from the ruined

Ahlhorn base to Noldholz and, with his typical fanaticism, rededicated himself to the task of bombing England. By this point, however, the United States had entered the conflict, Germany was losing its struggle against the Allies, and as a weapon of war, the value of the Naval Air Division's zeppelin was in steep decline.

The opening stanza of the zeppelin campaign against the British mainland, 1914 to late 1916, saw the zeppelin triumphant. Strasser's crews could expect plenty of potential problems due to mechanical failure, faulty navigation, and bad weather, but they could also expect to operate over England with relative impunity. Despite having long fretted about German airships and their ability to wreak destruction from the air, when hostilities commenced, Britain was caught unprepared. The only home-defense aircraft available to tackle the zeppelin menace were obsolete fighters, and these rickety craft took as many as sixty minutes to reach zeppelin altitudes. Once there, British pilots faced the prospect of being shot down themselves because the zepps bristled with machine guns, found on their observation decks, on their tails, and attached to their gondolas. Rather than risk getting in close enough to fire their bullets, therefore, the British attempted to fly above their target and drop a hand-held explosive called a Rankin dart—and then pray for the best.

During the middle stanza of the zeppelin campaign, late 1916 to 1917, however, there was a dramatic reversal of fortune, and British postcards now depicted zeppelins falling from the skies in spectacular displays of fire. British air defenses on the ground, now numbering over 17,000 men, had improved in both quality and quantity, as had airborne defenses. The RFC now assigned some of its best fighter planes to the cause and armed them with two new types of bullets, one type explosive and one type phosphorous. Seeded together in the drum of an RFC machine gun, the new ordinance spelled death to the highly flammable zeppelins; the explosive bullets ruptured the hydrogen cells while the phosphorous bullets set them on fire. "The only answer to this was height," explained historian Peter W. Brooks of the German response. "Hence the intensive effort in the last half of 1917 to provide zeppelins with greatly increased operating ceilings. Strasser's indomitable will gave this effort impetus; his refusal to admit that his beloved zeppelins were being defeated was absolute."[50]

London was now heavily defended against air attack and off limits to zeppelins, but at the concluding stanza of the zeppelin campaign, mid-1917 until peace in late 1918, Strasser's hopes rested on the "height climbers" of the L 48 and L 53 classes. The lower portions of these modern and sinister-looking ships were painted a matt-black for nighttime camouflage, and each proudly bore the giant symbol of the Iron Cross. The height climbers were super zeppelins stripped to the bone for lightness, and thus capable of cruising at incredible altitudes of over 20,000 feet. Frostbite and nausea in the cold and thin air at those rarified heights, however, severely affected Strasser's men, and these problems were only partly alleviated by warmer clothing and a rudimentary oxygen system. Tremendous winds in the sub-stratosphere were also new dangers, and landmarks on the ground were difficult to discern even in cloudless weather. In fact, if accurate bombing had been nearly impossible at ten or twelve thousand feet up, it was totally impossible four miles high.

After withdrawing from the airship campaign against England in 1915, the German army deployed its airships along the Eastern front against the Russians, but here too losses were unacceptable, and in August 1917 the army grounded its remaining inventory. This left only Strasser and his men to continue the zeppelin war, and a year later, August 5, 1918, he led a bold raid against England aboard the ultimate height climber, the brand-new, seven-engine, 1,715-horsepower L 70,

AUTHOR'S COLLECTION

First flown May 22, 1917, and commissioned the next day, four weeks later the "height climber" L 48 fell victim to the RFC at 13,000 feet while on its first mission over England. Of the nineteen men aboard, three miraculously survived the zeppelin's seven-minute flaming descent to earth.

capable of speeds of nearly ninety miles per hour. Whenever present on one of his airships, Strasser deferred to its commanding officer, in this case Johann von Lossnitzer, who inexplicably approached the English coast relatively low and slow. Lossnitzer was caught over the water by British aircraft, and of the twenty-two officers and sailors aboard L 70, all perished. The next day the supreme commander of the German navy, Admiral Reinhard Scheer, sent a telegram to all air bases. It read: "As Count Zeppelin will live forever in the grateful memory of the German people, so also will Captain Strasser, who led our airships to victory."[51] But as history would attest, victory for "our airships" was not achieved, and the zeppelin raid for which Strasser gave his life was to be the last one of the war.

For Count Zeppelin the years after being forced out at the Luftschiffbau might well have been quiet ones spent in retirement near the Bodensee of his youth, but that was not the case at all. The seventy-six-year-old man, who at the start of hostilities declared that the British must "be held in constant quivering fear,"[52] had convinced German industrialist Robert Bosch to join him in a private venture to build an aircraft capable of dropping twenty-two bombs, each weighing 1,000 pounds, on England. Bosch agreed, and the riesenflugzeug (giant airplane) was born. Ironically, though, officials in Berlin preferred zeppelins over airplanes in the bombing role, and were skeptical of the count's "R-plane." However, when zeppelin losses over England became intolerable his R-planes were received enthusiastically, especially by the army, and were soon blasting England. The count lived to see his newest aerial innovation in action but, perhaps mercifully for the old patriot, not Germany's defeat. On March 8, 1917, Zeppelin died in his sleep. The King of Württemberg attended his state funeral.

FOUR

In the immediate aftermath of the war a weary public on both sides of the Atlantic yearned for peacetime diversions, and one of these was to see who would be first to cross that ocean by air. The Luftschiffbau considered doing so in L 72, completed just after the war and now the most advanced airship in the world, but the question arose as to what kind of reception it might receive in the skies over the United States, a country still technically at war with Germany. Wisely, the idea was dropped. The British, on the other hand, knew that a warm welcome would await them in America, and thought they had a contender in His Majesty's Airship (H.M.A.) R 34, replica of German naval zeppelin L 33, which had, literally, fallen into their hands in 1916 after a forced landing in Essex. Therefore in June 1919 the British Air Ministry asked when R 34 would be ready for the trip, and in response its commander, Major George Herbert Scott, said no earlier than July because of various technical problems. While the English awaited the necessary fixes, the Americans on the other side of the Atlantic were waiting for nothing.

The United States had at its disposal three Navy Curtiss flying boats, NC-1, NC-3, and NC-4, and one four-man blimp, a motorized balloon of oblong shape akin to Walter Wellman's *America*. The goal was for all four of the navy's flying craft to depart Newfoundland together and head to the Azores, which, if reached, was far enough to count as "crossing" the Atlantic. In a display of raw power and might, the U.S. Navy planned to line the air route with no fewer than sixty-eight destroyers and five battleships, each vessel staged fifty miles apart and ready to assist the flyers if necessary.

The blimp and two of the flying boats made the initial passage from New York to Newfoundland without incident, but the third flying boat had to stop for repairs. Other delays followed and as the expedition sat grounded in Newfoundland the blimp, unmanned at the time, tore loose from its mooring and disappeared over the Atlantic. Now the squadron was reduced to just the flying boats and, with two pilots each and loaded to the gunnels with gasoline, they staggered into the air and headed toward the Azores. It was May 16, only weeks before the British were planning to launch R 34 in the opposite direction.

About fifteen hours later the pilots of NC-1 and NC-3, struggling with mechanical, navigational, and weather-related problems, gave up and landed, hard, in the ocean. NC-1 was rescued by a passing freighter, but NC-3 was not. Quite admirably, though, the duo aboard NC-3 taxied their stricken aircraft through the water until reaching the Azores, two and a half days later. With three of the navy's four hopes for crossing the Atlantic by air now dashed, it would be up to Lieutenant Commander Albert C. Read and Lieutenant Elmer F. Stone in NC-4 to make the United States proud; and this they succeeded in doing upon reaching the Azores by air fifteen hours after taking off from Newfoundland. Then, after a two-day pause for rest and repairs to NC-4, Read and Stone resumed their journey to Europe proper by flying along a chain of U.S. destroyers to Lisbon and then, to their ultimate destination, Plymouth, England, from where the Pilgrim Fathers had embarked for the New World. But the victory had not come cheaply. From start to finish, the expedition had taken twenty-three days to complete, cost the loss of one blimp and two flying boats, and could only have been accomplished thanks to the enormity of American naval power. And once safely in England, the idea that Read and Stone would fly NC-4 home was never even considered. Instead, the first to fly the Atlantic, along with their airplane, took a steamship back.

No matter how impractically attained, America's achievement meant for the British that the contest was lost. However, there was still the east–west crossing of the Atlantic to be done—the more difficult challenge because of prevailing headwinds—and with that goal in mind the dirigible R 34 was readied at the airship station at East Fortune in Scotland for a nonstop flight to New York. Among the twenty-two men (plus one stowaway) preparing for the trip was an American, Lieutenant Commander Zachary Lansdowne, who would represent the U.S. Navy, as well as General Edward Maitland, Britain's most senior airship officer and who once set a record by parachute jumping 11,000 feet over London. Although General Maitland outranked Major Scott he had complete trust in his captain, and looked forward to nothing more challenging than keeping a detailed dairy of the flight.

"Time, 1.23 a.m.," Maitland recorded of R 34's early morning departure on July 2, 1919, "Everything is now ready. The bugle sounds and the handling party commences to walk the ship slowly out of the shed stern first." And then, "At a signal from Scott, the bugle sounds the 'Let go,' the huge Airship slowly rises from the hands of the handling party, and is immediately swallowed up in the low-lying clouds at a height of 100 feet. Rousing cheers reach us through the clouds, and hearten us for the task we have in front of us."[53]

Airborne and moving in a westerly direction, Maitland noted that "When flying at night, possibly on account of the darkness, there is always a feeling of utter loneliness when one loses sight of the ground. We feel this loneliness very much tonight."

Burdened by 158 tons of fuel, Scott had to maneuver low over the

Scottish countryside, careful not to hit the surrounding peaks. "Passing under black ominous-looking rain-cloud 1,000 feet above us," Maitland jotted, "High hills on starboard beam causing bumps and making ship pitch slightly." Ten minutes later there was a "Magnificent view of Loch Lomond. Violent bumps off Dumbarton hills bring big strains on ship, particularly upon her elevators and rudders."

At 5 a.m. Scotland and its treacherous landscape lay astern, the ocean lay below, and Maitland had, "One last word with Meteorological Officer, who says weather conditions and prospects extremely good, and so to bed, with a comfortable feeling of confidence. Hammock berth No. 11 has been allotted to me; a nice deep, roomy hammock."

Maitland's repose in his hammock could only have been brief because he was back making weather observations an hour later, followed by breakfast at 7 a.m. The sun fully risen, Scott skillfully kept the ship in heavy clouds to avoid overheating the hydrogen, but navigator G. G. H. Cook needed to use his sextant, and so climbed the hundred-foot ladder from the bottom of the airship up past the gas cells to the exposed gun platform on the very top. Once there, Cook's body was concealed by mist but his head poked out into clear air, and from this vantage point he successfully took his reading of the sun. In 1919, R 34 had the entire sky above the Atlantic all to itself, but still Maitland wondered "What a strange sight it would have been to another passing aircraft to see a man's head skimming along the top of a cloud-bank at forty knots!"

By mid-afternoon the airship was in radio contact with the Azores and, using only three of its five engines, was cruising along at thirty-six knots at an altitude of 900 feet. Now that there was no chance of putting down on land, the stowaway, William Ballantyne, who earlier had been cut from the flight due to weight restrictions, emerged from his hiding place. "He says he could not bear the thought of being left behind," Maitland explained, "Cannot help sympathizing with his motive, but it is bad from a disciplinary point of view, to say nothing of risking the success of the flight. Without his weight we could have carried 200 lbs. more petrol, and of course he has been allotted neither food nor hammock." The general, though, forgot his ire and became enchanted with a "Very beautiful rainbow effect on the clouds: one complete rainbow encircles the ship, and another smaller one encircles our shadow on the water; both are vivid in their coloring."

Early in the evening of that first day of flight, Maitland noted that since lift-off nineteen hours earlier, R 34 had covered only 610 miles. However, "It must be remembered that Scott has to nurse his engines for the return journey," Maitland argued of R 34's performance, "and had it not been for this, our speed for this outward journey could have been as third as fast again." In fact, even though they were rated for 2,100 r.p.m., the five Maori 4 Sunbeam engines could not be safely run beyond 1,600 r.p.m. The engines, however, were only one of several things in need of improvement aboard the dirigible. For instance, the petrol tanks leaked when the airship went into an incline, infusing the crew's quarters with the smell of gasoline, and both the cooking arrangements and the food supply left something to be desired. The dirigible lacked a kitchen and what cooking could be done relied on engine heat. "No frying facilities," Maitland complained, "which would be a boon particularly for breakfast."

After dinner that day, Maitland recorded that, "Sun is now setting, and gradually disappears below the lower cloud horizon, throwing a wonderful pink glow on the white clouds in every direction; a very beautiful sunset, and very cold." He concluded by adding, "Turned in feeling very tired and sleepy."

All through the first night over the Atlantic the airship routine of navigating, steering, working the elevators, and attending to the engines continued, watch by watch, unabated, and by nine o'clock the next morning, Thursday, July 3, R 34 was twenty-four hours and 750 miles away from Cape Race, Newfoundland. Dank clouds dampened visibility throughout the morning hours, and lunch that day, Maitland said, was "cold roast beef with one cold potato each. We are short of potatoes, having apparently eaten too many yesterday!" Following lunch, he noted that "Clouds near surface of sea have cleared away, and we now have a visibility of about forty to fifty miles in all directions."

The shipping lanes below were teeming with vessels but, remarkably, none were ever sighted by R 34 during its sojourn across the ocean. The clear weather lasted only so long and, Maitland wrote, "It is raining very fast, driving through the roof of the fore car in many places, and there is a thin film of water over the chart table. The wind is roaring to such an extent that we have to shout to make ourselves heard."

Lieutenant Guy Harris, the meteorological officer, suggested that they climb higher to escape a low-depression weather system, and at exactly 3,400 feet, and just as Harris had predicted, the rain ceased and the flying was smooth. "To the west the clouds have lifted, and we see a most wonderful and interesting sky," Maitland marveled, "Black, angry clouds above us, giving place to clouds of a grey mouse color, then a clear and bright salmon-pink expanse, changing lower down the horizon to darker clouds with a rich golden lining as the sun sinks below the surface."

Darkness eventually spoiled the view although at daybreak, Friday, July 4, Maitland and the crew were treated to the spectacle of "Enormous pieces of floating ice under us now; small icebergs in themselves. The ice is blue-green under water, with frozen snow on top, and the whole sea seems to be full of little blobs of cream in every direction, very pretty sight." Congratulatory messages began to arrive in Morse code even before land was sighted, but then at 12:50 p.m. a few small rocky islands became visible through the clouds.

Small islands gave way to land and Maitland saw "Little groups of hutments at each harbor with piles of cut timber, which appears to be the principal industry in the country, bar fishing. Inhabitants gaze up at us in astonishment. They make no demonstration whatsoever. Nice little fishing village on promontory, a delightful collection of what look like tiny pink, blue and white, doll's houses. Miles away, out to sea, looking right across the peninsula to the East, we can see a huge iceberg, with the sun gleaming on its perpendicular walls of ice."

Leaving Newfoundland astern and heading southwest for Nova Scotia, the airship passed over the little French outpost in North America, the islands of Miquelon and St. Pierre, before being buffeted by strong headwinds, raising concern in the control car about diminishing fuel supplies. "If only we had sufficient petrol we would now change course to the westward," Maitland fretted, "crossing the American coast, and so get behind this barrage." Instead, the decision was made to plug along over Nova Scotia to conserve gasoline. Flying no faster than twenty-seven miles per hour, this leg of the journey took up all the next day, Saturday, July 5, but again the sights, and the smells, were wonderful. "Scott keeps the ship down to 800 feet, to avoid the wind at higher levels," Maitland wrote. "The trees each settler cut down last winter are neatly stacked, and look like little bundles of asparagus; and we see exactly where he gets his water, the extent of his housing accommodation, and the amount of land he has cultivated. The character of the soil is clearly visible to us, the natural drainage of the country stands revealed, and we get an insight into the rainfall, the types of trees which do best, the bird life and the depth of the lakes; whilst the glorious and invigorating fragrance of these enormous pine forests comes up to us as a refreshing tonic, putting new life into everyone on board."

With 500 miles between them and New York, Scott and his officers decided to run the ship on only three engines, so dire had the petrol

LIBRARY OF CONGRESS

A visitor from England: His Majesty's Airship R 34 *at Mineola, Long Island.*

situation become. "A signal is sent through to the U.S. Naval Authorities at Washington and Boston asking them to send a destroyer to stand by to give us a tow should we need one," Maitland noted, "Hope it won't be necessary." Severe weather of the kind that could wreck an airship was observed over New Brunswick to the north, and Maitland recorded that by mid-afternoon R 34 was "Caught in violent squall on extreme outskirts of the storm." Shortly thereafter a return message from the U.S. Navy stated that should R 34 need assistance "Arrangements have been made for destroyers to be south of Cape Cod." Scott opened up all five engines in an attempt to escape the storm, but the strategy failed, and precious petrol was wasted in the process. Close to midnight,

Maitland confided in his dairy that, "We wear our parachutes, and life-belts are all ready," and that "Our only bottle of brandy fell out of the chart locker with a crash during one of these vertical bumps."

In the early hours of Sunday, July 6, the storm had passed and R 34, with just enough petrol left, flew over Martha's Vineyard, Maitland observing that the island was "evidently a yachting resort, looks delightful," before favorable winds propelled R 34 clear over Montauk and straight for its destination, Hazelhurst Field in Mineola, Long Island. "As we skim over this American countryside," he said, "I confess to a delightful glow of satisfaction at gazing on American soil from the first time above. It brings home to me more than anything else could ever do, what a small place this world really is, what an astonishing part these great Airship Liners will play in linking together the remotest places of the earth; and what interesting years lie immediately ahead!"

Its epoch flight having concluded, Maitland looked down to see that most American of sights, a massive traffic jam. Autos were parked six deep at the field, with a stream of others, stacked bumper-to-bumper, arriving by the hundreds. Indeed, it was a momentous occasion because the future too had arrived—and had arrived by air. Befittingly, R 34's Special Duties officer, a man named Pritchard, parachuted out of the forward car to supervise the inexperienced American ground crew below.

The first-ever airmail between Britain and America was unloaded, and then while the U.S. Navy kept close watch on R 34 at Hazelhurst, the ship's officers and crew were treated by New Yorkers to two days of wining and dining. Free lodging at the Ritz-Carlton was given to the airship's officers and drivers were found to ferry the officers and men around town. New Yorkers also bestowed gifts upon them and General Maitland even got a sore tooth pulled by a dentist *gratis*. Alas, it was over all too soon and, minus the stowaway Ballantyne who had to return to

England by boat,[54] R 34 lifted off for the trip home on July 9 where, upon its arrival four days later, the *Illustrated London News* hailed it as the "Transatlantic Dirigible."[55]

In Germany, the unconditional success of the flight to America and back by their former foes had to have been difficult to accept. After all, the British dirigible was nothing but a "faux" zeppelin copied from a Luftschiffbau design and, if allowed, L 72 could easily have soared from Friedrichshafen to New York. German hopes that this might still be possible ended abruptly when the Allies awarded L 72 to the French as part of German war reparations. Renamed the *Dixmude*, the zeppelin came without an owner's manual and the French had to learn to operate it themselves. The zeppelin flew successfully on a number of occasions before, in December 1923, it and its fifty-three man crew vanished over the Mediterranean. That tragedy ended French enthusiasm for airships, but in the United States they had become a subject of great interest, especially to the military.

FIVE

In late 1919 when America and Germany were still technically at war, U.S. Army General William "Billy" Mitchell staged a coup against his rival the U.S. Navy by agreeing to buy L 72 from the Luftschiffbau. When the War Department in Washington, D.C. learned of this, however, it canceled the sale on grounds that this amounted to trading with the enemy (and thus L 72 would ultimately wind up in France). The War Department's veto was also necessary because Mitchell's opportunism had violated an earlier army–navy agreement that rigid airships were to be the navy's domain—a domain that would soon be jealously guarded by Admiral William A. Moffett.

Moffett, a son of the Confederacy, for which his father had bravely fought, hailed from Charleston, South Carolina, and attended the U.S. Naval Academy, class of 1890. While at Annapolis, Moffett battled hazing, physical ailments, mind-numbing naval studies, and the academy's system of discipline, a system which was as picayune as it was unfair. However, unlike the majority of his classmates who "bilged" before their four years were up, he soldiered on to graduate thirty-first out of a remaining class of thirty-four. Leaving Annapolis, Moffett immediately proved himself to be a highly capable naval officer, and one of his many early career accomplishments involved the clearance of Manila harbor of ships sunk during the Spanish-American War. Later, in 1900, he met Sultan Abdul Hamid II in Constantinople as part of a U.S. Navy delegation, and the Sultan became so taken by Moffett that he offered him captaincy of a Turkish warship. Moffett declined, but rose rapidly in the ranks of his own navy and by 1913 was commanding the cruiser *Chester*. In a fortuitous bit of timing for an ambitious officer like Moffett, Mexico was just then in the throes of revolution and President Woodrow Wilson, reacting to a rebel threat, ordered an invasion of Veracruz. In the action that followed, April 21–22, 1914, Moffett from the bridge of the *Chester* directed shell fire to good effect and for this was awarded the Congressional Medal of Honor (in an era when that medal was rather freely distributed). During the subsequent American occupation, the navy shipped several seaplanes down to Veracruz where they conducted reconnaissance missions over the area. Watching from his bridge, therefore, Moffett would have witnessed the first use of American air power in combat. While undoubtedly impressed, Moffett knew, as any naval officer at the time would have known, that the future of the U.S. Navy, and of one's career *in* the U.S. Navy, belonged squarely to the battleship.[56]

His next assignment sent him to the Great Lakes Naval Training Station near Chicago to be commandant. This was certainly not battleships, nevertheless it was an opportunity for Moffett to demonstrate his myriad leadership skills in the build-up to America's entry into the European conflict. Great Lakes under Moffett's command saw dramatic expansion, particularly so after the U.S. declared war with Germany on April 6, 1917. Tens of thousands of recruits and tens of millions of dollars poured into the station almost all at once, and Moffett handled the challenges and crises that accompanied this explosive growth adroitly. Admiral W. S. Benson paid a visit and declared, "It is hard to say too much in praise of Captain Moffett and the way he is conducting the Station. I am speechless. The spirit that pervades this Station is so fine that it is hard to put it into words. Every element fits in exactly in the teamwork of the whole. Every man feels his individual responsibility."[57]

Great Lakes also gave Moffett the opportunity to showcase his penchant for politicking and publicity. In Chicago, for example, Moffett mingled with the city's elite, men such as the pork baron J. Ogden Armour and chewing gum tycoon William Wrigley Jr., and was careful to maintain these civilian ties long after leaving Great Lakes. At the training center he organized a multitude of athletic clubs, many led by the nation's best coaches, and some of these clubs toured the country carrying with them the Great Lakes banner. Moffett's football team bested the Naval Academy squad and his baseball team beat the Chicago Cubs. On Wednesdays and Sundays, Moffett opened wide the training ground gates, and as thumping bands and marching sailors entertained the public, he stood in the reviewing stand next to such luminaries as former presidents Theodore Roosevelt and William Howard Taft. The grand finale of these events occurred when several thousand sailors, dressed in red, white, and blue, took to the parade ground and formed a human American flag. Moffett also did not neglect the arts, and requested $40,000 from astonished navy officials for musical instruments. In a major catch, Moffett persuaded the great John Philip Sousa to be his musical director. Sousa joined the navy and soon had bands, orchestras, and other musical troupes from Great Lakes touring the nation. Sousa held his boss in the highest esteem, recalling that, "During my service in the Navy, from May 1917 to March 1919, I learned to love and admire Admiral Moffett. Every man who had the honor to serve him felt the same. His own hours for work were all hours. He asked no man to do more than he was willing to do himself. Certainly his executive ability was unusual and although he was a great disciplinarian, he had nothing of the martinet about him."[58]

In addition to its dozens of other functions, Great Lakes served as an important training facility for aviation mechanics, and before the war was over would turn out 3,350 of them. Moffett's sights, though, were still set on battleships, and his wish was granted when made commander of the super-dreadnought *Mississippi* just after the war. During fleet exercises off Cuba shortly into his command he came to appreciate the value of the airplane in the spotter role, yet did not specifically request his next posting, which sent him to Washington to take charge of naval aviation. From commanding a battleship to sitting behind a desk might have been seen by Moffett as a demotion, but seven months into his new job, July 1921, Congress passed a measure creating the Bureau of Aeronautics, and this would elevate his profile immensely. President Warren G. Harding promptly named him Bureau Chief, and along with the appointment came a flag rank, meaning that Moffett was now an admiral.

A seafarer of the old school, Admiral Moffett at age fifty-two defied expectations by not only making a rapid conversion to aviation, but also by being its most tireless proponent. Richard E. Byrd, who would earn world fame as an arctic aviator, remembered that "Flying stock went up in the Navy Department. With an admiral to fight our battles we began to get things done. We soon had more money, safer planes, bigger fields, better experimental laboratory and other lesser things that we so vitally needed."[59] In his new job Moffett wasted no time by wanting to see naval aviation everywhere. He wanted to see it on submarines, destroyers, cruisers, fleet auxiliaries, and battleships; he wanted to see it not just on flat-tops—existing ships modified to launch airplanes—but on purpose-built aircraft carriers as well; and he also wanted to see it in the form of dirigibles capable of playing the aerial-cruiser role in the upcoming war that he, as many in the navy did, thought would eventually break out with Japan. "In the rigid airship we have a scout, capable of patrolling the Pacific in the service of information for our fleet," he wrote his superiors, capitalizing for emphasis, "THE USE AND DEVELOPMENT OF RIGID AIRSHIPS IS A NAVAL NECESSITY."[60]

When appointed aviation chief in January 1921, Moffett inherited an ambitious dirigible program, a program predicated on the American and British belief that during the war German zeppelins had performed brilliantly in the reconnaissance role, and had nearly tipped the balance of sea power from the Allies to the Germans. Indeed, veterans of the German Naval Air Division boasted of this in their memoirs, but the reality was entirely different. Zeppelins, as Peter Strasser discovered, were ill-suited for sea patrols because they were only able to fly in good weather, meaning that over the turbulent North Sea, where German air patrols were most needed, they could only fly a quarter of the time. And even then, their reconnaissance effectiveness was negligible, and not a single sinking of an Allied ship or submarine could be attributed to a zeppelin. In fact, during the seminal naval engagement of the war, the Battle of Jutland, May 31 to June 1, 1916, Strasser's zeppelins failed to locate the English fleet, and played no role in the battle (other than to confuse the German navy with inaccurate sightings). The U.S. Navy's subsequent ardor for the airship may have therefore been misplaced, but in 1921 a gargantuan shed, representing the largest enclosed space in the world, stood newly built at the Lakehurst Naval Air Station in New Jersey, awaiting the arrival of Zeppelin Rigid 1 and Zeppelin Rigid 2.

The two dirigibles were to be the navy's first zeppelin-type airships, ordered in 1919 at a total cost to the U.S. taxpayer of four million dollars. After assuming his new duties, Moffett learned that at the League Island Navy Yard in Philadelphia where it was being fabricated, the completion of Zeppelin Rigid (ZR) 1 was held up due to technical problems but that fortunately ZR-2, the biggest airship ever built, had just been completed by the British at the Royal Airship Works in Cardington, and was ready for delivery.

A year earlier, twenty-two American officers and sailors, led by Commander Louis H. Maxfield, had steamed across the Atlantic for training at the Royal Navy's Howden Airship Station. Nicknamed the "Howden Detachment," the Yanks had tired of their long deployment in England and were impatient to take possession of the giant dirigible and fly it home. With this in mind, the planned number of test-flights for R 38 (which was to retain its British designation R 38 until hand-over) was therefore limited to just four, and at midnight during its fourth flight, August 24–25, 1921, a series of vigorous course alterations at full speed and low altitude was made over the city of Hull with catastrophic consequences.

Propelled by six powerful Sunbeam Cossack engines, and pushed hard by its English commander, Flight Lieutenant Archie Wann, the bulky airship, as large as the *Lusitania*, executed a zigzag course through the dense air. During one particularly hard turn the frame buckled and the hull split in two. One half exploded in flames, the other half did not, but both fell into the river Humber. The toll was horrific: twenty-six British and sixteen Americans killed. General Maitland, aboard as an observer, was one of them, as was Commander Maxfield and a man named C. I. R. Campbell, the person who had designed R 38. Miraculously—as seemed to happen fairly commonly with dirigible disasters—some men survived the explosion and four were plucked from the Humber; one being the airship's commander, Wann, who had little recollection of what had happened.

Stung by the magnitude of the disaster and in particular the loss of Maitland, a bulwark of the British airship program, England scrapped its remaining dirigibles. Moffett and the U.S. Navy, though, were relieved that an inquiry absolved the R 38 crew of improper handling, meaning that the appalling incident could be blamed on faulty British engineering and nothing more. In fact, except for the tragic loss of life, the Americans were secretly glad to be rid of R 38, which had shown evidence of structural problems even before the disaster.

With blame for the debacle having been placed on foreigners, America's slow-moving but indigenous ZR-1 project was allowed to proceed apace. Parts were fabricated at the navy yard in Philadelphia and then shipped to the hangar at Lakehurst for assembly. In building an airship from scratch, the inexperienced but enthusiastic Americans had to do everything themselves, although chief of construction, Commander Ralph D. Weyerbacher, did manage to lure a zeppelin training pilot, Anton Heinen, from Friedrichshafen to Lakehurst for guidance, and he also convinced several workers from the former British airship program to lend him their expertise. Meanwhile, in Philadelphia the navy was having difficulty transforming duralumin, the advanced alloy developed by the Germans, into the 400,000 girders needed for completion. Concurrently, in Washington bureaucrats insisted on reviewing and debating every aspect of the project, further delaying the program. Finally, though, after several years in gestation, "Fleet Airship Number One" was set for its debut, August 20, 1923.

From the moment ZR-1 took to the air at Lakehurst in front of 15,000 enthusiastic spectators, though, it was obsolete. The person in charge of design was named Starr Truscott, and while he had advanced notions regarding dirigibles, Truscott was also risk averse, and so for America's first "rigid" had insisted upon making a copy of L 49, vintage 1916 and captured a year later in France during the "black day for zeppelins". But not only was Truscott's replica height-climber outmoded the minute it was launched, because of the availability of helium it was also never capable of being the Pacific-spanning air cruiser once promised. This was as a direct consequence of the R 38 conflagration in England, followed by the explosion of the U.S. Army blimp *Roma* in Virginia resulting in thirty-three deaths less than a year later. Both hydrogen calamities came as ZR-1 was only half-built, forcing Moffett instead to use a different, new, gas called helium, just then becoming available but only in minute amounts.

From a safety standpoint there could be no argument, since hydrogen when mixed with air, as had been so amply demonstrated over the years, is extraordinarily flammable, while helium will not burn under any conditions, making it a miracle-gas for airships. Helium, however, has not quite the lifting power (97 percent) of hydrogen, and while seemingly inconsequential, for ZR-1 this translated into a steep, 40 percent, penalty in terms of its ability to carry fuel, oil, provisions, and other things necessary for extended flight. So with a helium-filled ZR-1, the possibility for long-range ocean patrols was no more, casting doubt on the entire naval airship program. Moffett, however, was unperturbed since he had other things in mind for the ZR-1.

First was a tour of Lakehurst for reporters of the *Philadelphia Bulletin*, Universal Press, *Saturday Evening Post*, and *Aviation Magazine*. The scribes were shown the massive doors of Hangar Number 1, each weighing 1,300 tons, and the trolley tracks (just as Santos-Dumont had envisioned) that guided the airship in and out of the hangar, then the reporters were ushered to an elevator that took them to a construction bridge next to the roof. There, hundreds of feet above the hangar floor, they got a bird's-eye view of the airship, silvery in its sun-reflecting aluminum paint. Their guide here, Lieutenant Mayer, told the reporters that while the outsides of the helium cells within the airship were made of everyday cotton, the insides were lined by a far more exotic material. "Goldbeater's skin—the stomach lining of oxen—is used to make the bags leak-proof," Mayer said, explaining that, "Three-quarters of a million oxen gave their 'tummies' so our helium won't leak out." Cost of the cells, he continued, ranged from a low of $12,961 for the small cells in the nose up as high as $15,000 for the bigger cells amidships. The reporters then took the elevator down, and at ground level entered the airship's control car. Here they were shown the accouterments of dirigible control: components such as altimeters, barometers, toggles, wheels, thermometers, annunciators, compasses, switches, pulleys, levers, and telegraphs. The control car, even minus engine and generator, the reporters were told, cost a small fortune, nearly $49,000.

Another lieutenant, Edgar Sheppard, took over the tour from there and stated that, "There's nothing so sweet as a motor that's right—and nothing so irritating as one that's balky. Let's go to the power cars and see them." Leaving the control car, Sheppard walked his tour to the first engine gondola, which was aerodynamically shaped like an egg. "We number the cars in order from the stern forward," he said, "on this side are numbers three and five, and on the port side are the even-numbered gondolas. Each engine car is six feet wide and twenty feet long, and uses the Packard IA-1551 engine, weighing 1,060 pounds and delivering 325 horsepower at 1,400 rpm's." When asked, Sheppard estimated fuel consumption to be a gallon per mile, less than some airplanes used, and added that oil consumption was about 7 percent of the gasoline expended. Then he revealed something that was probably also not known to the reporters. "We've devised a recovery unit which condenses the water from engine exhaust and stores it," he said, "thus taking the place of weight lost when fuel is burned—so we keep our buoyancy the same. Saving helium is important, in a financial way."

Standing at the stern of ZR-1 and looking lengthwise to the bow of the ship 682 feet away, the reporters could see that the five engine cars were not equally spaced. "The staggered arrangement of the cars," Sheppard explained, "distributes the stresses and eliminates any overlap of slipstream from the wooden propellers, each of which is 18 feet in diameter." The reporters scribbled on their notepads and were then hurried on to the next leg of the tour, because there was just so much more to see: the forty 113-gallon hanging fuel tanks that could be cut loose by wire cutters in an emergency; the crew's quarters, furnished with hammocks and a couple of benches; the food locker; the mess table, galley, and electric stove; the officer's ward room; the mooring equipment; the hatches; the water ballast bags; the telephones; the radio that could beam out messages 1,000 miles away; the internal catwalk three blocks long and nine inches wide running the length of the ship; a sample of duralumin (strong as steel but one-third the weight); the twenty gas cells; the eighteen helium maneuvering valves; the pneumatic bumpers; and, of course, the lavatory. "Thank you so much for your interest in the ZR-1," Sheppard concluded, "we can use the publicity."[61]

Test flights over New York and Philadelphia, with the press in both cities given ample advance notice, were capped with a splashy aerial entrance to Washington D.C. There the men who controlled the nation's purse strings, members of Congress, could look to the sky and admire the pride of the U.S. Navy, soon to be given the heavenly name *Shenandoah*, Native American for "daughter of the stars." Dropping flowers on the Tomb of the Unknown Soldier at Arlington, and then later shedding silver leaflets proclaiming October 27 Navy Day, and also more personal messages dropped by tiny parachutes to prominent persons and local organizations, the rigid was greeted by tens of thousands of people waving from the ground in Pennsylvania, Maryland, Virginia, New York, Connecticut, and other eastern states. A jaunt out to Saint Louis in time for the international air races, and then return by way of Chicago, caused a national sensation—as did a completely unplanned trip that began on January 16, 1924.

With a skeleton crew aboard, USS *Shenandoah* was moored to the new mast at Lakehurst and, engines running, enduring a vicious wind and rain storm. The mooring mast was a futuristic sky dock, 165 feet high with an elevator to bring crew and equipment from the ground to a hatchway in the bow of the airship. The mast also had pipes for helium, fuel, oil, and water, meaning that the airship could be serviced high on the mast instead of being returned after every flight to the giant shed, a laborious and tricky process involving hundreds of men. But the concept had yet to be fully tested, and so as an endurance trial the *Shenandoah* had spent the previous four days continuously on the mast.

As the storm raged on, Captain Frank McCrary, reluctant commander of the *Shenandoah* and no fan of airships, could be found at home enjoying a hot meal. Then at around half past six in the evening a particularly strong gust of wind wrecked the airship's top vertical fin and, in the twisting motions that followed, the dirigible ripped itself free of the mast. Number one and two gas cells in the bow of the ship collapsed during departure and, now bow heavy, the *Shenandoah* sank nose down while being carried toward nearby trees by winds of sixty-eight miles per hour. Navigator Maurice Pierce, as the most senior officer aboard in McCrary's absence, assumed command while the veteran zeppelin pilot Anton Heinen, who luckily was also on board, grabbed the wheel. Orders were given to empty all ballast bags, cut away three fuel tanks, and dump 454 pounds of spare parts. Lighter, the ship gained altitude and, with engines brought up to cruising speed, maintained a holding position over the New York and New Jersey shores. At 9:10 p.m. the radio, disassembled for repairs, was made to work and the message "All okay, will ride out storm" was transmitted from the airship and, fortunately, received at Mitchel Field on Long Island. A powerful radio station in Newark, WOR, interrupted its regular programming to communicate with the airship, giving listeners the opportunity to tune in to the unfolding drama. By 3:30 in the morning, though, the radio show was over and the ship back safely at Lakehurst with all hands accounted for. The airship's elopement cost the navy $78,000 in repair bills, but the publicity generated made it well worth the expense. Literally overnight, the *Shenandoah* was a celebrity worthy of Hollywood status, and America had caught what was popularly called "dirigible fever."

Repairs took all winter, and when the airship emerged from its shed the "Iron Horse," as it was nicknamed, was significantly heavier because of structural strengthening and other modifications, but ready to report to duty. Before flying resumed in the spring Moffett gave the dirigible both a new captain, the highly capable Commander Zachary Lansdowne (aboard during R 34's transatlantic flight), and an ambitious agenda. According to the admiral, the *Shenandoah* was to demonstrate docking at sea, fly round-trip across the continent, return to the West Coast again, sail to Hawaii, and finally conquer the North Pole. Lansdowne got to work. In August, he eased the giant ship to a perfect rendezvous on Narragansett Bay with a mast affixed to the fuel tanker USS *Patoka*, and in the wee hours of October 7, 1924, he and his men prepared for the transcontinental journey. If weight allowed, the *National Geographic Magazine*'s Junius B. Wood hoped to join them.

The dirigible emerged from the humongous hangar at Lakehurst at the break of dawn and, held to the ground by 300 sailors, marines, Filipino mess boys, and civilians, waited for the sun to "superheat" the helium and thus expand the gas cells. Patience was needed since this would take several hours, but patience would be rewarded because for every one degree Fahrenheit rise in temperature, the airship's helium could lift an additional 300 pounds. By ten o'clock that morning and after several hours basking in the sun, the *Shenandoah*, its bow now clamped to the mast, had sufficient lift to begin accepting men and materials.

Embarkation, the *Geographic*'s Wood explained, was a slow and strange affair. One by one officers and sailors rode the tiny cage elevator up the mast, and one by one they entered the bow via a small gangway. The first men aboard stood at predetermined spots along the keel's narrow catwalk, because so delicately balanced was the craft at mooring that human ballast had to be carefully allocated, lest the tail dip and hit the ground. Oil was piped aboard in driblets for the same reason, and only when Lansdowne was convinced that the *Shenandoah*, getting lighter by the minute in the sunshine, could sustain the weight of another body, would he permit the next man to walk the plank. Wood waited his turn and, knowing that of all those wanting to fly that day he was the most expendable, pondered his fate. "To be all ready for a cruise into the great unknown," he reported, "to get within one step of it, and then, perhaps, to get no further, provides an anxious moment." The journalist had come prepared for the trip, although packing, he noted, had been minimal. "Personal baggage was limited to six pounds. A pair of socks, a suit of underwear, two handkerchiefs, a towel and cake of soap, and an expurgated assortment of toilet articles had replaced a wardrobe trunk. A typewriter had gone aboard as ship equipment."[62]

Wood was finally invited to follow the others, numbering eleven officers, Admiral Moffett among them, and twenty-seven sailors. Despite all being aboard, however, lift-off was delayed as men were shifted back and forth along the keel in a continuous balancing act until the sun could fully heat the helium. Minutes passed while measurements from the mast indicated that the ship was still too heavy to fly, so in the control car Lansdowne ordered Lieutenant Houghton to open the ballast tanks for five seconds. The correct levers were pulled and instantly the ship became hundreds of pounds lighter and, freed from its mooring, the dirigible teetered up and down like an airborne seesaw. More water ballast irrigated the sandy soil below as Houghton attempted to steady the ship and men scurried to different places along the keel for the same purpose. Then, to clear the mast, which was about to impale the dirigible, still more water was dropped and two fuel tanks cut away. As intended, the 724-pound steel containers tore through the cotton cover and shot to earth—no ground casualties reported. Now safely airborne, the five idling engines were brought up to "standard speed," meaning 1,200 r.p.m., the bow was raised to thirteen degrees, and the gathering airstream under the hull gave it lift and stability. The graceful *Shenandoah* was now fully dirigible and its men free to go about their aerial business.

Inside the *Shenandoah*'s twenty goldbeater-lined bags was stored nearly all the world's extracted helium, an element prolific in the universe but scarce on earth, and only found in any quantity in the United States. The *Shenandoah*'s helium came from certain Texas natural gas wells that contained trace amounts of the element, and in 1924, just as now, the refining process was complex and costly. This, naturally, gave Lansdowne great pause whenever he needed to valve helium, and to avoid this he had a number of strategies. One was that he kept his cells at only 85 percent capacity and, as the *National Geographic*'s Wood had observed, relied on the sun's rays to expand them fully for flight. Then during flight, Lansdowne was careful to maintain a level course and not exceed the *Shenandoah*'s 4,500-feet "pressure altitude," the height at which its ventilators automatically opened and at which helium would be released. Helping him avoid this event was the "condenser unit" mentioned to the press by Lieutenant Sheppard, which cooled the water vapor in the engines' exhaust until it became liquid. Unlike any airship captain before him, therefore, Lansdowne could both release and add ballast while in flight. Lastly—and for the opposite reason why departures took place well after daylight—Lansdowne preferred to land well after dark. First he would "bull" the ship downwards by using all engines at maximum power, and then hover in the cool night air and wait for the helium to contract.

From Lakehurst the rigid passed over Pennsylvania and Delaware, and four hours later and at 3,000 feet, flew a photogenic line between the White House and the Washington Monument, all the while beaming out the first of hundreds of radio messages to the press. By nightfall the *Shenandoah* was over North Carolina where some of those on board, based on personal experience flying balloons over the same area, grew wary of bullets from suspicious moonshiners below. Thankfully, no shots were fired as the dirigible floated ghostlike in the dark overhead.

"The ship is not wired for lights," Wood reported, "Only those in the navigating room, in the radio shack, and the running lights are on batteries." Otherwise, he stated, flashlights provided illumination. According to Wood, "The long keel is eerie with phosphorescent figures and letters, which glow from every latticed frame or piece of emergency gear, with lights which flash in the distance and disappear and lights which suddenly appear from nowhere, while one fur-padded form leans at a dangerous angle and another passes on the ribbon of a runway." A misplaced step could send a man tumbling right through the cotton beneath and into thin air but, Wood remarked, "No admonitions are needed to walk the straight and narrow path. The crew, as nimble as structural steel workers, trot along, pass each other, and even stop to wrestle."

Accommodations were spartan, one twelve-feet-square plywood platform along the runway serving as officers' quarters, and another one a short distance away as quarters for the crew. The men, who worked in shifts of four hours on and four hours off, dressed in layers of clothing and donned fur-lined flight suits, mittens, and boots as protection against the cold. In terms of sustenance, the only hot food available was coffee and soup prepared on a small stove; otherwise the fare was cold sandwiches, beans, sardines, and chocolate cake, served whenever anybody had time to eat.

On the second day of the journey the dirigible reached Fort Worth, Texas, home of the navy's helium gas plant. Presumably after topping off its cells, the *Shenandoah* spent the night on a mooring mast before lifting off the next morning, headed for a course over the Rockies, and loaded with 17,016 pounds of fuel, 850 pounds of oil, and 2,500 pounds of water. Navigating over canyons and between treacherous peaks,

Lansdowne was forced to climb well above pressure altitude and could only grimace as precious helium escaped from the ventilators. Once past the mountains, he was able to resume a lower altitude, while a train kept the airship company for a couple of hours through Arizona before it slowly pulled ahead. Sunny California was reached through a rain and snowstorm, and the airship arrived at San Diego on October 10, just three days since departure from Lakehurst. Then after five days spent on the mast so repairs could be made (on landing the rear gondola had thumped the ground), the dirigible journeyed up the scenic coast to Seattle, returned to San Diego, and followed its tracks back across the country to Lakehurst where a new navy airship, delivered from Friedrichshafen, awaited it in the hangar.

This upstart dirigible rudely requisitioned *Shenandoah*'s helium, and the older ship spent a flightless winter in the shed before getting its gas supply back in the spring. There would, however, be no trips to Honolulu or the Pole for the *Shenandoah*, because while last October's twenty-day, 9,000-mile journey had been a publicity coup, it was also proof that the eighty-three-ton Iron Horse, denied the hydrogen for which it was designed, could never carry a full load; hence the stops every other day or so for fuel and provisions. So instead of heading to distant lands for 1925, Lansdowne and his men could only look forward to a busy domestic schedule of "hand waving" flights. There would be the intercollegiate crew races at Poughkeepsie on the Hudson in June and the Governor's Convention in Portland, Maine on the Fourth of July, followed by test flights and naval training exercises in August. Then at the instance of local congressmen, in early September six days of hand waving over state fairs in Ohio, Iowa, Wisconsin, Minnesota, and Indiana were planned. Lansdowne, a native Ohioan, had reservations about flying at the height of the Midwestern thunderstorm season, but kept them to himself. His reservations, it turned out, were prescient.

The commander said goodbye to his young wife Betsy and their little daughter Peggy at Lakehurst on Sunday, September 2, 1925. At 2:52 p.m., Lansdowne ordered the standard order for ascent, "Stand by—*up ship!*," and with that the dirigible was released by the ground crew and twelve hours later was dodging black clouds over Ohio. Surrounding Lansdowne in the dark control car, illuminated only by flashes of lightning, were officers whose watch had ended but who remained on duty to help. Strong headwinds eventually reduced ground speed to near zero, although in the distance the sky appeared to be clearing. At around twenty-five minutes after four on Monday morning, however, the *Shenandoah* was caught in a line squall and, propelled by winds of fifty miles per hour, rose unexpectedly. Lansdowne ordered the elevator man to bring the bow down eighteen degrees and rang for all engines full speed. Engine number two quit under the strain and along the tilted catwalk men slipped and fell while others were tossed out of their hammocks: "Am losing my seat,"[63] were the last words broadcast from the radio operator George Schnitzer. Control was regained at around 4,000 feet followed by six minutes of level flight before the ship shot up to over 6,000 feet in a matter of two minutes.

Lansdowne did everything he could to arrest the ascent and then, so as not to go into a free fall, retard the descent. Helium was valved, the remaining engines kept wide open, the nose directed down twenty-five degrees, and water ballast dumped. Under the strain, engine number one seized up but the remedy worked and at 3,000 feet control was restored—that is until another powerful gust threatened to send the dirigible stern-over-bow. For the next ten minutes the storm toyed with the airship, putting it into near loops and exerting upward forces of 30,000 pounds on its duralumin frame, already burdened with tons of rain water that had soaked into the outer cover. The combined pressures proved too much and suddenly there was "that unmistakable 'cry' of metal under

The bow section of the USS Shenandoah, *picked bare by looters, on the Nichols farm in Sharon, Ohio.*

severe stress," the navigator, Lieutenant Charles E. Rosendahl, recalled. "It was as though a thousand small metal pieces had been thrown in a heap and violently tramped on; as though a thousand panes of glass had been hurled from on high to pavement beneath."[64] At approximately quarter to five in the morning, and over the skies of Ohio, the *Shenandoah* had split in two with a big chunk of the mid-section containing the control car and two of the engine cars hurtling to earth.

The horror above was witnessed on the ground by a surprising number of early-risers, and the bodies of Commander Lansdowne and thirteen of his men, Lieutenant Sheppard included, were quickly gathered where they fell. The dead were laid out on a farmhouse porch before being taken to a local funeral parlor to sit all day in the heat until Washington, D.C., shut down for Labor Day, wired permission to embalm.

LIBRARY OF CONGRESS

Terrible as the fatalities were, though, two-thirds of the crew, twenty-nine men, reached the ground alive and with minimal injury; and this gift was owed entirely to helium, because on a hydrogen-ship there most assuredly would have been explosion and fire following the break-up.

Twenty-two of the survivors happened to be in the stern section which, after separating from the rest of the dirigible, contained sufficient helium for some degree of buoyancy. Coming to earth after several minutes of descent, the stern was blown by the wind for 200 yards before losing both engine cars, hitting some trees, spilling out four of its men, sailing on for another third of a mile, and then coming to a halt. Badly shaken but able to walk, the ship's cook located the nearest telephone and called Lakehurst to report that the bow portion of the ship was still in the air, last sighted at 8,000 feet and rising.

In the free-ballooning bow were seven officers and sailors clinging to the girders. At first unaware of each other's existence, they formed an impromptu flight team and, led by Rosendahl, initiated a controlled descent that ended over an hour later at the front door of farmer Ernest Nichols's house. Now that all of the *Shenandoah* had come to earth, news of the tragedy spread from farm to farm and village to village. Soon, nicely turned out folk, enjoying the holiday and on their way to county fairs, stopped by the three crash sites where, in the hours before some army troops arrived, they stole whatever they could.

As with the loss of R 38, a board of inquiry absolved the ship's crew of any wrongdoing and blamed the incident on structural failure. "All was done for security that human skill could accomplish," the U.S. Navy said of its men, "but no talent can meet the freaks of nature. We must have dirigibles and the only thing is to go ahead and build another before our nerves become flabby."[65] Moffett, however, did not escape the episode unscathed and had to endure criticism that the dirigible's planned tour of the Midwest was just a publicity stunt, and something that his officers and sailors had paid for with their lives. There was no danger, though, that the accident was going to end Moffett's career or the U.S. Navy's airship program, as the admiral was far too savvy to let that happen, but he knew that he needed safer airships.

England's R 38, of course, was a deadly disappointment and then, even before it crashed, Moffett had been under no illusion that America's *Shenandoah* was of any use to the fleet either, and had, in fact, shielded it from participating in naval exercises in which its performance would only have been an embarrassment. What the admiral was impatiently waiting for at the time of the Ohio accident were capable aerial cruisers that would once and for all demonstrate the utility of the airship in the reconnaissance role. To his satisfaction, it was arranged that these new cruisers were to be built by the Goodyear-Zeppelin Corporation, a joint enterprise between Goodyear Tire and Rubber of

Akron, Ohio, and Luftschiffbau Zeppelin of Friedrichshafen, Germany. As it turned out, the first Goodyear-Zeppelin airship was still some years away, but already Moffett had received a dirigible from Friedrichshafen. In place of $800,000 still owed to Washington as part of Germany's interminable war reparations, Berlin had instead offered an airship, the result being LZ 126.

Germany's enormous 2,472,000-cubic-feet "Amerika-Zeppelin" represented the last word in airship technology, and reached Lakehurst after a flawless and record-breaking nonstop flight from Friedrichshafen. Christened USS *Los Angeles* (ZR-3) after delivery by its German crew, this was the ship that had earlier appropriated the *Shenandoah*'s helium. As could be expected, Moffett gave the *Los Angeles* a hectic schedule, having it crisscross the country, fly to Bermuda and Panama and back, test new types of masts that were both closer to the ground and self-propelled, take scientists aloft to view a solar eclipse, land on an aircraft carrier, and launch and retrieve airplanes in flight. There were also plenty of hand-waving tours, and the zeppelin even starred in Frank Capra's talkie *Dirigible*, with Emmet Corrigan playing the Admiral Moffett character who sends his prized airship on a desperate rescue mission to the South Pole, with a romance thrown in for good measure.

Whenever aboard the *Los Angeles*, built by a disarmed Germany to civilian passenger standards, the real Admiral Moffett traveled in style, and the crew also enjoyed luxuries never before found on other military airships, such as food prepared in a modern galley with running water, a commercial stove for hot meals, and a baker's oven for fresh bread. Admiral Moffett and Captain Rosendahl (*Shenandoah* hero and now commander of the *Los Angeles*) each had their own stateroom, the ship's two lavatories were of the best quality, and the baggage room commodious. While the fifty sailors aboard the *Los Angeles* bunked more modestly within the canvas-covered duralumin hull, the airship's eleven officers

COURTESY NAVAL HISTORICAL FOUNDATION

Rear Admiral William A. Moffett as Chief of the Bureau of Aeronautics, 1929.

could avail themselves of the control car's comfortable sofa-fitted compartments and gaze out the large windows at the moving panorama below. Still, the floating hotel could only be used for training purposes, something stipulated by the British and French in allowing the Germans to sell the zeppelin to the United States, and as Moffett was in desperate need of dirigibles that would be of value to the fleet without dispute, in November of 1925, and just a month after the *Shenandoah* loss, he had proposed his bold Five Year Plan.

This ten-million-dollar plan called for a thousand-acre Pacific Coast airship base, a 1,250,000-cubic-feet training dirigible, and best of all, two seven-million-cubic-feet cruisers to be built by Goodyear-Zeppelin. The proposal was taken up by a Moffett ally, Thomas S. Butler, Republican Congressman of Pennsylvania and Chairman of the Naval Affairs Committee, and a year later the sum of $200,000 was appropriated to

COURTESY NAVAL HISTORICAL FOUNDATION

USS Los Angeles *moored to USS* Patoka.

begin implementation. Moffett, though, could work only so many wonders, and political and budgetary hurdles were to delay completion of the first cruiser, ZRS-4, until late 1931.

The Germans, reeling from their nation's post-war economic and social woes, had hardly been in a position to bargain when from the start Goodyear insisted on total control. The Luftschiffbau, relinquishing its engineering patents to the company, would play no role in the development of the ensuing airship, ZRS-4. In 1929, construction of the new airship commenced at the vast Goodyear hangar in Akron, Ohio, and Dr. Karl Arnstein, associate architect of no fewer than sixty-eight zeppelins for the Luftschiffbau, then quit his former employer and immigrated to America to lead the project.

Comforted by the safety margin that helium afforded, Arnstein placed the engines, notwithstanding their sparks and hot exhaust, within the hull instead of hanging them in gondolas on the outside, as was mandatory for hydrogen ships. This change not only made engine maintenance easier, but led to it being the most streamlined airship ever built. The control car, dwarfed by the gargantuan 6,850,000-cubic-feet frame, 785 feet long and 133 feet wide, was kept small for the sake of aerodynamics, and Arnstein utilized swiveling propellers (as Melvin Vaniman had done twenty years earlier) for greater maneuverability. The new airship also had three internal keels, instead of one, for additional strength, and in another departure from the standard, ZRS-4 relied almost entirely on duralumin framework for structural integrity instead of wire bracing. The huge and futuristic craft had an internal hangar for fighter airplanes and, driven by eight 570-horsepower V12 Maybachs for a speed of eighty-four miles per hour, had an incredible range of nearly 11,000 miles. The ship additionally boasted an internal communications system of eighteen telephones, improved condenser units, eight 30-caliber machine guns, and a $25,000 radio apparatus able to transmit messages 5,000 miles away. The cost to the U.S. Treasury for the newly named USS *Akron* came to a shocking $5,375,000. To avoid any appearance of profiteering, however, Goodyear promised to bill just under half that amount, $2,450,000, for the second airship of the navy's two-airship order.

Throughout construction and attendant difficulties, many criticized the *Akron* as being a multi-million dollar boondoggle, but when the dirigible was finally unveiled the reception, as Moffett predicted, was phenomenal. An enthused crowd of 200,000 people gathered to see the first flight on September 23, 1931, and wherever on the ground the *Akron* cast its long shadow everything—traffic, commerce, farming, housework, education—came to a halt as all eyes turned up, mesmerized, to the sky. For those not lucky enough to have had the monstrous dirigible pass over their hometown, Moffett's close ties with the NBC radio network assured that its every milestone was broadcast live to listeners nationwide.

Captained by Rosendahl, the dirigible gave joyrides to congressmen, and for publicity's sake once set a record by airlifting 207 men, but it also practiced with the fleet. In one exercise over the Atlantic, it was *Akron*'s job to find the "enemy" and this it did undetected, although during another exercise over the Pacific the dirigible was ignobly "shot down" by opposing aircraft. Unfortunately the *Akron*'s own airplanes, three gnat-sized F9C-2s, had not yet been delivered by their builder, Curtiss, and hence could not repel the predators. However, when the fighters did arrive from the factory they transformed the *Akron* into an untried but promising weapon, the likes of which history had never witnessed.

Rosendahl practiced relentlessly with the F9Cs, capturing and launching them from the airship's "trapeze," a ladder-like structure on which the fighters hooked and unhooked themselves. The hope was that the fighter-bearing *Akron* could scout a line many hundreds of miles wide, creating a reconnaissance net from which an enemy armada could not escape. At first the midget fighters lacked radios and compasses, meaning that they dared not lose sight of the mother ship over the ocean lest they get lost, but with the addition of this equipment, flying from the *Akron* the Navy Curtiss aircraft once conducted a seven-hour, hundred-mile-wide sweep off the northeast coast—a feat not surpassed until the 1950s when airplanes equipped with super-long-range radar became available.[66]

After nineteen months and some tentative successes, the aerial cruiser, now captained by Commander Frank C. McCord, had still not found its footing with the fleet. There were a number of reasons for this. For example, to serve over both the Atlantic and Pacific as required, meant shuttling across the continent on a regular basis, but *Akron*'s operating ceiling of around 3,000 feet made traversing the far higher Rockies, standing in the way, possible but dangerous. Another problem was that on the West Coast mooring arrangements were rudimentary, meaning that the zeppelin would have to abandon the Pacific for the risky flight back to Lakehurst whenever major repairs were necessary. And then there was the sheer size of the thing, making the beautiful but bulbous *Akron* such a tempting aerial target that the Navy Department and battleship admirals dismissed it as hopelessly "vulnerable."[67] However, Moffett disagreed, and were it not for his fierce advocacy, his genius for publicity (and his additional hope that naval dirigibles would pave the way for commercial airships), the entire dirigible program would surely have been canceled. But then tragedy struck, robbing America of its most powerful proponent of the airship.

It was in the early morning hours of April 4, 1933, when the Navy Department called Admiral Moffett's residence in Washington D.C., and the phone was answered by his wife.

"The Akron has just gone down," the voice said. "Will you notify the admiral?"

"The admiral is on the Akron," she replied.[68]

The previous day, and with A. F. Masury of the Mack Truck Company (and a great supporter of airships) as his guest, Moffett had gone along for the ride as the *Akron* departed Lakehurst for a publicity swing around Philadelphia before heading north to New England for radio calibration work. Weather reports, however, failed to predict one of the worst thunder and lightning systems to hit the East Coast in years, and in the final hours of April 3, 1933, Captain McCord was caught by surprise while over New Jersey. McCord headed the *Akron* out to sea in an attempt to ride out the storm, which in retrospect was not a wise decision because about twenty miles off the coast, and shortly after midnight, violent turbulence forced the ship's altitude down from 1,100 to 700 feet. With rain pouring through the open windows of the control car, McCord hollered at his elevator man to lift the bow, called for full power, and ordered water ballast bags emptied. The situation was stabilized and level flight resumed, but this lasted no more than a minute. At 1,600 feet the dirigible was again pushed down by an invisible hand, stern first and at a rate of 800 feet per minute. Fearing the worst, McCord ordered "landing stations" and each of the ship's eighteen telephones rang the alarm. At 800 feet, as measured by the altimeter, a jolt shot through the *Akron* but the descent ended and the airship seemed to regain trim. Oddly, though, the helmsman reported that the controls were slack. Equally oddly, the airship assumed a forty-five-degree upward angle yet, despite engines at full power, was not gaining any altitude. Moments later the nose dropped precipitously, and through the fog and darkness McCord could see white-tipped waves coming at him at a fantastic rate. "Stand by for a crash!," he shouted.[69]

Whether McCord realized it or not, his altimeter had been faulty—undoubtedly skewed by extreme changes in barometric pressure caused by the storm—and instead of leveling off at 800 feet, as he had thought, the *Akron* was speeding in a nose-up but descending course toward the Atlantic. Just three short minutes elapsed between sounding the initial alarm and the ocean surface being littered with floating wreckage and swimming survivors. Negligently, not one life preserver had been stowed aboard, and only three men managed to swim long enough in the cold water to be rescued (one of them being Boatswain's Mate R. E. "Lucky" Deal, a survivor of the *Shenandoah*). Admiral Moffett's body was one of the few recovered, and the death toll, seventy-one officers and sailors, staggered the nation.

Just one month earlier, Jeanette Moffett, the admiral's wife and now widow, had christened the *Akron*'s sister ship, ZRS-5, the USS *Macon*

AUTHOR'S COLLECTION

AUTHOR'S COLLECTION

The USS Macon *arrives at NAS Sunnyvale, California, October 15, 1933, after a nonstop flight from the east coast.*

amidst optimistic pronouncements as to the future of naval dirigibles; but in the wake of what had just happened, naval support for that future had evaporated. The *Macon*, however, had already been delivered and could not be returned, and although it achieved the fastest speed of any airship in history, eighty-eight miles per hour, nevertheless the new ship was still the subject of intense scrutiny by a navy that did not want it. Indeed, the dirigible fared poorly during fleet war games in 1934, being "shot down" and having to re-enter the exercises each successive time with a new identity, "ZRS-6," "ZRS-7," etc. Its defenders, however,

OPPOSITE: *ZRS-5 under construction in Akron, Ohio.*

COURTESY NAVAL HISTORICAL FOUNDATION

An F9C-2 hooked on the trapeze.

strenuously objected that the ship was not being used for its intended purpose, namely long-range reconnaissance, operating by itself far from shore and releasing its scout airplanes to search vast stretches of ocean. Instead the dirigible had to perform tactical duties close to shore and in coordination with the fleet, and indeed in this role it was very vulnerable. The argument was made moot, though, on February 12, 1935, when America's rigid airship program was to die forever.

The *Macon* was captained that day by Commander Herbert Wiley, who with "Lucky" Deal was one of only three to have survived the *Akron* tragedy. Having been newly released from fleet exercises off Point Sur, California, the *Macon* was broadsided by a gust of wind on the return journey to Moffett Field (named in honor of the late admiral) south of San Francisco. This set into motion a series of interconnected events. First there was the loss of the *Macon*'s upper fin just after the wind burst hit. Then there was structural failure at Frame 17.5 as a result of the destroyed fin. Following that was deflation of helium cells one and two because of the failure of Frame 17.5. Finally, and due to excessive dumping of ballast in the chaotic seconds just after the incident, there was the ascent to heights above pressure altitude, causing more helium to be lost through the safety ventilators.

Inexplicably, the engines were kept running at full speed, which kept the stricken *Macon* at high altitude, venting helium all the while, for an entire sixteen minutes. But by the time the mistake had been realized and throttles pulled back, too much helium had been lost and the *Macon* began its final descent. Fortunately, though, the descent took as long as fifteen minutes, giving Wiley ample time both to send out an S.O.S. and for his crew to don lifejackets (which, after the previous disaster, had become mandatory). It was 5:40 p.m. when the airship came to rest upon the ocean, and the ship did not sink for a further forty minutes. All aboard were life vested and had been prepared for a dunking, and two navy cruisers were already on the scene by 6:40 p.m. By rights, therefore, all eighty-three officers and men should have survived, but instead two sailors somehow went missing and were never found.

Extensive hearings and investigations after the loss of the *Macon* focused intently on an April 1934 incident in which the ship was caught in severe turbulence over Texas, suffering damage at the point where the port horizontal fin met the frame. That the airship might have been improperly repaired afterward, or that there was an inherent defect in the airship's design, were two of the contending theories regarding the crash off Point Sur a year later. By this time, however, it was all academic since two more airship fatalities were two too many for a hostile Congress.

Moffett's original Five Year Plan called for the construction of a single training dirigible, and phoenix-like this request had been revived by President Franklin D. Roosevelt after the loss of the *Akron*. Now with the *Macon* lying at the bottom of the Pacific, however, not even the benign *Los Angeles* would be spared. In 1940 the venerable "LA," which had enjoyed that rarest of lives for an airship, a long and successful one, was dismantled for scrap, netting the U.S. Navy less than $4,000. A year later America went to war in the Pacific without any of Admiral Moffett's airships—because there weren't any—but it did, at least, go to war with the sea-going aircraft carriers *Langley*, *Saratoga*, and *Lexington*, which a decade earlier the admiral had insisted upon, and which in the early days of the war held the line against the Japanese.

SIX

The quest to fly to the top of the world that had obsessed Walter Wellman also obsessed Norway's Roald Amundsen, the first to navigate the Northwest Passage (in 1906) and to reach the South Pole (in 1911). As early as 1909, Amundsen had been making plans to reach the North Pole by airplane, but intervening events prevented this; until, that is, he had the financial backing of a wealthy and adventurous young American, Lincoln Ellsworth, who wanted to fly along with him. While their subsequent flight from Kings Bay, Spitsbergen, in the spring of 1924 ended short of its goal, Amundsen discounted the significance. "I had not any great interest in reaching the Pole," he said afterward.[70] However, for a driven man like Amundsen who had a lived a life in pursuit of world fame, this modest assertion belied the truth.

Later that same year, 1924, the Italian airship builder Colonel Umberto Nobile received a telegram from Amundsen suggesting that they meet in Rome for, the Norwegian said, "an important and secret conference." Nobile explained that "A few months previously Amundsen had returned from an expedition in which he had unsuccessfully tried to reach the North Pole with two Dornier Wal seaplanes, built in Italy at Mariana di Pisa. When one of them was damaged, both had been obliged to alight on the ice north of the Spitsbergen islands, in 87° 40' latitude N. Twenty-five days later, abandoning the wrecked machine on the pack, Amundsen and his five companions had all crowded into the other and flown back to their starting-point at Kings Bay. Having failed in this attempt to reach the Pole by seaplane, Amundsen had thought of an airship—the advantages of which over an airplane as a means of polar exploration were obvious even to a layman."[71]

This obviousness, of course, rested in the airship's ability to span vast distances that still eluded the airplane, and now Amundsen proposed not only to reach the Pole, but to soar over it and continue thousands of miles beyond until reaching the North American continent on the other side, the exact same thing attempted by the, at that point, still-missing Andrée nearly thirty years before. Amundsen convinced the tiny Aero Club of Norway to be his official sponsor, and also recruited several Norwegian colleagues from past adventures to be his crew. Money for the venture—$120,000—would again come from the American Ellsworth, and the piloting would come from the Italian Nobile, hired as an employee of the expedition. Five of Nobile's mechanics, who were the only other Italians Amundsen permitted on board, would see to the engines and do other chores during the flight, such as scraping ice off the top of the dirigible.

Amundsen, an old sea salt at age fifty-two, and Nobile, an aeronautical engineer who was thirty-nine, made for an unlikely pair. The hearty Norwegian had a lifetime's share of outdoor adventures behind him, while the intellectual Italian had been turned down by the army during the war as being too frail. By both men's accounts, however, their partnership was a highly productive one, with Amundsen in charge of organizing the overall expedition and Nobile in charge of readying an airship in just eight months.

Eight months proved insufficient to design and build a dirigible from scratch, so the Italian chose one of his existing ships, the N 1, a 654,000-cubic-feet semi-rigid built for continental passenger service.

Being "semi-rigid" meant N 1 was not just a car and engine hooked to a gasbag, such as Santos-Dumont's No. 6 or Wellman's *America* had been, nor a vessel of duralumin framework, like the zeppelins and their British and American counterparts; rather, it was a hybrid of both types. The dirigible had a triangular metal-and-canvas keel attached to an oblong hull above, and attached to the keel was the pilot cabin and three motor gondolas, but the hull itself had little rigidity and kept its shape mostly from the pressure of hydrogen (helium not being available in Italy) and air inside. Because the flight across the Pole necessitated mooring at masts and the need to carry much petrol, Nobile strengthened N 1 by adding a rigid bow and made it 3,500 pounds lighter by removing its kitchen, salon, and an elegantly decorated bedroom.

When the refurbished airship stood ready for delivery, ownership was handed over by Italy's powerful Benito Mussolini to the Aero Club during a formal ceremony in Rome, and its new owners christened it the *Norge* (Norway). Italian Air Ministry officials were skeptical of the polar flight, but Mussolini (*Il Duce*) fully supported the venture, and in Italy his was only opinion that counted. He met with Nobile and, as Nobile recalled, "He asked what provisions we were taking." Just as Nobile answered, "Pemmican, biscuits, chocolate, tea," Mussolini remarked, "But then it's not necessary to eat." According to Nobile, "He seemed convinced of that—and almost succeeded in convincing me, who would willingly have left food behind in order to take on more fuel."[72]

For the first portion of the long journey to Spitsbergen, where Kings Bay would again serve as Amundsen and Ellsworth's base, the flight took on a thoroughly international flair. There were not only Norwegians and Italians on board, but also English and French military observers, a Russian radio operator, and a Swedish meteorologist. Theoretically, English was the official language of the expedition, but in practice the crew of twenty-one men, while perfectly amicable, could not understand each other. With all in readiness, on the morning of April 10, 1926, the dirigible rose from Ciampino and then, Nobile recalled, "The *Norge*'s prow was turned toward the heart of the city, to salute it. We looked down upon the Quirinal, the Capitol, the Vatican, and the workshops where we had designed and built our ship. I am told that the bells of churches rang out in salutation and good wishes, and that an unknown priest, when he saw us pass high above him, knelt down in the street to pray."[73]

Nobile also looked around at the scenery inside and saw that "The interior of the airship looked distinctly picturesque. We had distributed an enormous quantity of materials in the various sections of the hull, using girders to support them. But the little pilot cabin was equally cluttered. When the kitbags and suitcases of some of the crew were added, there was hardly room to move. Among the many things on board I will mention, as a curiosity, were two armchairs in steel tubing covered with velvet, intended for Amundsen and Ellsworth."[74]

Mention of the armchairs in these otherwise uncomfortable surroundings was perhaps more than a "curiosity," and instead a dig at the great Amundsen and his rich American benefactor, both of whom had seen fit to take a steamship to Kings Bay where they would await the arrival of the dirigible in relative comfort.

After a rough passage over France through squally weather, the *Norge* crossed the English Channel and landed with some difficulty in Pulham, ninety miles northeast of London. British authorities quarantined Nobile's flying companion, his little dog Tatina, threatening a minor diplomatic scandal. However, on April 13 she was reunited with her master when the airship, this time without the military observers, lifted off for Spitsbergen via Oslo, Leningrad, and Vadsö. Seven hundred miles later, Oslo was reached the following afternoon, and after a few hours spent at mast to show itself off to the citizenry, the airship ascended into darkness and fog. At daybreak on April 14 the weather cleared to reveal a nondescript landscape.

Where, Nobile and his men wondered, were they? Finland? Estonia? Latvia? Russia? "At last we found a farmstead, lost in the wide colorless plain," Nobile said. "A group of peasants stared up at us. I had the idea of questioning them. I prepared a message: '*What country is this? Finland? If so, raise your arms in the air.*' I had it translated into Swedish (which most Finns understand), Russian and German, and threw it down. The astonished peasants, gazing at the airship that was circling over their heads, did not notice the message and nobody picked it up."[75]

The lost airship followed a railway until a town was sighted. Genadii Olomkin, the Russian radio man, was called forth and he concluded from the shape of a church that this was his country. It was 3:27 p.m. and, carried along by a favorable tailwind, the expedition reached Gatchina near Leningrad after an impressive day of flying: 738 miles in just seventeen hours. The Soviets were friends of Nobile, who had spent time in Leningrad four months earlier in preparation for this trip, and they placed soldiers, an airship hangar, and the Imperial Palace at his disposal. He was also honored with a reception at the Academy of Sciences. Despite the hospitality, Nobile was anxious to be off, but difficulties in completing the airship base at Kings Bay forced him to wait. The delay was frustrating, and then Amundsen telegraphed to say that the venture should be put off until June, causing Nobile further annoyance. "I was completely taken aback," Nobile recalled, noting that Amundsen's advice "was altogether opposed to the convictions of the experts on Arctic weather conditions; and even to his own previous declarations. In fact, if we were to postpone the flight by a whole month it would, in my opinion, be equivalent to giving it up."[76] Faced with this argument, Amundsen relented and agreed to the original plans. On May 5 the *Norge* set sail for Vadsö while the Soviets below yelled "*Viva l'Italia!*"[77]

The Norge *in flight.* AUTHOR'S COLLECTION

Leningrad to Vadsö represented a distance of 840 miles, and Vadsö to Spitsbergen an additional 780. Flying at an average speed of forty miles per hour over forests, frozen seas, and islands, the dirigible tossed and turned nauseously, or else droned along monotonously. The temperature inside the pilot cabin was a miserable twenty-one degrees Fahrenheit. Along the way the left engine went to pieces, yet Nobile pressed on and the *Norge* arrived to a warm welcome from Amundsen and Ellsworth at Kings Bay on May 7. Also at Kings Bay was U.S. Navy Lieutenant Commander Richard E. Byrd with his trimotor Fokker airplane, the *Josephine Ford*. Byrd kept his intentions to himself, but anyone could see he intended to take off for the Pole at the first opportunity.

Prior to the arrival of the *Norge*, the Amundsen-Ellsworth and Byrd parties had maintained a mutual suspiciousness of each other, and when Byrd roared off in the *Josephine Ford* on the morning of May 9, just two days after the arrival of Nobile, he did so in secret. Byrd returned to base earlier than expected but claimed to have reached the Pole (a claim that soon became highly controversial, with most experts today considering it false).[78] To mark his supposed success, the Navy commander invited the dirigible men to a celebratory dinner. There, Byrd told Nobile and Amundsen that the only reason he left for the Pole before them was so the *Norge* could rescue him should he crash. While Nobile and Amundsen tried to swallow this excuse, Byrd assured that he and his airplane would remain at Kings Bay after they left, should something happen to them. Complimenting Byrd on reaching the pole, Amundsen and Nobile could at least look forward to being first to traverse the top of the world.

For its upcoming voyage, the *Norge* was laden with seven tons of gasoline and 800 pounds of motor oil, and to save weight the crew, now whittled down to sixteen men, carried no extra clothing and took only what they were wearing, the most important items being thick underwear and good fur-lined clothes. There was sufficient food for several days of flight, with provisions including sandwiches, fruit, hard-boiled eggs, thermos flasks of coffee, and more thermos flasks filled with a mix of bouillon and terrible-tasting meatballs. The Norwegians, with their arctic expertise, were responsible for emergency rations and packed enough for everyone to last a month on the ice, should it come to that. Consideration was also given to drinking water, but after the ascent from Kings Bay, May 11, it was discovered the water had been left behind. But no matter, because, according to Nobile, "The weather was magnificent, the sky cloudless. The impressive Spitsbergen peaks glittered snow-white in the sunshine. I felt deeply happy; the malaise and weariness that had oppressed me on the previous evening and during the night had vanished as if by magic. How light I felt! A few hours previously I had been shivering with cold; now I would have liked to take off my furs . . . Our lovely ship was sailing along at nearly 50 miles per hour toward the Pole—and beyond the Pole, into the Unknown."[79]

A fox, bear prints, and white fish were spotted from the air at low altitude before Nobile climbed to 3,650 feet in an effort to escape strong headwinds. With the change in height, ground speed increased to a respectable fifty-two miles per hour, a clip that lasted until the left engine quit. Ice, it was discovered, had fouled the fuel line. The line was cleared and the motor restarted. Thick, cold fog, the bane of Andrée's expedition, froze on the exterior of the airship and coated the celluloid windows, although the Norwegian navigator, Hjalmar Riiser-Larsen, was steadily narrowing the distance between the *Norge* and the Pole. There were just two more hours to go. "As we approached, the excitement on board was growing," Nobile recalled. "No one spoke, but one could read the happy impatience in their faces."[80] Flags were unfurled, and at 1:30 a.m. on May 12, Riiser-Larsen, taking sextant readings every time the sun poked through the clouds, confirmed the unbelievable: at ninety degrees north, they were on top of the world!

Although the scenery below consisted of nothing more interesting than flat ice disrupted by pressure ridges, all aboard felt the moment profound, and the airship loitered over the Pole for a couple hours. From here, of course, the *Norge* could only go south, and a track twelve degrees left of the meridian that had brought the dirigible up from Spitsbergen was set. Then at 2:39 p.m., Nobile and his men flew into the only blank spot remaining on the map of the globe.

Over the next few hours, pieces of ice that had formed on the hydrogen envelope fell periodically into the spinning propellers and were sent flying dangerously against the sides of the airship. Wind whistled through every joint in the pilot cabin and, Nobile recalled, "We had been in the air 32½ hours. The cabin was horribly dirty. The dozens of thermos flasks heaped on the floor, near the little cupboard where we kept the charts and navigation books, presented a particularly sad spectacle: some of them empty, others overturned, others broken. Coffee and tea had been spilt everywhere, and all over the place were the remains of

LIBRARY OF CONGRESS

Departing for the Pole and the unknown beyond, Colonel Umberto Nobile looks out from the control car of the Norge, *May 11, 1926.*

food. In the midst of all this mess there stuck out picturesquely Amundsen's enormous feet, with his grass stuffed shoes, his diver's gaiters and red and white gloves."[81]

With a minimal crew, no one could be relieved of his duties and all were totally exhausted, except perhaps for the man in gaiters and gloves, whose burden was light. "Nobile and I spent most of our time in the pilot's cabin," Amundsen recalled nonchalantly. "Naturally, I had the easiest task of all on board. The others did the work of keeping the ship going, and going to the right objective. My function was solely that of the explorer, watching the terrain below, studying its geographical

LIBRARY OF CONGRESS

Roald Amundsen in his special armchair of steel tubing and velvet.

character, and especially keeping an alert eye out for any signs of a possible Arctic continent."[82]

If there was any disappointment at this stage in the journey, it was the failure to see land, yet for Nobile this again was no matter. "The vast expanse of frozen sea, with its shadows, dark patches, embroidery of blue, was truly fascinating," he said. "From time to time there appeared long serpentine channels, dark grey in color; and once, what looked like a wide black river, its banks formed by layer on layer of blue-sprinkled ice. The airship itself had toned into the polar landscape, now that ice had formed on almost all its metal parts—sometimes half an inch thick or more . . . It was as though the ship had been festively decorated, now that the polar crossing was on the point of being achieved."[83]

The north coast of Alaska was sighted early in the morning of May 13, followed by Eskimo villages and their awestruck inhabitants staring up at the silvery craft, but many more hours of difficult and dangerous flight remained through dense fog and bad weather until the *Norge* could land at Teller, population fifty-five, located a hundred miles from Nome. The trip had lasted seventy-two hours, covered 3,391 miles at an average speed of forty-seven miles per hour, and was an unqualified success. The explorers had done exactly what they set out to do: they reached the North Pole and did so convincingly, and they confirmed that there was no hidden continent between northern Europe and Alaska—just water and ice. Additionally, the *Norge* had given exemplary service on a trek for which it was not designed; although slumped over on its side after a rough deflation, it was now a wreck. At Teller, Amundsen and Ellsworth made for the local telegraph office to rush off the first of their exclusives for the *New York Times*, for which they would receive a total of $50,000. Ellsworth may not have needed the money but Amundsen, whose past expeditions had brought him fame but not fortune, was counting on it. However, it transpired that he and Ellsworth were not the only ones who intended to profit from the flight.

"A thing that was perfectly clear in my mind as in Ellsworth's," Amundsen later complained, was "that we regarded Nobile solely as a paid employee, and that at no stage of the preparations nor during the flight did we ever consent that he should be regarded otherwise." Amundsen continued that "Certainly, we never intended and did not consent to his sharing in any financial returns from the expedition. Our money had paid for the expedition, including the payment of a salary to Nobile. If there were to be any financial returns, as from a book or other writings, certainly we had no reason to share these returns."[84] Nobile, however, did not share this opinion, and to Amundsen's utter horror, sold his own exclusives to the press and, while he was at it, audaciously claimed victory for Italy.

"We of the Italian contingent are especially proud that it was Premier Benito Mussolini who fostered the undertaking and gave for it the ship and the men to command her," Nobile wrote for *National Geographic* magazine. "After centuries, the dream of old Italian navigators to reach the Pacific across the north, starting from the Mediterranean, is at last realized . . . We are happy and proud that all along the aerial route of 8,500 miles across Europe, the Barents Sea, the Polar Sea, the Bering Sea, and Alaska, we carried on the front of our commander's cabin the 'fascio littorio,' symbol of the old, eternal Rome and of the new Italy."[85]

For the staunchly nationalistic Amundsen the seeds of this treachery were, in retrospect, evident back when he was negotiating the purchase of N 1, and the airship was offered to him free of charge by Mussolini as long as it flew the Italian flag. "I did not realize that significance at the time," Amundsen confessed of his naiveté, "but it is now clear that it was a deliberate effort on the part of the government to gain for the present Italian political regime in particular, and for the Italian people in general, a world-wide advertisement. My idea of a transpolar flight was thus subtly to be appropriated as their own by the Italians, and my skill in Arctic exploration was to be utilized as the means of a dramatic achievement for which the Italians would take the credit."[86]

Unable to stop the expropriation of his story and forced to share victory with another country, the Norwegian resorted to maligning Nobile in his 1927 memoir *My Life as an Explorer*. Amundsen began his treatment of Nobile by, among other things, accusing him of being a lunatic when behind the wheel of a car. "So long as we were proceeding on a straight and level stretch of highway he drove steadily at a rational speed," Amundsen recalled. "The moment, however, we approached a curve in the road where an ordinary driver would slow down as a matter of course, Nobile's procedure was directly the opposite. He would press the accelerator down to the floor, and we would take the blind curve at terrific speed. Halfway round, as I was convulsively tightening my grip on the seat with my hands and shuddering with fear of disaster, Nobile would seem to come out of a cloud of abstraction, realize the danger, and frantically seek to avoid it."[87] Amundsen also charged that Nobile deprived the Norwegian members of the crew on the journey from Rome to Spitsbergen of their cold-weather suits on the account of weight, yet allowed unnecessary guests to accompany him on the flight. Such behavior on the part of Nobile, Amundsen said, was testament to "his arrogance and egoism and selfishness."[88]

Continuing his literary assault, Amundsen lampooned Nobile for insisting that he and Mussolini had initiated the arctic venture. "I remember on one occasion," Amundsen explained of skiing in Kings Bay, when "Nobile fell on smooth ground and could not get up, so that he had to be assisted to his feet. It is merely amusing to suppose that men of this semitropical race, who had not the most rudimentary idea of how to take care of themselves in a cold country, could ever have conceived of the notion of undertaking on their own account an expedition which required as its most elementary qualification an ability to survive on the ice in an emergency. Indeed, before the *Norge* left Italy, Nobile took Riiser-Larsen to one side and made him promise 'if we have to get down on the ice you will not leave us Italians and save yourselves.'"[89]

And there was more about Nobile, according to Amundsen's book: before the flight, Nobile had been incapacitated by fear; thrice during the flight he had lost his mind and nearly crashed the airship; he lacked a basic understanding of navigation; at Teller, he removed Riiser-Larsen from the most comfortable lodgings and took them for himself; he had secreted a heavy and resplendent Italian colonel's uniform aboard the *Norge* to wear when he arrived in America, and so forth.

A final thing Amundsen griped about was that "Ellsworth and I had each, of course, brought a flag to be dropped overboard as we crossed the Pole—Ellsworth the Stars and Stripes and I the national flag of Norway. In keeping with Nobile's injunctions, we had each brought a little flag not much larger than a pocket handkerchief. As we crossed the Pole, we threw these overboard and gave a cheer for our countries. Imagine our astonishment to see Nobile dropping outside not one, but armfuls, of flags. For a few moments the *Norge* looked like a circus wagon of the skies, with great banners of every shape and hue fluttering down around her. Nobile produced one really huge Italian flag. It was so large he had difficulty in getting it out the cabin window. There the wind struck it and it stuck to the side of the gondola. Before he could disengage it we must have been five miles beyond the Pole. When it finally flew free, it hurtled back to the rear gondola and there for an instant it seemed that it would become entangled with the propeller and give us serious trouble. At length it fluttered free and sank swiftly to the surface of the ice below us."[90]

Undeterred by Amundsen's scathing criticism, Nobile—now, thanks to Mussolini, *General* Nobile—had a dirigible built along the lines of N 1 for a return voyage north. "Many persons have asked," he told the Milan Geographical Society in March 1928, shortly before departing for Kings Bay, "why we are going up there. Was not one successful trip sufficient? Was not that which was done at that time sufficient for Italy? And would it not be better to give up this new undertaking?" Answering his own question, Nobile said, "I, however, look upon the expedition of 1926 merely as a beginning of a new era in polar exploration."[91]

Il Duce once again gave the venture his hearty approval, the new airship was christened the *Italia*, and this time there was no doubt that the expedition was a state-sponsored enterprise to be leveraged for maximum propaganda value. In April the Italian steamship *Città di Milano* (City of Milan), under the command of Captain Giuseppe Romagna, barged into Kings Bay before being stopped by a thick layer of fjord ice.

Sailors streamed off the ship to plant 200 bombs between it and the shore, but when the bombs were detonated they did little to break up the ice. Norwegians from a local mining operation were then asked to help, and their dynamite—one and a half tons of it—did the trick. Romagna reached shore, where provisions, motors, spare parts, and innumerable other items needed for the dirigible, including 4,005 heavy gas cylinders, were hauled by tractor a short distance through the snow to the airship base, still standing after two years' vacancy. With preparatory work not yet completed, the *Italia* arrived on May 6. "From the deck of our ship," the Norwegian journalist Odd Arnesen recalled, "we observed the airship fighting wind and weather, unsteady as a drunkard, but slowly advancing. A head wind was handling the airship roughly, and it did not augur well for the coming flights in the polar regions. We heard subsequently that Nobile indeed contemplated returning to Vadsö after the ship had reached Spitsbergen, as there appeared to be little hope of effecting a landing."[92] Nobile, though, stuck it out and, after seven weary hours of trying, the airship came safely to ground.

Sharing Amundsen's prejudices against the Italians in that their "race" was inherently unsuited to cold weather, Arnesen noted that in unloading the *Città di Milano* all toil ceased whenever it snowed. But Arnesen did find the Mediterranean invaders colorful. "There are all sorts of Italian military uniforms," he exclaimed, "common soldiers in grey, picturesque Alpini, naval officers in brilliant uniforms with masses of decorations, and marines in fluttering cloaks."[93] He also thought the Italians "the queerest conglomeration of warring opinions. Some of them were fanatical Fascists who shot up like rockets and saluted in Fascist manner whenever the general appeared at the staff mess of the mining camp, while the Fascism of some others was lukewarm, and yet others were entirely uninterested in the question."[94]

Arnesen was on hand to chronicle the flights of the *Italia*, but not many other reporters bothered. One reason for this was that Nobile, whose own newspaper contracts were rumored to be worth three million lira, was a formidable competitor who kept his sources to himself. Another was the desultory nature of the expedition, one that seemed to lack any purpose other than to poke around the icy environs and hope for a discovery that could be trumpeted by Rome. Most of civilization, therefore, was ignorant of events taking place above eighty degrees north that spring.

The first exploratory flight, on May 11, was destined for a distant point to be determined along the way, and vast amounts of fuel and supplies were loaded aboard the dirigible in expectation of a prolonged mission. Instead the *Italia* encountered fog and winds and returned some hours later. Upon landing, the rear-motor gondola hit the ground and needed major repairs. Heavy snow and fierce winds then canceled the second scheduled flight, which was to have gone to Nicholas II Land, an uncharted archipelago east of Spitsbergen. That flight got underway a few days later, but it too was a disappointment. Fog concealed Nicholas II Land, Nobile came within 300 feet of hitting a mountain, he got lost, and it was so cold aboard the *Italia* that the Chianti froze. Nobile, though, promised that on the next flight he personally would stand on top of the world with a large wooden cross, bestowed upon him by the pope.

This third—and what was expected to be the penultimate—trip of the expedition was scheduled to last thirty-five hours, and it began at 4:28 a.m. on Wednesday, May 23. Radio messages from the airship were in cipher and presumably meant for Mussolini in Rome, but in the early-morning hours of Thursday, May 24, Arnesen was told by officers aboard the *Città di Milano* that the general had reached the Pole. Conditions had prevented a landing with the cross, but, Arnesen also learned, "While the *Italia* circled round the point of the Pole, Nobile ordered the Fascist hymn to be played on the gramophone, and all the Italians raised their right hands in the Fascist salute. Afterward the gramophone played, 'Beautiful Italy, with all my heart.'"[95]

The dirigible was expected back that evening, yet nightfall came and went with no sign of the *Italia*. Reports issued by the *Città di Milano* were that Nobile and his crew of sixteen were having difficulty navigating and that ice was forming both on the inside and outside of the airship; also, headwinds were reducing forward speeds by half. At 10:30 a.m. on Friday the airship radioed that its position was north of Moffen Island and due north of Wood Bay. After that, nothing more was heard from the *Italia*.

Suddenly, the world's largest newspapers demanded the latest on the lost airship from Arnesen, and he was soon joined by hordes of reporters who got to Kings Bay any way they could. In the midst of this press frenzy there was panic aboard the *Città di Milano* as the Italians, poring over maps of this foreign and forbidding land, realized they had no means of finding the dirigible and rescuing its crew. Just to do something, anything, the unhappy ship steamed out of the bay to scout the shoreline but, stymied by ice, was back again in a few days. Then a party of Alpini troops set out on foot and nearly came to grief. There was gloom and doom all around, and this lasted until June 8, two weeks after the airship disappeared, when the *Città di Milano* picked up a faint signal. "It is Nobile! It is the *Italia!*"[96] the wireless operator cried as several more messages came in confirming that this was so. Nobile, with a tent for shelter and enough food for himself and his men to last only so long, radioed from his position on a drifting ice floe that he was stranded off the coast of North East Land.

When the *Italia* had first gone missing, the Norwegian government dispatched a ship to Spitsbergen with two airplanes, one of them piloted by Riiser-Larsen, former navigator of the *Norge*. As soon as he was able, on June 17, Riiser-Larsen took to the air and flew over the area where the general and his men were supposed to be, but in the vastness of the Arctic wastes could not see their pinprick of a tent. Major Umberto Maddalena, just in from Rome piloting an exotic Savoia-Marchetti twin-hull flying boat, was the next to fly over the area, but he too came back with nothing. Nobile radioed afterward that he had seen both airplanes, and so a simple set of codes was developed with which to communicate with the pilots next time. The system worked, and on Maddalena's second attempt he was directed over the tent and able to drop 600 pounds of supplies, most of which scattered and smashed all over the ice.

Although erroneous reports had the USS *Los Angeles* joining the effort as well, Swedish and Finnish aircraft were arriving at Kings Bay and more aircraft from other countries were on their way, including that of Roald Amundsen, who was expected at any time. Since the flight of the *Norge* the famous explorer had gone into a cranky and impoverished retirement, but upon learning of the plight of the man he detested, proclaimed that he would save him. Amundsen asked Ellsworth for money, but for reasons unknown the still-wealthy and once-generous American turned him down. Then in a stroke of amazing fortune, from France came an unsolicited offer of not only a French Navy Latham 47 flying boat, but a crew of five to fly it, and within days Amundsen was preparing to leave Tromsö, where he and the Latham 47 had landed. Planning to fly across the Barents Sea for Kings Bay, the flying boat took off on June 18 but never arrived. One theory held that Amundsen made straight for Nobile instead, but when this turned out not to be the case, another massive search effort had begun.

As some of the pilots now went off to look for the Latham 47 and its famous passenger, there was intense rivalry among the remaining ones over who would rescue the first men of the *Italia*. Then, on Sunday, June 24, the *Città di Milano* began to sound its horn to announce that the competition was over. The Swedish airman Einar Lundborg had landed on the ice floe and returned with a man and a dog: the general and Tatina.

Aboard the *Città di Milano*, now anchored farther north in Virgo Harbor where the remains of Andrée's balloon-house were still discernible, Nobile lay convalescing, a virtual prisoner of Romagna. The captain accused him of abandoning his men and forbade him to take any part in the rescue effort. Nobile argued strenuously that Lundborg, who could only carry one passenger, had insisted he fly out first, and that he, Nobile, would be of far more use to his men aboard the base ship directing things than stuck out on the ice. Nobile then berated Romagna for the painfully slow pace of the rescue process and wondered why, among other things, he had failed to detect his distress signals for an entire two weeks. Becoming defensive, Romagna told Nobile that he was not listening for them because he had mistakenly assumed that the *Italia*'s sole wireless operator, Giuseppe Biagi, had been killed in a freak accident. According to Romagna's scenario, Biagi had stuck his head out the cabin window only to be decapitated by the wind-driven propeller used to generate electricity for the radio.

For Nobile, this excuse was absurd, yet he did not care to argue the point because on the ice pack there were two, and possibly three, groups of survivors in need of immediate rescue. The crash had occurred forty-four hours after leaving the Pole, and during most of those hours the *Italia*, flying through freezing fog and the occasional snow squall, had strained against headwinds, raising concerns that the fuel would give out. Then without warning, from an altitude of 1,500 feet the airship fell precipitously. "Instinctively I grasped the helm," Nobile recalled, "wondering if it were possible to guide the ship onto a snow-field and so lessen the shock. . . . Too late! . . . There was the pack, a few yards below, terribly uneven. The masses of ice grew larger, came nearer . . .

A moment later we crashed."[97] It was 10:30 a.m. on May 25, and the event—caused perhaps by ice on the envelope, or perhaps loss of hydrogen, or perhaps both—had lasted two minutes.

"When I opened my eyes," Nobile continued, "I found myself lying on a hummock in the midst of an appalling pack . . . I noticed at once that some of the others had fallen with me. I looked up to the sky. Towards my left the dirigible, nose in the air, was drifting away before the wind. It was terribly lacerated around the pilot-cabin. Out of it trailed torn strips of fabric, ropes, fragments of metal work. The left wall of the cabin had remained attached. I noticed a few creases in the envelope. Upon the side of the crippled, mutilated ship, stood out the black letters I T A L I A."[98]

Around Nobile were scattered nine men, meaning that six more were still with the free-ballooning dirigible. Of those on the ice four were seriously wounded—all of them, coincidentally, veterans of the *Norge*. There was Nobile with leg, rib, and arm injuries that made him an invalid; Natale Cecioni with a broken leg that made him similarly incapacitated; Finn Malmgren, a Swedish meteorologist, with a dislocated shoulder; and Vincenzo Pomella, who appeared to have no serious injury but later collapsed and died. The *Italia*, stripped of its pilot cabin, had quickly vanished in the Arctic sky, and the situation for Nobile on the ice was dire but also remarkable in that, while one of his men died, five of them suffered only minor injuries or none at all. Equally remarkable was that navigational items, tins of fuel, 280 pounds of food, and an expertly selected assemblage of emergency equipment that included a pistol, a tent, and a radio, had spilled out of the dirigible. Biagi got the radio to work and for the next fortnight the stranded men were able to hear the nine o'clock news from Rome detailing their disappearance, but were unable to get anyone to respond to their broadcasts for help.

Ice was melted for drinking water and there was enough food to last forty-five days if mealtime rations were limited to a half-pound of pemmican and a few pieces of chocolate per man. Although water would always be in short supply, the food situation brightened on the fourth day when a polar bear made the mistake of becoming too friendly, and sacrificed itself for 400 pounds of fresh meat. Heartened by this lucky incident, Nobile had the tent painted with red dye to increase chances that they would be seen from the air. (The dye was from glass balls, meant to be dropped from the airship and timed until impact, giving an indication of altitude.) The men nicknamed their cramped little home the "Red Tent,"[99] and although the ice floe on which it was situated appeared to be sound, astronomical observations determined that it was quickly drifting due east, a trend that if unchecked would take them away from North East Land and out into the Arctic Ocean.

Although designated a general in the Italian Air Force, Nobile's rank was largely ceremonial and his leadership style decidedly democratic. Therefore, when Adalberto Mariano and Filippo Zappi, both young and fit and also both naval officers, announced they wanted to strike out on their own, he counseled patience but did not stop them. Food and equipment were divided up and on May 30, five days after the crash, the two little groups of survivors bade each other farewell. One group would remain, while the other—consisting of Mariano, Zappi, and a third man, the Swede Finn Malmgren, chosen because of his knowledge of the Arctic—would try to rendezvous with searchers and lead them to the tent.

For the six who stayed behind, their little world was soon littered with the debris of human habitation, and living in the same clothes day after day and unable to bathe, the men became unspeakably filthy. "If we did not—and could not—worry about our bodies, it must not be imagined that the elementary canons of hygiene were applied even to eating and drinking," Nobile explained. "To tell the truth, I must admit that the simplest rules of cleanliness, partly from necessity and partly through laziness, were neglected by everybody, and even considered quite superfluous. Thus we did not hesitate to drink water soiled with reindeer hairs, soot, or bear-fat; nor were we surprised to see men using fingers instead of forks, or (worse still) carefully licking the chocolate from their fingers, so as not to lose the tiniest taste of this precious food, or even picking up a scrap of meat that had accidently dropped on the filthy floor of the tent, so that it should not be wasted."[100]

Life on the ice quickly settled into a daily routine. Biagi vainly sent out S.O.S. signals, bear meat cooked over a small fire was the main meal, everyone listened intently to the nightly news from Rome, and bearings were taken of the ice floe's position. Within days of the departure of Mariano and the two others, it was determined that the floe's eastward drift was not inexorable, and that in fact it was being blown by the winds in a counter-clockwise rotation. Although preferable to being swept out to sea, this also made for disquieting scenery, as sometimes the shores of the islands of Foyn and Broch would appear close enough to walk to, while other times they would vanish over the horizon as if never to return.

The first, and wonderful, intimation that salvation was at hand came on June 6, when the news from Rome was that an amateur radio operator in Archangel, Russia, heard the call signs of the *Italia*. Still, there was a frustrating delay of two more days until the *Città di Milano* responded to Biagi, which was followed by an interminably long wait—sixteen days—before Lundborg landed in his airplane to take Nobile off. Cecioni, whose injuries were the most severe, was the second man scheduled for evacuation that day, but when Lundborg, apparently drunk, returned a few hours later, he flipped his airplane upon landing. Horrified at the living conditions on the ice floe, he gladly departed when

LIBRARY OF CONGRESS

His inverted Fokker behind him, Einar Lundborg (left) poses with Italia *survivors (left to right), Francis Behounek, Giuseppe Biagi, and Natale Cecioni.*

another Swedish airplane picked him up twelve days later, leaving Cecioni and the rest of the Red Tent occupants to their own devices.

Despite Nobile's constant hectoring that more must be done, Captain Romagna aboard the *Città di Milano* in Virgo Harbor had actually fewer options now than before. Due to his dithering, the small international air force at his disposal could no longer land on the ice pack because, in the summer warmth, it had become soft and was breaking apart; it was also too late to organize dogs and sledges for a long march to reach the survivors. Such an effort should have started weeks earlier, and in reality one had been, against Romagna's direct orders, by a lone Alpini, Captain Gennaro Sora. The Alpini captain was joined on his illicit enterprise by a twenty-two-year-old Dutch explorer named van Dongen and a Danish engineer named Warming.

The three men, along with nine huskies, a sledge, and hundreds of pounds of supplies, were carried by the whaling ship *Braganza* as far as it could go, to Cape North on North East Land, and then on June 18, the same day Amundsen departed Tromsö, the trio set out on their own toward Foyn Island. Four days later, Warming became ill at Cape Platen and was left with food and a sleeping bag, while the other two sledged on until a blizzard stopped them for two days. On the third day they discovered that two of the dogs were in a bad way and had to be shot. The march resumed, although two more dogs had to be euthanized and then three more drowned when the sledge fell through the ice. Sora and van Dongen finally reached Foyn Island on July 4, where the last of the dogs were eaten. Van Dongen came down with a fever and lapsed into delirium while airplanes passed overhead, yet none spotted the two men. Then, on July 12, when their food had run out, a dark ship belching black smoke appeared, shrilled its whistle in greetings, and continued on its way.

It was the *Krassin*, a 10,000-ton, 10,500-horsepower, steel-armored Soviet icebreaker. For two years the ship had sat idle in Leningrad when, with only five days to prepare, it hastily left port on a desperate rescue mission funded by the Italian government. For this the icebreaker was carrying a Junkers airplane on deck and 138 souls below decks, all practically living on top of one another. The men (and one woman) were officers, sailors, pilots, mechanics, doctors, scientists, radio operators, and journalists. The icebreaker refueled in Norway before crossing the Barents Sea, cruising up the west coast of Spitsbergen past Virgo Harbor, and, on June 30, heading east and into thick ice.

"The spectacle of this struggle of man against the forces of Nature was deeply impressive," noted an Italian correspondent, Davide Giudici, who accompanied the *Krassin*. "For hundreds of yards around, the pack-ice crumbled beneath the formidable blows of the ice-breaker. Great hummocks of fantastic shape were pushed up like feathers, afterwards overturning and disappearing in the sea amidst columns of white foam. The white expanses seemed to be in convulsion as from the effects of a frightful earthquake, and while the *Krassin* laboriously advanced, noisily opening for herself a passage, the eyes of all on board scrutinized the shining ice-fields." They were now in the region where Mariano, Zappi, and Malmgren could possibly be, and "Every ten minutes the sirens of the *Krassin* emitted piercing blasts in the hope that these might be heard," Giudici said, "but it was our fate to see nothing, with the exception of some seal sleeping in the sun."[101]

By July 3 the icebreaker, just fifty-five miles from the Red Tent, came to a virtual halt, having managed just one mile in four hours, at an expenditure of twenty tons of coal. July 4 was taken up by sport hunting since the ship was icebound anyway, and the next day, when forward movement could resume, it was discovered that the rudder was damaged and one of the ship's three propellers had a lost a blade to the ice. Retiring to a quiet inlet for repairs (the *Krassin* carried a spare propeller) would have been the regular course of action, but under orders from Moscow the ship instead searched for a suitable site from which to launch the Junkers, upon whose wings the lives of Nobile's men now depended.

A young Soviet aviator named Boris Chuchnovsky and a crew of four prepared for a test flight three days later. A smooth area on the ice had been found and the airplane unloaded from the icebreaker. The flight was a success, and two days after that Chuchnovsky left for the Red Tent on a reconnaissance mission to ascertain how he was going to extract the survivors. The aviator, however, could not find the tent, whose redness had long since faded to white, but after turning around and heading back to the *Krassin* he spotted two men standing and one man lying on a small floe. It had to be Mariano, Zappi, and Malmgren. There was not enough space to either land or drop supplies, so Chuchnovsky circled in recognition before continuing homeward. Thick fog, however, had rolled in, which now concealed the icebreaker, and six hours later the pilot radioed that while he and his four crewmates were unharmed, the Junkers was down and damaged near Cape Platen. He assured, however, that emergency rations, plus parachute parcels intended for the Red Tent, would keep them alive for two weeks. Denied the services of its airplane, the *Krassin* fired up its ten boilers and moved at a snail's pace, one and a half miles per hour, through ice six feet deep toward Mariano, Zappi, and Malmgren.

Thursday, July 12, 1928, turned into an amazing day in polar history. At 5:30 a.m., a lone figure was sighted scrambling toward the icebreaker. "On board all were seized by deep emotion," said Giudici. "But where were the other two men? Nothing was to be seen of them. A sailor in the crow's nest shouted out that he could see a dark form on the ice, lying still in the shelter of a hammock. When we were about half a mile away, the man we had first sighted stretched out his arm in the Roman salute. All doubts vanished; the party was Italian."[102]

The momentum of the *Krassin* threatened the integrity of the ice, so the icebreaker stopped and a rope ladder was lowered. Sailors and the ship's doctor reached the first man, who turned out to be Zappi, his face blackened by the sun, while others raced to where the other man lay prostrate in a pool of water. It was Mariano, barely alive and covered by a wet blanket. Malmgren was not with the two survivors; the third figure Chuchnovsky had thought he saw from the air was actually a blanket thrown on the snow to attract attention.

The march of Mariano, Zappi, and Malmgren, begun six weeks earlier, had been an unmitigated disaster. They walked toward shore but the ice, propelled by the wind, drifted in a different direction and they never even reached land. Malmgren succumbed at some point, although Zappi, who was in comparatively good shape upon rescue, could not give a consistent account as to when this happened, how it happened, or what had become of the body. There were other mysteries concerning Zappi. For example, why was it that, when brought aboard the *Krassin*, he was wearing in addition to three wristwatches, long underwear, good outerwear, and a double layer of boots, while his comrade Mariano, both feet frozen, only had wet stockings? Also, although Zappi was strong enough to climb the rope ladder into the icebreaker unassisted, he claimed not have eaten for thirteen days. The ship's doctor, however, estimated that Zappi had been without food for three days, while Mariano had gone without for five days. Why the vagueness surrounding Malmgren's demise and his mortal remains? Had there been, as some whispered, cannibalism? Why the disparities between Zappi and Mariano's clothing and sustenance? While intriguing, these and other questions were never answered, and in any event were not a detriment to Zappi's military career, as he later became a general.

With Zappi and Mariano being tended to below decks, the *Krassin* made straight for the Red Tent, and along the way sighted Sora and van Dongen waving frantically from Soyn Island. There was no time to stop, although the duo's position was relayed to Swedish and Finnish flyers and they were rescued eventually. As instructed by radio, the five remaining inhabitants of the tent built a fire, and at eight o'clock that evening smoke was visible to the icebreaker from a distance of four or five miles away. Making steady progress, the *Krassin* neared, and when the encampment hove into view the ship stopped a hundred yards short. There the Soviets were greeted by four bearded men: three Italians plus a Czech scientist named Francis Behounek who had spent his time on the floe measuring cosmic rays. Cecioni, with his game leg, was still unable to leave the tent.

In savoring the moment, Biagi proudly showed off his radio, the most famous radio set in the world, while the other survivors offered a tour. Despite a lack of facilities, the minuscule community on the ice floe now boasted Lundborg's upturned Fokker, from which parts could be salvaged for various purposes, plus a bearskin rug the survivors had made for the tent. Because of regular air drops, in the latter stages of their adventure the survivors had not been wanting, and were in receipt of such items as Swedish delicacies, inflatable boats, a gas stove, and first-rate arctic gear. Still, the summer ice was rapidly disintegrating and, forty-nine days since being erected, the Red Tent was in danger of sinking into the sea.

Lundborg's airplane and everything else was taken aboard the *Krassin*, and it was decided to steam directly to Kings Bay. All would have preferred to remain in the area and search for the missing men of the flyaway dirigible, but one of Mariano's feet had developed gangrene and it was imperative to get him to the *Città di Milano*'s operating table right away. The next day the downed Junkers and its crew were reached, but at first glance there seemed to be three too many survivors—that is, until the puzzle was solved. It turned out that two young men, university students and members of the Italian Alpine Club, along with their Norwegian guide, had chanced upon the Junkers while searching the coast for *Italia* survivors.

With cessation of the various rescue efforts in and around Spitsbergen, the world's attentions turned to other matters, although reports three months later that a fuel tank from Amundsen's seaplane had been found in the Barents Sea was a stark reminder that he and his crew, one Norwegian and four Frenchman, were still missing. Also still missing were the men who had floated away with the dirigible. The six from the *Italia* and the six from the Latham 47, including Amundsen, would never be found.

Umberto Nobile, whose failed expedition was an embarrassment to Mussolini, returned to Italy as *persona non grata* and, stripped of his rank, went into self-imposed exile. He designed semi-rigid dirigibles in the Soviet Union before returning home in 1936, but three years later moved to the United States where he taught aeronautics in Illinois until the middle of World War II. Then, for family reasons, he returned to Rome for a second time. After the war Nobile's full military rank was restored to him, plus back pay, and he was elected to the Italian parliament. The general died at age ninety-three in 1978, having both lived to see man walk on the moon as well as the half-century anniversary of the flights of his airships *Norge* and *Italia*.

SEVEN

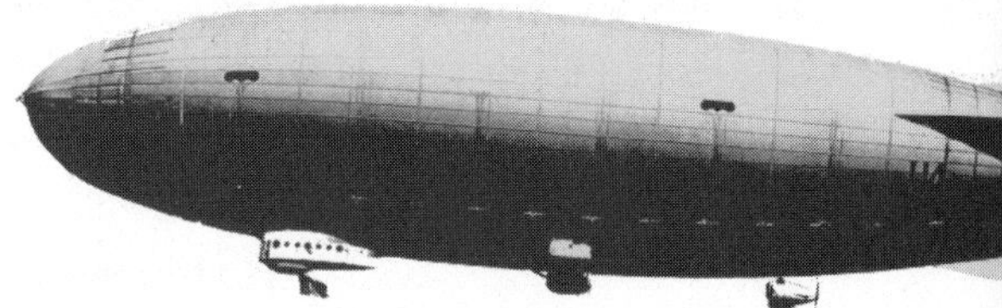

Secure in the knowledge that long-distance passenger flight would never be feasible by airplane, Britain's Conservative government initiated the Imperial Airship Scheme in 1923. This came just two years after the R 38 disaster had abruptly consigned the country's remaining dirigibles to the scrap heap, but now the push was on for a new fleet to connect the red parts of the globe, those that made up the British Empire, by air. The aviation concern, Vickers Ltd., was prepared to accept £4,800,000 in taxpayer money to meet this demand, yet before the Conservatives could act, the Labor Party were swept into power and preferred to give the Air Ministry a chance at the business too. Hence it was announced by the Cabinet Committee on Airship Development that Vickers would be paid to build one dirigible, R 100, while the Air Ministry would build another, R 101. A contract for the rest of the fleet would then be awarded to the maker of the better craft.

Hoping to be the maker of the better craft, and thus win years of lucrative work, in the autumn of 1924 Vickers advertised for new hires, and a young engineer at the de Havilland aircraft firm named Nevil Norway responded. Norway, who would later earn world fame using the pen name Nevil Shute, was ready for a change in employment, and accepted Vickers' offer to join the R 100 program.

When he first started, Norway was tasked with calculating the forces and stresses that would be put on every frame of R 100, and for a budding novelist who was writing fiction by night this assignment may have sounded dull. He, however, found it exciting, and also knew that the job was vitally important. Accurate stress calculations were something only recently made possible due to advances in aerodynamic theory, and prior to this, airship designers had been forced to rely on educated estimates. Usually the estimates were satisfactory, but there were unfortunate exceptions such as, of course, R 38 whose frame had crumbled in a tight turn, and also Britain's first rigid dirigible, Royal Naval Airship No. 1, the *Mayfly*. Built by Vickers in 1911, the ironically named *Mayfly* was found to be structurally unsound and, confined to ground testing, one day split in half. Vickers had learnt its lesson from this failure, and so for eighteen months straight, Norway kept his pencil sharpened and slide rule handy, checking and rechecking his calculations for R 100.

Preparations to begin construction started in 1925 when Vickers took over the abandoned Howden Airship Station, then overrun by wildlife. "The rough shooting was quite good," Norway recounted. "Rabbits infested the enormous piles of steel and concrete debris formed by the demolition of the other hangars; partridge, hares, and duck were common on the aerodrome immediately outside the shed, and we got many snipe. This state of affairs continued till the day we left, though the game moved out a few hundred yards from the shed as the work got under way."[103]

The enormous but derelict shed was restored to the point where it could again house airships, although the roof leaked prodigiously and conditions were icy in wintertime. Vickers had agreed to a fixed price of £350,000 for R 100 from the Cabinet Committee on Airship Development, but was now projecting a loss, and so did everything to keep costs down. According to Norway, the joke going around Howden was that

"R 100 was getting along rather more quickly now that one of us had bought a car and lent the tool kit to the workshops."[104]

Comprised of just fifty standardized parts, R 100 began to come together like an overgrown Erector Set. The first girders were fabricated and ready by the autumn of 1926, and the first transverse frame was completed by Christmas. Norway and his fellow workers, though, were learning as they went along, and there were many frustrating delays—delays made even more frustrating by the knowledge that at the Royal Aircraft Works at Cardington, where R 101 was being built with public monies, civil servants enjoyed unlimited funding. "We learned that at Cardington an entire section of their ship had been erected for experimental purposes and scrapped, at a cost to the taxpayer of £40,000," Norway recalled. "The designer of the capitalist ship could take no such refuge from responsibility."[105]

Vickers was an innovative firm, yet concepts found lacking were dropped. Initially, for example, the company had intended to use engines that ran on hydrogen and kerosene, and a good deal of effort was put into their development. It was also thought that servo motors were needed to aid the helmsman at the controls because of the enormity, over a thousand square feet, of the rudder surface area. Both ideas, however, were eventually dropped. Rolls-Royce Condor engines (bought secondhand at knock-down prices) were found to be just fine for R 100, and the rudders turned out to be perfectly movable by hand without any mechanical assistance. Also, when fabricating automatic gas valves proved too much for Vickers, some were simply ordered from Germany.

With the stress calculations complete, Norway was frequently called upon to inspect parts of the airship as it gradually took shape in the shed. "I remember, sick with fright, watching the riggers clambering about on the first frame to be hoisted," Norway said, "carrying out their work a hundred feet from the floor with the girders swaying and waving at each movement that they made. Within a year I, too, was clambering with them."[106] The airship had fourteen bags in which to hold its hydrogen, a gas that was just as dangerous as ever. Helium from the United States, of course, would have been infinitely preferable, but every square inch was needed by Admiral Moffett, and the British were resigned to do without. Therefore, Norway spent many days during the summer of 1929 making sure that R 100's hydrogen bags, made of thin fabric and goldbeater's skin that easily tore, were safely inflated. The work went off with barely a hitch, and soon the hundred-ton dirigible was as light as a feather.

A silvery cover of doped-cotton fabric was affixed to the exterior of the frame, but before the dirigible was ready for daylight its six Rolls-Royce Condor engines had to be tested in the shed by running two hours at forward cruising power, and a half-hour in reverse. For Norway and those watching this was an earsplitting event fraught with danger. The Condors, housed two apiece in the airship's three engine cars, roared with thunder while their giant wooden propellers, whipping up an indoor hurricane, spun madly only inches from the concrete floor. "All my life I shall remember the sight of those engine cars leaping and straining at their cable wires with terrific force," Norway said, "suspended from a hull that was completely full of hydrogen, each car with smiling men gesticulating with thumbs up out the window in the deafening clamor, myself gesticulating back thumbs up to them and with a cheerfulness I could not feel."[107]

The engine trials were concluded without catastrophe, but it was R 101 from Cardington that flew first, on October 14, 1929. Predictably, perhaps, the government ship made a point of flying over Howden, but Norway and his fellow workers did not wave their congratulations, and in fact had utmost disdain for their rivals. "Most of those men are now dead," Norway stated unapologetically in 1954, "killed in the accident to the airship they designed in competition with us, the R 101, and it may be that these acerbities ought not to be revived twenty-five years later. If I revive them for the moment now it is because there are still lessons to be learned from this peculiar experiment of Government and private enterprise working in direct competition on constructions of the same specification, and because the bitterness, almost amounting to direct hostility, between the competing staffs had its effect on history; if there had been more friendly cooperation between the design staffs the disaster to R 101 might not have happened."[108]

Throughout the five years that both airships were under construction, Vickers and the Air Ministry mostly ignored each other, while the men of Howden and Cardington were totally non-communicative, never visiting one another's workshops, or discussing how to overcome mutual problems. "If the Cabinet Committee wanted competition they got it with a vengeance," Norway concluded, "but I would not say it was healthy."[109]

A month after R 101's introduction to the world, R 100 was also ready to be unveiled. Vickers was a manufacturing outfit and not an operator of airships, and so under the auspices of the Air Ministry a scratch crew consisting of Royal Air Force (RAF) officers led by Squadron Leader Ralph S. Booth and Captain George Meager, both recipients of the Air Force Cross, along with upper-class types from Rolls-Royce, and more plebian types from Vickers, were gathered together. Norway earned a spot on the flight team after becoming the de facto chief engineer of R 100 late in its development, and he marveled at the competence of this disparate group of men; yet he also noted that when left to their own devices, individualism prevailed and all discipline was lost.

The dirigible itself was a marvel to behold. Although its length, 709 feet, was not remarkable for a rigid airship, it was its enormous girth, 133 feet in diameter, which gave R 100 the distinction in its day of being the largest object ever flown. Yet for all its bulk the leviathan appeared almost gaunt, its tightly fitting cover exposing widely spaced ribs of duralumin stretching from its tapered stern to its pointed bow. Like a giant dart, during speed trials the airship reached eighty-one miles per hour and, shooting through the air, would be able to fly a distance of 6,338 miles without stopping. As if out of a Jules Verne novel, thanks to R 100 countries like Canada, South Africa, India, and Australia were now only days, and not weeks, away from London.

Upon entering commercial service, R 100 would be able to transport 140 people housed within the frame next to the girders and hydrogen bags. The officers' and crew's quarters in this three-story structure were on the first floor, and consisted of among other things a pantry, mess hall, and cabins. Accommodations on the second and third floors were more sumptuous because these areas were reserved for passengers. Two forty-feet-long promenade decks graced each side of the second floor, and a triple row of windows tilted downwards to reveal the scenery below. Between the two promenade decks were located a service hutch and bar, passenger cabins, and a dining salon that could seat fifty. With the exception of the tinkling of glass and the sound of polite conversation, meals would be taken in the dining salon in relative quiet, the roar of the six Condors, located well aft and outside the hull, barely audible. At one end of the dining salon was a double staircase leading passengers to the third floor, where they would encounter a veranda lounge and more cabins. A unique aspect of third-floor cabins was their access to a narrow balcony overlooking the second-floor promenade deck and its windows. There were still some reminders, though, that this luxury liner was a ship of the air and not of the sea. For example, to save weight, walls were of painted cloth and cabin doors were cotton curtains, limiting privacy, and although water, hot and cold, was available, there was not enough for a bath. Additionally, R 100's guests would undoubtedly be complaining bitterly to the captain about that strictest of airship rules—no smoking.

The new dirigible had its share of problems as it completed a series of test flights around England, but these were overcome except for an odd tendency for the outer cover to undulate when R 100 was at speed. Flying alongside, the RAF took pictures of this deformity, and while no cure was found, it was determined not to be a hazard. With everything shipshape, therefore, by the summer of 1930 the dirigible was ready for its ultimate proving flight, as stipulated by contract, to Canada and back. The Air Ministry's R 101 had also to complete a lengthy voyage, in its case to India, but Cardington was hesitant and suggested both flights be postponed. Howden demurred. "Perhaps if we had realized at the time how, very, very bad their ship was, how real the danger of complete disaster if they started for India, we might have taken a different attitude to this approach," Norway explained of rival R 101 and its builders. "Their own secrecies concealed the real facts from us: we guessed that their ship was a bad airship, but we did not know the whole story."[110]

The flight to Canada in modern R 100 was a more certain enterprise than had been the journey taken by Maitland eleven year earlier in the primitive R 34, but R 100's venture was still pathbreaking to the extent that before 1930 only one airplane had ever flown in the east–west direction across the Atlantic; and then only barely, because it came to grief on an island off Newfoundland.

R 100 departed in the wee hours of July 29 with six officers, thirty-one crew members, and seven officials from the Air Ministry on board. With no duties to perform, a few of the officials had earlier located their cabins and settled into bed, the sublime sensation of an airship at mooring lulling them to sleep. Upon awaking they were somewhat shocked to learn that they had left the mast hours ago, and it was now time for breakfast. The Irish Coast passed beneath the ship, and the last outpost of the British Isles, Tory Island, disappeared from view just before a lunch of tomato soup, lamb chops, peas, potatoes, and coffee was served. This proved that the electric stove for preparing food was working well, although the electric heating system for the passengers was never made to work successfully, and for all aboard it was best to keep mittens on. Over the next forty-eight hours, Squadron Leader Ernest Livingston Johnston expertly navigated R 100 across the Atlantic to the Gulf of Saint Lawrence. All was smooth sailing over the Gulf toward Quebec when, at a height of 1,200 feet and at a speed of seventy knots, the airship was hit by a cold north wind that ripped the four huge fins that graced its tapered stern. Norway, who up to now had been kept busy pumping gas from the lower to the upper tanks, or by scrambling along the top of the airship to inspect this or that, strolled along the top of the port fin to ascertain damage. Soon he was joined by no fewer than fifteen men crawling around and stitching up the fabric, with nothing but their grip on a piece of wire and thin air between them and the waters a thousand feet below.

The airship flew near Quebec City early that evening, August 1, to the sound of distant sirens and cheers, and headed for the Montreal airport at St. Hubert, still some 140 miles distant. After visiting with the ship's commander, Major George Herbert Scott, down in the control car, Norway went up for a glass of sherry in the dining salon with two other crew members. Just before this, Scott, former captain of R 34, had rashly opted to go through rather than around a line squall. Suddenly the dirigible was driven by a wind gust from 1,200 to 4,500 feet. To keep from rising further, Scott had the elevators put hard down, with the unintended consequences that dinner, which had been laid out on the salon's center table, shot down a corridor and ended up near Frame 2 in the bow. Of more concern, new rips in the fins occurred that needed mending, and the electricity was knocked out, plunging everything into

AUTHOR'S COLLECTION

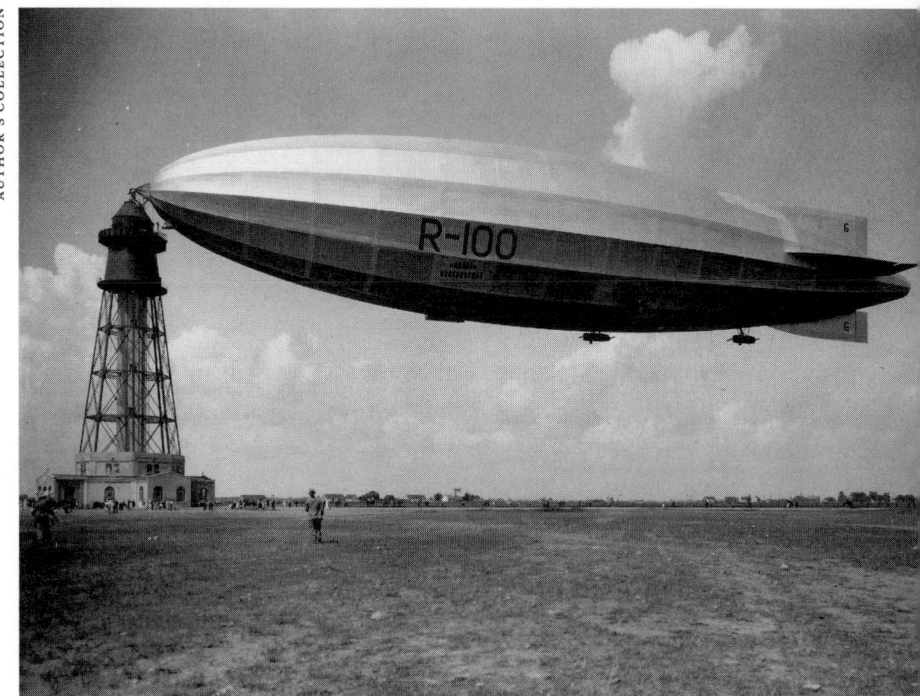

The "capitalist" R 100 *on the mast at St. Hubert, Quebec.*

darkness. Then at two o'clock in the morning the crew was greeted by a ghastly visage: a glowing cross floating in the night sky. To laughter and relief, it turned out to be Montreal's famous monument of steel atop Mount Royal, illuminated by lights. The trip was completed in seventy-nine hours, and with 1,505 gallons of fuel left, could have gone on much longer.

Delighted to be on the ground, perhaps, was Reginald Colmore, chief of Cardington's R 101 program and purportedly anxious before embarking upon R 100 bound for Canada. Also pleased to be in one piece on this side of the Atlantic was another passenger, Archie Wann, former captain of R 38 and one of only four men to have survived that disaster. When he wasn't busy with repairs, another arriving passenger, Norway, took the opportunity to visit friends from his Oxford days. "I like this place," he said of his host country and its people, "I like the way they go about things, and their vitality . . . I have never been in a place that has got hold of me so much as this has done."[111]

The airship spent twelve days on the mast at St. Hubert, and during this time perhaps as many as one million people came out to see R 100. Throngs in Ottawa, Toronto, and Niagara Falls also greeted the ship as it flew over their cities during an aerial tour of eastern Canada. Having picked up eleven happy Canadian passengers in Montreal, the airship was over Britain again shortly after breakfast on August 16, and with the shout "Ship secure!" was on the mast in Cardington, its new home, by lunchtime. Norway was irritated at the modest reception awaiting R 100. Even though the BBC was on hand to describe the arrival, the fact that there was only a small crowd in attendance demonstrated that the Air Ministry had done little of the publicity work it had lavished on its own airship, R 101.

Such publicity included a fly-over for the benefit of King George V and Queen Mary, in which R 101 had dipped its nose in salute, and the promise to take one hundred members of parliament on a flight around the country; a promise Secretary of State for Air Lord Thomson later called "the greatest error of all my life." Indeed, when the flight for the one hundred members of parliament never occurred, Thomson minimized expectations, explaining that "the airship programme which I had the honor to introduce in this House in 1924" had always been "experimental and tentative" and that "It was never claimed that we were going to build two commercial airships which would at once take the air as their native element and fly to all parts of the globe." He also noted in the same speech, that in the near future "it may be urged that the construction should . . . proceed forthwith of a 7,500,000-cubic-feet ship as that would be about the size of an airship to be a commercial proposition."[112]

In distancing himself from just-completed R 100 and R 101, and by urging their quick succession, Thomson had given the impression that somehow both were a disappointment. The reality was, however, that while the R 101 program was in deep trouble, there were no obvious obstacles preventing R 100 from being the "commercial proposition" for which it was designed. Nevertheless, when R 100 had safely completed its flight to Canada and back (a flight in which not one person had even become airsick), it was handed over by Vickers to the Air Ministry. The ministry promptly relegated it to No. 2 Shed, from whence it would never reappear. R 100's neighbor in No. 1 Shed, meanwhile, was in the middle of an extensive rebuild for an inaugural run to India. The fact that this maiden voyage would turn R 101 into the *Titanic* of the skies has, fairly or unfairly, generally been blamed on Lord Thomson.

Christopher Birdwood "C. B." Thomson was a military man who, like Count Zeppelin and Admiral Moffett, converted to aviation later in life, and then became its most tireless proponent. Thomson was born in Bombay and, immigrating to the home country, entered the Royal Military Academy at age seventeen. The cadet graduated as a second-lieutenant in the Royal Engineers in 1894, and for the next twenty years saw extensive overseas service, including South Africa (where he helped with British observation balloons), the Balkans, Mauritius, and Sierra Leone, as well as bureaucratic postings at the Staff College and the War Office. He was in France during the early part of World War I before becoming a military attaché, and then head of the British Military Mission in Romania. Thomson next found himself in Palestine where he was decorated for valor during the capture of Jerusalem. Afterwards, he was present at the signing of the armistice with Turkey in October 1918 and, the following year, the Treaty of Versailles. At one point the youngest major in the British army, Thomson left the service at the rank of Brigadier General to become a civilian. Displaying an idealistic side few could have guessed at, in July 1919 he was drawn to the socialism of Britain's new Labor Party, and intended to stand for office.

The retired army officer made for a most unlikely Labor candidate. Reed thin, he was six feet five inches tall, had a patrician's bearing, was aristocratic in both dress and manner, a confirmed bachelor, and often seen in fashionable places with a certain married woman (a Romanian princess, no less). As unlikely a Laborite as he appeared, Thomson ran a hard race during the elections of 1922, and although failing at the polls, earned the respect of Party leader James Ramsay MacDonald. "It needed a rare courage to enter a sphere of activity for which he had no experience," MacDonald said, "and in which he had no influence—especially as he was to enlist in the ranks of a Party whose creed and personnel were anathema in those circles in which he had hitherto moved."[113] When MacDonald came to power in 1924 as Britain's first Labor Prime Minister, the man with "rare courage" was given a seat in the House of Lords, and additionally made member of the Cabinet as Secretary of State for Air.

Airships were only one part of Lord Thomson's Cabinet portfolio, being also accountable for the RAF, civil aviation, and Britain's aircraft and air transportation industries, but like Admiral Moffett, it was airships for which he cared most. Thomson had, it transpired, only nine short months to get his fledgling airship program off the ground, but in this he was successful. By the time Labor fell from power that November, he was able to hand over to his Conservative predecessor and successor, Sir Samuel Hoare, a viable dirigible program. Over the next five years Hoare would make no changes to Thomson's template, and in 1929 when Labor again pushed the Conservatives out, and Thomson

AUTHOR'S COLLECTION

Secretary of State for Air Lord Thomson.

was again made Secretary of State for Air, Hoare was able to hand the R 100 and R 101 program over to his successor. Both ships were badly behind schedule, 1927 being their original delivery dates, but almost complete.

The two craft had been broadly designed to Thomson's original specifications, that is, that they be 5,000,000 cubic feet in size, weigh ninety tons empty, and be able to lift sixty-two tons including cargo and one hundred passengers. The mandate had also called for the airships to cruise along at sixty-three miles per hour, and to do so, non-stop, for 3,500 miles. Vickers' R 100 fit the bill. It had a hydrogen capacity of 5,158,060 square feet, it weighed 106 tons empty, it could lift fifty-one tons, and it had accommodations for one hundred passengers. Although only seven passengers were aboard the proving flight to Montreal, the 3,874 miles were covered safely and at an average speed of sixty-two miles per hour. On the strength of this flight, Vickers received final payment for R 100, and hoped orders for many more dirigibles would be forthcoming. The Air Ministry, though, was too preoccupied by the development of its own airship to give Vickers another thought.

That something was not right with R 101 was evident even before its first ascent. For one thing, at a cost to the Treasury so far of £527,000 it was far more expensive than R 100, whose costs had run to just £337,000, and for another thing it was greatly overweight. The second revelation came about shortly after R 101 emerged from its shed and calculations for gross lift were made. This came to 145 tons—an impressive number, except for the fact that almost all of this would be consumed by having to lift the frame, engines, cabins, control car, gasbags, outer cover, electrical system, and everything else that was a permanent part of the airship. With "fixed weight" being so high, this left only a scant thirty-three tons available to loft "useful weight," which constituted things such as crew, passengers, luggage, cargo, drinking water, food, fuel, and oil. Then as now, fuel was the largest component of useful weight for long-range flight, and in R 101's case meant that for a 3,500-mile trip the fuel load would come to twenty-six tons. With Air Ministry estimates that a hundred passengers and their baggage would alone total fourteen tons, not to mention a sixteen-ton allowance for cargo, and however much more than that officers, crew, and provisions weighed, it was clear that as an airborne carrier, R 101's current potential was woefully inadequate.

In trying to figure out what had gone so very wrong, engineers in Cardington returned to their adding machines and revised their original calculations to show that R 101 empty of hydrogen had tipped the scales at 113 tons, 26 percent higher than anticipated. Apparently during its five years of development in Cardington, the airship had suffered from previously undetected but serious weight overruns. One culprit, it turned out, was the dirigible's frame, made of 60 percent stainless steel and only 40 percent duralumin, and another offender was the mansion-sized, 7,780-square-feet passenger compartment, also over the weight limit. But as feared, the worst miscreants were the engines, five diesel Beardmore Tornados, built for railroads and heavier than comparable gasoline engines built for aviation.

The choice of diesel power even at the expense of more weight reflected the Air Ministry's obsessive worry that gasoline was too volatile a substance for use in tropical climes, like those of India, the country for which R 101 travel was mainly intended. The concern was that in the heat of the sun petrol fumes would build up in the tanks and then leak out, find a spark, and destroy the airship. Diesel fuel, on the other hand, is an oil and inherently less explosive than gasoline, and so the choice of the Beardmore Tornados. In addition to being weighty, the engines also had the nagging problem that they did not run in reverse. This second drawback meant that one of the Beardmore Tornados, the aft one, had to be reserved solely for backwards thrust, which was a wasteful expenditure of poundage (4,733 pounds to be exact) on an engine that would only be used when maneuvering on and off the mast. The Air Ministry, however, could come up with no better solution.

Despite R 101's crippling weight handicap, it was thought that by scrapping Thomson's 1924 requirements the dirigible could instead act as a demonstration ship of sorts. To do this, three sacrifices would need to be made. First, cruising speed would have to be slowed to fifty-five miles per hour, saving fuel and eliminating the need to fly with tanks full. Second, only twenty-four passengers and their bags could be permitted on board. And third, cargo must be kept to just one ton in weight. There were numerous minor amendments that could be made to further lighten the ship as well, and Cardington was planning for these, but then to the Air Ministry's horror, when R 101's hydrogen bags were filled to capacity, it was discovered they held 102,620 square feet less hydrogen than expected. This decreased the airship's already reduced

AUTHOR'S COLLECTION

Lighter-than-air but still tons overweight, the Air Ministry's R 101 *on the mast at the Royal Airship Works in Cardington.*

lifting capacity by a further three tons which, for all practical purposes, sounded R 101's death knell.

To outward appearances, and also from enthusiastic press reports, there seemed to be nothing wrong with the beautiful airship, and Cardington gamely put the craft through its paces in trips around England. Yet top Air Ministry officials knew that the 5,000-mile flight to India, scheduled by Christmas, was sheer fantasy because a fully loaded R 101 would have never have gotten off the ground. The India venture was postponed indefinitely, and the dirigible quietly parked in No. 1 Shed. To divert attention from this embarrassment, Thomson announced "Project G" and "Project H," which, if he secured the funding (£950,000), would become dirigibles R 102 and R 103 that, at 7,500,000 cubic feet, would be larger than the American's new *Akron* and *Macon*.

With the Secretary of State for Air's sights set on the future, engineers in the present got to work lightening R 101. Out of the airship came twelve passenger cabins and miscellaneous engine accessories, out came two water ballast tanks and two lavatories, cello windows were substituted for glass, and the amount of kitchen equipment was reduced. These and other measures lopped almost three-and-a-half tons off the airship's weight, and then to increase lift, the engineers "let out" the hydrogen bags by three inches, resulting in a net gain of 104,760 cubic feet for an added three tons of lift. This was a good start but hardly sufficient, and so the Air Ministry ordered radical surgery. R 101 was severed at Frame 8 and an extra bay with an extra hydrogen bag grafted into place. With the weight reductions, plus the added hydrogen capacity, gross lift grew to 167.3 tons and, more critically, useful lift came to 49 tons, almost equaling that of R 100.

Work in No. 1 Shed had been slow in completion, though, and by mid-August when R 100 had triumphantly returned from Canada, and with Germany's newest airship, the *Graf Zeppelin*, making globetrotting look easy, there was intense pressure on Cardington to ready R 101 for Lord Thomson's trip to India. That flight was nearly nine months behind schedule, and the Secretary of State for Air, fretting about the Imperial Conference that was shortly to convene in London, was extremely eager to get underway.

The Imperial Conference was an event held every few years in which the British Commonwealth's prime ministers came together to discuss mutual concerns, and the 1930 Conference would be an opportunity for Lord Thomson to deliver his paper titled "The Progress of Imperial Communications." The paper was written with the aim to impress upon the premiers the vital importance of airships for their far-flung dominions and colonies and, especially, to persuade Canada and India on the notion of subsidizing proposed airships R 102 and R 103 to the tune of £600,000. Certainly, the trip to Montreal in R 100 was proof positive that Canada would only benefit from more and better dirigibles. Now Thomson's goal was to reach India in R 101, turn around for England, and then, making a dramatic entrance to the Conference, present himself as tangible evidence that swift air travel to and from the subcontinent was possible.

The timing was extremely tight, but the Air Ministry thought that if R 101's refit was completed by September 26, then Lord Thomson could fly out and be back in London before the Conference adjourned. Fortunately, two of the Tornados had just been reengineered to run backward, liberating the aft engine to help propel the ship forward, but Cardington still had work to do on a new outer cover, and September 26 came and went with the airship stuck in No. 1 Shed. Finally, five days later, on Wednesday, October 1, the opening day of the Conference, R 101 emerged into the early morning mist for its second unveiling.

The heavily modified craft was essentially a brand-new vessel, but there would be no time for an exhaustive program of aerial evaluation, and in fact there was only just time for one test flight, scheduled to start that very afternoon. If all went smoothly, by Friday the dirigible would be well into the first leg of its journey to India, the 2,235 nautical miles from London to Ismailia, on the Suez Canal, where a giant airship mast had been built. After refueling on the mast, the second leg would take R 101 another 2,125 nautical miles over Baghdad and the Persian Gulf to Karachi, where an identical mast awaited. None of the routes, over land, sea, desert, or mountain, had ever been flown by dirigible before.

The scheduled departure date slipped a day to Saturday, October 4, because R 101's officers and men, harried to be off and having had to complete a thousand tasks at once, had become too exhausted to fly on Friday. Knowing that the fight had been briefly postponed, Prime Minister MacDonald asked Thomson to come to his house, 10 Downing Street, and inquired of his Secretary of State for Air if the danger were worth it. "C.B. brushed aside any risk," MacDonald recalled of Thomson, "He had set his heart on the flight, he said. It was the right thing for him to do. He believed in the ship. It was his child. He had watched it grow. How could he stay at home whilst it went on its way to attainment?" MacDonald advised Thomson, for his own safety, to remain behind, but "He was confident. Feeling I was doubtful he chaffed me about my earlier desire to cross the Atlantic in R 100 and said that I was the last man on earth to hold him back." Then in a more serious vein, Thomson told his boss, "You know I have never let you down. I shall not do it now." The last MacDonald saw of Thomson was when "Later, as he descended the stairs and I leant over the balustrade at the top . . . he stopped and called up in lightsome words that, if the worse came it would soon be over and that the Fate of all of us was written."[114] That night, Thomson wrote out a brief will leaving everything to his brother.

The test flight of October 1 stretched into October 2 and lasted sixteen hours, thirty-two hours less than the recommended minimum of forty-eight, yet if Thomson's schedule was to be met, could last no more than that. Winds during the truncated evaluation were very calm, which should have allowed for speed trials, but one of the Tornados burst its oil cooler and instead R 101 had to move along at a sedate forty-four miles per hour. No written report of the test flight was filed because, again, there was simply no time, but the crew's word that all had gone "really well"[115] was good enough for the Air Ministry, and a Certificate of Airworthiness was issued on the spot.

By delaying Friday's start Thomson had permitted his subordinates one day's holiday, but was in no mood to indulge them in another, and so he ordered that R 101 be off for India. Embarkation commenced at 6 p.m., Saturday, October 4, when fifty-four men in twos and threes took the lift up the mast and, like animals entering Noah's Ark, walked the plank into the airship's nose. Aboard for the flight would be six representatives of the Royal Airship Works, three of them being those most responsible for R 101's conception and development: Reginald Colmore, chief of the entire program, Vincent Crane Richmond, designer of the airship, and Michael Rope, Richmond's very able assistant. Also among those scheduled to fly that night was a select group of aviation authorities: Sefton Brancker, Britain's director of civil aviation, Percy Bishop, Britain's chief aeronautical inspector, William H. L. O'Neill, India's deputy director of civil aviation, and William Palstra, Royal Australian Air Force officer and Australia's liaison to the Air Ministry. Of course, also on board would be none other than Brigadier General, The Right Honorable Lord Christopher Bird Thomson of Cardington, His Majesty's Secretary of State for Air. Thomson would be carrying with him his ceremonial sword, his two large trunks, his favorite carpet, and two cases of his best champagne for the small, but exclusive, dinner parties he planned aboard R 101 whilst on the masts in Ismailia and Karachi.

The highly experienced Flight Lieutenant H. Carmichael Irwin was designated captain of R 101 and Lieutenant Commander Noël Grabowsky Atherstone would be his first officer. The third-in-command would be Flying Officer Maurice H. Steff, and Squadron Leader Ernest Johnston was to be, just as he had been on R 100, navigator. A civilian named Maurice Giblet, a highly qualified meteorologist, would round out the officer contingent. Slated to be aboard as crew were thirty-three men of lower ranking plus a cook, two stewards, and a galley boy named Thomas Megginson, just eighteen years of age but a veteran of R 100's flight to Montreal. From Irwin to Megginson, these forty-two men were to be entrusted with the safety and comfort of the six representatives from the Royal Airship Works aboard, as well as the six observers riding along as passengers. Thomson and his young valet, James Buck, were among them, as was Major Herbert Scott, who came aboard in full dress uniform and let it be known that he, as Britain's most senior airship officer, was now in charge. This pronouncement undoubtedly was made to Irwin's astonishment, if not outright ire, but according to England's arcane rules governing the captaincy of dirigibles, Scott trumped Irwin in seniority, and there could be no argument.

Everyone was aboard by half past the hour and, amid intermittent winds and a light rain, the airship slipped the mast six minutes later, and headed north toward Bedford. This was in the opposite direction of the plotted course, but Bedford was home to the thousand men and women of the Royal Airship Works and, by tradition, R 101 always first circled the village. With two straight days of hard flying to go until reaching the mast at Ismailia, perhaps this gesture could have been skipped just this once, but the excursion was over in less than an hour and, burdened by its enormous amount of fuel and oil, R 101 throbbed south toward London.

Giblet the meteorologist predicted that weather over southern France and the Mediterranean would be fine, although there might be some adverse conditions before then. Almost immediately, it was evident that this was indeed the case, as strong and gusty winds, accompanied by heavy rains, battered the airship and showed no sign of abating. The mast at Cardington was still at hand and, it being obvious that these were conditions fit for neither man nor bird, Scott should have turned his ship around and waited for the morrow (and, had he done so, would have been greeted by perfect-flying weather). However, the airman who had so skillfully managed R 34's fuel-starved final hours back in 1919 failed to make the correct call, and ordered the dirigible to "press on" regardless.

Quite quickly the aft engine showed low oil pressure and had to be shut down for a prolonged period, but Scott radioed not a word of this back to Cardington. Making decent headway on four engines, though, by 10 p.m. the 777-feet-long ship had reached the outskirts of London, and then virtually skimmed 200 to 300 feet above the metropolis, bringing throngs out into the rain-splashed streets to see the spectacle overhead pass by. Rolling and pitching considerably, the dirigible, with its red and green navigation lights glowing, double rows of brightly lit picture windows shining, and searchlight beam emanating from the control car, made for an unforgettable sight in the dark and stormy night. Equally unforgettable was the airship's manner of forward movement as it dealt with a stubborn crosswind: to slide along at right angles to its intended path like a crooked arrow in flight. In this strange attitude, R 101 passed over villages to the east of the city so low that locals feared it was going to sail right through their living room windows, however at 10:35 p.m. the dirigible, flying nearly sideways into the wind, was sighted over the cliffs of the English coast as it headed out into the Channel. Passengers could be discerned silhouetted in the huge windows while music could be heard as the band (actually, it was the dining room radio) played on.

A formal meal, on Royal Airship Works crested china, had been served at 7:30 p.m. for the dirigible's distinguished guests, and now these men with their cigars and brandies took advantage of what promised to be R 101's most popular innovation: a fireproof smoking room. With asbestos and metal separating the smokers from 5,509,753 cubic feet of hydrogen all around them, down in the control car Johnston was dropping calcium flares into the water to determine wind drift. Calculating this drift to be quite substantial, he ordering the necessary course corrections, taking the ship over the French coast and then to Paris, southern France, and across the Mediterranean to its first stop, Ismailia.

After a two-hour crossing, R 101 made landfall at Point de St. Quentin, at the mouth of the Somme, shortly before midnight while, because of its now rain-soaked outer cover, flying three-and-a-half tons heavy. This meant that stopped, or "static," R 101 would have settled slowly to earth of its own accord, but motoring forward with bow up a few degrees, the underside of its hull acted as a giant airfoil, giving the craft "dynamic" lift, proving that airships can not only float but fly (a fact well known by dirigible captains).

Tired by an eventful day, by 1:30 a.m. the airship's senior officers, Scott, Irwin, Atherstone, and Johnston, had gone to bed, leaving the relatively inexperienced Maurice H. Steff down in the control car. Giving directions to his steering coxswain, who controlled the right and left direction of the airship, and his height coxswain, who controlled the up and down motion, Steff had to cope with heavy rains and violent winds. And he had to do this at full speed, since Lord Thomson, before retiring to his two-room suite, had worried that arrival at Ismailia would be too late for the intended dinner party to which his guests had already been invited.

In the smoking room a lone occupant, an engineer from the Cardington contingent named Harry J. Leech, was puffing on a cigar when, at about five minutes after 2 a.m., the ship went into a dive that caused the room's furniture to slide across the metal floor and into the forward bulkhead. This incident lasted perhaps thirty seconds and, although Leech had no way of knowing it, the dirigible had dropped hundreds of feet. The ship then seemed to regain trim for several seconds before going into another dive that ended in what witnesses on the ground at Beauvais described as a "crunch." Later it was determined that at the first indication of trouble, Steff had called for elevators full up, and had also moved the engine telegraphs dials to "slow." Nose up and diesels throttled back, the ship hit the earth quite slowly, maybe only at ten miles per hour, and at a glancing angle. Still intact, R 101 made one bounce of about sixty feet before resting astride a meadow and a wood of small trees. The flight to India had lasted all of seven and half hours, covering just 397 nautical miles.

Assuming there need be a death toll at all, the reason it was so appallingly high is because something ignited the hydrogen seconds after the soft crash. Leech, lucky enough to be caught in the fireproof smoking room, miraculously made his way through the inferno, as did four engineers sheltered in their metallic engine cars at the time of impact. Besides these five fortunate ones, three others made it out alive, but two of the three would succumb to their injuries.

In the aftermath of the tragedy, British authorities were denied the benefit of hearing from either Lord Thomson or Major Scott, or the heads of the R 101 design team, or the ship's officers, or any of the aviation experts aboard as passengers, since all had died at Beauvais. Investigators did, though, glean useful information from the handful of survivors, and particularly from statements made by one of the two surviving crew members before he too passed away.

The official "Report of the R.101 Inquiry" was released in March 1931. Earlier that year, Britain's remaining airship, R 100, had been ordered broken up for its duralumin (netting the government all of £450). Norway had already left Vickers for a new career, and was thus spared the pain of watching his airship being deliberately destroyed by the Air Ministry.

The R 101 inquiry concluded, more or less to everyone's satisfaction, that the most likely cause of the accident was a rip due to wind and rain damage to the outer cover near the second and third frames in the bow.

This rent in the envelope, it was theorized, left several of the fragile hydrogen bags inside exposed to an airstream in excess of sixty miles per hour, and caused them to tatter and release their gas. The sudden loss of lift in the forward part of R 101, already flying heavy, proved too much, and despite Steff's quick response the craft pitched down once and, perhaps aided by a shove of the wind, went down a second time and landed on the ground. One of the airship's hot engines probably went up into the frame, igniting a hydrogen cell. No fault was found with either R 101's basic airworthiness or with the behavior of its crew, although the report was critical of the abbreviated test flight beforehand, and especially the failure to stress the ship at speed, which had it been done, might have revealed the weakness to the bow cover. The report also noted disapprovingly that Lord Thomson's "policy decision," that is, his need to make the round trip to India in time for the Imperial Conference, had dictated the timing of the voyage to an adverse extent.

On the day of the crash, Sunday, October 5, the dead had been collected on the ground before being shipped back on the destroyer HMS *Tempest* to a grieving England. There forty-eight coffins lay in state in Westminster Hall before being put on a train for Cardington and their final resting place. Many bodies had been burnt beyond recognition, the remains of the galley boy, Thomas Megginson, being among them. At the mass burial his father asked that a wreath be put "on one o' the larger coffins [because] he were a tall lad."[116]

EIGHT

And so the British had given up on dirigibles, following the French who quit after the loss of the *Dixmude* in 1923 and also the Italians whose airship program died along with the *Italia* five years later. Besides the French and the Italians, the Japanese had been interested in but never started an airship program, and the Soviets dabbled in dirigibles in a minor way. The only nations really left in the game, therefore, were the United States and Germany, and then when the *Macon* went down in 1935 it was just Germany; and this despite earlier Allied efforts to have the Count's former firm, the Luftschiffbau Zeppelin, euthanized. The threat to the Allies was that at war's end the Luftschiffbau had wasted no time in resuming production, and the brand-new *Bodensee* was ready for its first flight by August 1919. Flying for a revived Delag, the small but speedy zeppelin kept up a regular schedule by ferrying two dozen passengers the 370 miles from Friedrichshafen to Berlin before making the reverse trip the next day. The pocket airship, just half the size of the wartime zeppelins, was no "baby-killer," and its innocuous flights gave hope to Luftschiffbau employees that their vocation had a future. As important, the success of the *Bodensee* gave hope to the company's board of directors that it would interest others in buying a larger zeppelin to be flown on a grander scale. The company was set to deliver a sister craft, the *Nordstern*, to the Delag when in early 1920 the French and English demanded a stop to all flights and surrender of the two zeppelins. While the victorious powers further debated the merits of having the giant sheds at Friedrichshafen torn down, the Zeppelin factory turned to making aluminum pots and pans. By all rights, this should have spelled the end for the company's production of airships, yet it was not to be, largely because of the determination of Dr. Hugo Eckener.

In 1892 Eckener had earned his Ph.D. in psychology, but by 1900 had tired of the subject and was submitting short articles on various subjects for the *Frankfurter Zeitung* from his home in Friedrichshafen. The newspaper offered him the job of covering Count Zeppelin's airship flights, then taking place over the Bodensee, and Eckener accepted. Having been on vacation at the time, he missed the inaugural ascent of LZ 1 in July, but the count's experiments nevertheless interested him and Eckener was present when another flight took place that October. "I adopted a rather cool and critical tone in my story," Eckener admitted of what he wrote afterward, but argued that "It is not correct, as was stated later about me, that I was at first an 'opponent' of Count Zeppelin, and later was 'converted like Saul into Paul.' I merely asserted that the heavy ship with her metal framework had actually risen into the air and had attained a certain speed, naturally showing herself to be controllable also, but that the speed of 13–16 miles per hour which she had attained was much too slow for her to withstand even a moderate wind."[117]

Five years later Eckener was again on the shores of the lake, this time to report on the first flight of LZ 2. Like tens of thousands of other spectators that day he watched as the craft gracefully took to the air only to lose all power and control. The next day he visited the spot where it landed and also where, while tethered to the ground, it had been wrecked by overnight winds. There Eckener saw "The old Count quietly and calmly standing beside the badly damaged hull and giving orders for it to be dismantled."[118] Eckener may have been moved by the count's setback, but in his subsequent story for the *Frankfurter Zeitung*, which appeared under the byline "Dr. E.," he had no choice but to declare the flight a disaster. Some days later Count Zeppelin appeared at the doctor's front door and politely inquired if he was "Dr. E." and if he had written the story. "I said I had," Eckener admitted, "whereupon he said he wanted to thank me for the friendly tone in which I had written about him personally, but that he wished to discuss further with me some inaccurate statements included in my article."[119]

After setting the doctor straight on certain technical particulars pertaining to airship flight, the count invited him for dinner several days later. At that dinner the host regaled his guest with complaints about the military, civil, scientific, industrial, and other forces that were conspiring against him. The count also complained that the failure of LZ 2 had caused disillusionment among his public and that the German people had lost interest in him and his work. Eckener thought he had the answer, and this was, he recalled, "that only a steady and unremitting educational and publicity campaign could revive this interest. Clearly the Count's appealing personality, which aroused respect and admiration, would be an important factor in this publicity effort."[120] The doctor offered to help and, becoming the Luftschiffbau's publicity agent, led a public relations offensive that culminated in the enormous enthusiasm with which the mayors of such cities as Berlin, Düsseldorf, Munich, and Hamburg thrilled at the prospect of being linked together by air. However, when the Delag demonstrated an embarrassing inability to make this happen, Eckener said "It presently came about that I personally had to assume the difficult task of proving the capabilities of the Zeppelin airships. This caused me many sleepless nights, and tortured hours, before success was achieved."[121]

The very first humiliation was the crash of the *Deutschland* in June 1910. This led to the dismissal of the airship's commander and also to a vacant captaincy position, which the business manager of the Luftschiffbau, Alfred Colsman, picked Eckener to fill. "Naturally I had to accept," Eckener explained, "since I had always championed the usefulness of the Zeppelin airships."[122] Right out of the starting gate, though, the doctor stumbled badly by running his mount, the second *Deutschland*, hard against its shed, and as a result the zeppelin had to be completely rebuilt. Colsman, however, maintained faith in his new captain and Eckener continued flying right up until the beginning of World War I. Then with cessation of passenger flights, Eckener volunteered for the Naval Airship Division. Although denied a combat command, while training new zeppelin crews he also advised Captain Peter Strasser, whom he greatly admired, on the best use of airships for the navy. Busy as he was, Eckener must have additionally given considerable thought to the subject of Afrika-Zeppelins and what they portended for peacetime flight.

The original Afrika-Zeppelin was the height-climber L 57, conscripted for a desperate attempt to resupply German forces in East Africa. Unfortunately, no sooner had the kaiser given his approval for this daring plan than the airship was accidently set on fire. A replacement Afrika-Zeppelin, L 59, emerged from the sheds at Friedrichshafen to take its place, and on November 21, 1917, the airship, loaded with fifteen tons of arms and provisions, arrived over Africa via Turkey and the Mediterranean. By this time, however, the German forces had moved elsewhere and it would now be impossible for L 59 to find them. Radio messages to this effect finally reached the zeppelin when it was near Khartoum, and the mission was aborted. Although the four-day, 4,200-mile sortie was ultimately of no military value, it surpassed—to put it mildly—all previous records for aerial endurance and distance. "The transoceanic ship was here!" exclaimed Eckener of the feat, "But the conditions of peace at first forbade us to build and fly it. What more could we do? Was the Zeppelin idea dead, at the very moment when its realization was possible? The task now before me was to try to overcome the restraints."[123]

The Allies ultimately spared the sheds at Friedrichshafen and even allowed the Luftschiffbau to resume construction of airships, as long as they were for civilian use and did not exceed 1,100,000 cubic feet in capacity. The first restraint, Eckener was willing to accept, but not the second since it meant he could build no airship large enough for oceanic air travel—and specifically for Atlantic travel, which was where the commercial market existed. Again, it would have been reasonable at this juncture to assume that the Luftschiffbau would be out of the dirigible business forever, but ironically it had been the purposeful destruction of zeppelins by die-hard officers of the Naval Airship Division that would change everything.

Inspired by the example of Scapa Flow, where the German sea fleet was scuttled by its own men, the Airship Division officers sought to do the same two days later, June 23, 1919, when they let seven of their huge zeppelins, cells empty of hydrogen and hanging from the rafters, smash to the shed floor. The Allies had wanted some of those ships, the newer ones, and Germany was held liable for their loss. A deal was reached whereby France, England, Italy, and Japan received four surviving zeppelins (the Japanese were never to fly theirs), while the United States was promised the equivalent of $800,000 in gold-backed marks in compensation. Fortuitously for the then bankrupt German government, the Americans were in the midst of their own naval airship program, and reacted positively to the offer of being given a new-built zeppelin instead of cash. In a complex round of diplomacy, U.S. military representatives negotiated directly with the Luftschiffbau on the delivery of the airship, while Washington persuaded Paris and London to agree that the ship could exceed the size limitation so as to reach America.

While the U.S. Navy's zeppelin, known by its builders as LZ 126, was in construction at Friedrichshafen, officers of the U.S. Army under orders of General Billy Mitchell snooped around the sheds and asked the German workers a number of detailed questions. The U.S. Navy got wind of this espionage, registered its outrage, and Mitchell was put in his place. That matter taken care of, the navy maintained a small number of representatives in Friedrichshafen who were in daily contact with Eckener, now head of the Luftschiffbau.

In late August of 1924 Eckener took LZ 126 out on a series of pre-delivery flights, being careful to pass over Germany's most heavily populated areas and always to carry a score of reporters with him. Eckener knew what he was doing, and what the effect would be: "Yes," he exclaimed, "the Zeppelin frenzy was here again, and apparently stronger than ever!"[124] His public, though, would have the joy of seeing his marvelous zeppelin only briefly, since soon it was destined for a one-way flight to the States to become the USS *Los Angeles*.

Having had no sleep the night before, Eckener reached the Friedrichshafen field at 6 a.m. on October 12 and saw that his dirigible was ready to depart. Then over the next ninety-five hours he guided LZ 126 nearly 5,000 miles eastward without once touching earth or water. The dirigible neared Lakehurst on the fifteenth, but before landing the doctor just had to dally over Manhattan a few hours so as to whip up a little zeppelin frenzy on this side of the Altantic. The frenzy was contagious and quickly spread to the rest of America. Millionaire yachtsmen wanted the mighty VL 1 Maybach engine, exactly like the ones on the zeppelin, for their boats, and Henry Ford, hoping to lure the dirigible to Dearborn, had a $400,000 mooring mast built at Ford Airport.

Not long after Eckener returned to Europe (having, of course, to travel back by boat), the Allies lifted all restrictions on German civil aviation. He was now free to create an airship of any size he wanted, and he envisioned a three-million-cubic-feet zeppelin, to be numbered LZ 127. The ship would be an elongated version of the *Los Angeles*, thus reducing development costs, and although able to carry twenty passengers, was intended as a training and demonstration craft. Still basking in the afterglow of his triumphal flight to America, Eckener thought funding would be forthcoming, but in this he was mistaken. "The Zeppelin," he bemoaned, "in spite of all its accomplishments, was considered a mistaken idea, at least in the circle of aviation experts. Count Zeppelin had had to combat this attitude from the beginning, and, as I found out, there had been little change since."[125] Looking to the past, Eckener organized a national appeal for money, just as the count himself had done before the war, and called it the "Zeppelin-Eckener Fund of the German People."[126] This strategy may have worked in the good old days of national prosperity, but the German people were now economically on their knees, and only two and a half million marks were contributed against the seven million required. Taking what resources he had, however, the shrewd Eckener began building LZ 127 anyway, figuring that Berlin would eventually capitulate and give him the remaining sum he needed; and in this he was right.

Unlike British and American airship builders who had to learn as they went along, the Luftschiffbau could call upon a deep reservoir of expertise. This expertise resided in men and women who had spent their entire adult lives with the company, and none more so than Dr. Ludwig Dürr. An engineer, Dürr had begun working with the count in 1899 and was to be the architect for every Luftschiffbau ship, with the exception of LZ 1, that would ever be built. Not all of Dürr's designs, of course, made it from drawing board to construction shed, but LZ 127 was mostly complete by July 8, 1928, the ninetieth anniversary of the count's birth. Appropriately enough, on that day his daughter, Hella, christened the ship the *Graf Zeppelin* (Count Zeppelin). A series of high-profile flights followed and by October that year the already-famous *Graf*—as it was fondly called—was set to fly the Atlantic.

Eckener, whose adult son Knut was part of the crew, made himself commander of the flight and appointed a seasoned airship officer, Ernst A. Lehmann, to be his captain. And to promote press coverage Eckener invited no fewer than six correspondents along for the ride, including two representatives of the influential Hearst newspapers in the United States. They were Lady Grace Marguerite Hay Drummond-Hay and her colleague and companion Karl H. von Wiegand. His reporting on the voyage was without fault, but it was her prose that history remembers. "The Graf Zeppelin is more than just machinery, canvas and aluminum," Drummond-Hay famously wrote upon reaching America, "It has a soul." She continued that, "every man who worked to build it, every man who worked to fly it, every one of us who have made this journey has contributed to the humanization of the aerial colossus. I love the airship as if it were something living—a being animated by life, responsive, grateful, capricious, loveable in the sense that it can give as well as receive."[127]

Having been aboard the *Graf* twice before during test runs, and knowing that the *Graf* lacked heat, Drummond-Hay had sacrificed much of her fifty-pound baggage allowance to a gray squirrel coat, wool-lined boots, thick woolen stockings, sleeping socks, a warm jumper suit, and woolen underwear. She also knew that high-heels easily punctured the zeppelin's thin aluminum flooring, and so had packed more sensible shoes. Suitably prepared, Drummond-Hay welcomed news that the airship, delayed twenty-four hours due to bad weather, would leave early in the morning of October 11.

"Suppressed excitement was inevitable, no matter how calm or confident we felt about the matter," she said of departure. "To watch the Zeppelin officers, alert, giving orders, moving about with precision and animation—the passengers installed at the windows taking photographs, calling to friends or investigating the living quarters of the airship to be their home off earth for three or four days—the groundsmen holding the long ropes, slinging to the sidebars of the monster which seemed even more impatient than ever before to be released into the immeasurable vastness of space, and last, but not least, those we were leaving behind."

Some of her fellow passengers had arrived by train late the night before and were curious to meet the only woman aboard. Lady Drummond-Hay, or "Lady Zeppelin" as she was nicknamed, must have also been curious to meet them as they were an eclectic bunch. There was, in addition to her and von Wiegand and the four other reporters on board, people such as the Count's son-in-law, Count Brandenstein-Zeppelin, five German dignitaries, a newsreel man, two artists to capture on paper what could not be captured on film, a passenger who had survived a recent airplane crash in the Azores, a wealthy American named Frederick Gilfillan, and a U.S. Navy observer, Charles E. Rosendahl of the late, great *Shenandoah*. Introductions complete, Drummond-Hay inspected her cabin and found that its "walls were no more than flowered chintz stretched from floor to ceiling" but that it had "almost every comfort and convenience one can wish." Taking inventory, she noted: "There is a luxurious silken covered settee, at night is converted into the two sleeping berths. Two suede cushion covers disguise the pillows. Wardrobe, ample for the journey, rack for hats, table, pouches for shoes, etc." The only things wanting was a bell to summon the attendant (if there was one), a looking glass, and, she said, "facilities to open at least one of the tiny panes in the cabin windows."

Instantly, many of her fellow passengers got down to something which would obsess them for the entire trip, and this was writing hundreds upon hundreds of postcards. Each card was rubber-stamped

"Graf Zeppelin" and the crew dropped them to earth by the bagful without bothering with postage, knowing that the prestige of the ship was enough to guarantee delivery. (Most times the airdrops were successful although, remarked Drummond-Hay, "At Schaffhausen the mail bag fell into the famous Falls.") Flying over Switzerland shortly after take-off, the reception from those in the fields and villages was enthusiastic, but later over France she said "we were ignored, or even worse." Their feelings from the last war still raw, French women refused to acknowledge the Teutonic monster and the men turned their backs to their former foes. Meanwhile French officials kept the *Graf Zeppelin* from restricted areas, which according to them meant most of France.

That afternoon's lunch for Drummond-Hay and her fellow travelers was a formal affair. They dressed for the occasion and enjoyed a view of Mont Blanc between the soup and meat course. However, from then on all formality was dispensed with as passengers took to wearing sleeping gowns and pajamas and holding little parties in their cabins. By the end of the first day of flight the *Graf* reached the shores of Iberia, where Spaniards below were ecstatic at the sight above, crowding the streets, plazas, and parks to have a look. Barcelona was brilliantly lit in the night and another bag of mail was dropped. Soon the Rock of Gibraltar was beneath and sunrise for the airship's crew and passengers was over the Atlantic. Next the Madeira Islands came into view around lunch time, to then be followed by endless ocean.

While British plans for R 100 and R 101 called for promenade decks, dining rooms, staircases, balconies, and lounges, guests aboard the *Graf* had only a sixteen-by-sixteen-feet salon in which to eat, congregate, and generally pass the time of day. When things became dull, Drummond-Hay would remove herself to the chart room behind the control cabin where, she said, one could watch "the 'works' of this giant airship." She found these to be "as exquisite, as perfect, as minute in their beauty as those of my tiny platinum and diamond wrist watch. Yet they look so simple and uncomplicated. Two men at two small wheels, turning, turning, letting go, turning again. Dr. Eckener, ever watchful as an eagle, moving here, there, glancing at the chart, glancing at his men. Knut Eckener in overalls, perched upon the window ledge, trying to snapshot his papa unawares, waiting for his watch to come. They seem devoted, father and son. One seldom sees fair-haired Knut anywhere except as near his forceful-looking fine father as possible."

She also made a mental sketch of the other personalities who ran the ship. There was: "Capt. Ernst A. Lehmann, Dr. Eckener's staff captain, small, nimble, keen as a gimlet, always brimming over with good humor and dry wit," and "Capt. Hans Flemming, tall and handsome, serious, he who borrows every aspect of the visionary directly he leaves the earth," as well as "Capt. Hans von Schiller, ever active, courteous, charming, with sea-deep eyes." She added to this list the "Navigations Officer Walter Scherz and G. A. Wittemann, both delightful in manner and striking in personality; Max Pruss of long experience, an expert helmsmen as well as navigator. The moment any emergency threatens, Pruss is called out to take charge." Lastly, she made note of "Chief Engineers Siegle and Beuerle, upon whom rests all responsibility outside the navigation department."

Drummond-Hay and, as could be expected of a navy man, Rosendahl were in good humor, but others became irritated by privations such as no baths or showers, no attendants to make the beds, no wine (that soon ran out), and no smoking. The last hardship was too much for Gilfillan, whose habit ran to over a hundred cigarettes per day, and he spent the voyage in bitter complaint. The trip was also hard on Eckener and his crew, none of whom managed to get any sleep during the crossing. "Although traveling on an airship is comfortable," Drummond-Hay said of her situation, "It is a strain on the nerves of those who have any set work to do—the constant vibrations, the ever present hum of the motors, the changing altitudes, the desire to see everything and to miss nothing of the outside keeps one tense and alert."

The voyage would have been incomplete for Drummond-Hay, or for her readers, without at least one brush with danger, and this came on the third day of flight just as breakfast was served. Without warning, the *Graf Zeppelin* pitched up fifteen degrees causing passengers to fall on the floor or land in each other's laps. "Breathless moments passed," Drummond-Hay recorded, "leaving not a few blanched faces and the thought—we were facing death." The ship's china had been reduced to fragments, butter and marmalade covered the passengers, all the coffee had been spilt, and the upholstery and carpet soiled. Thankfully, though, there were no injuries save for Gilfillan who was hit in the head by a heavy movie camera. There was, however, damage to the ship. The unexpected gust, coming as the dirigible was nearing a black squall, had ripped much of the canvas cover off one side of the stabilizing fin. Eckener radioed the U.S. Navy to stand by while also ordering a repair party that included his son Knut to the stern of the *Graf*. "Little imagination is needed to picture the task before them," Drummond-Hay said of the open-air surgery on the fabric, "The huge airship, hundreds of feet above the sea, a certain amount of wind inevitable in spite of the slow speed, the danger of falling, the urgent necessity of mending the fin, the possibility of a fresh gale to wreck still further havoc, pressure of time. It was a noble piece of work."

When lunch was supposed to be served and was not, it became evident that another part of the dirigible had suffered, and this was the electrical system. Power out, when lunch eventually emerged from the darkened galley it consisted of bread and cold sausage. The *Graf* had lavatories but no showers, and early the next morning Drummond-Hay attempted to wash herself using paper towels "which," she said, "melt

AUTHOR'S COLLECTION

Dr. Hugo Eckener and his Graf Zeppelin.

to pulp in one's hand," and looked forward to the comforts of a proper hotel room in New York. However, after breakfast as she rushed to write her last fifty postcards the news came that, due to headwinds, there would be another day or two of flying. The early attempts at culinary variety had long since given way to bread, butter, ham, and sausage at every meal, and for the unwashed voyagers the flight must have gotten tiresome. Finally, "Monday morning . . . Land!," Drummond-Hay wrote, "Land at last!" Arrival over the United States was dramatic; first Chesapeake Bay, then Washington D.C., Philadelphia, and New York, and finally Lakehurst, where 30,000 people awaited their first glimpse of the *Graf*.

This time around, Eckener returned to Germany bringing his airship with him, but he had no funds to conduct other flights. How to raise money? To do something, anything, he conjured up a ploy to impress

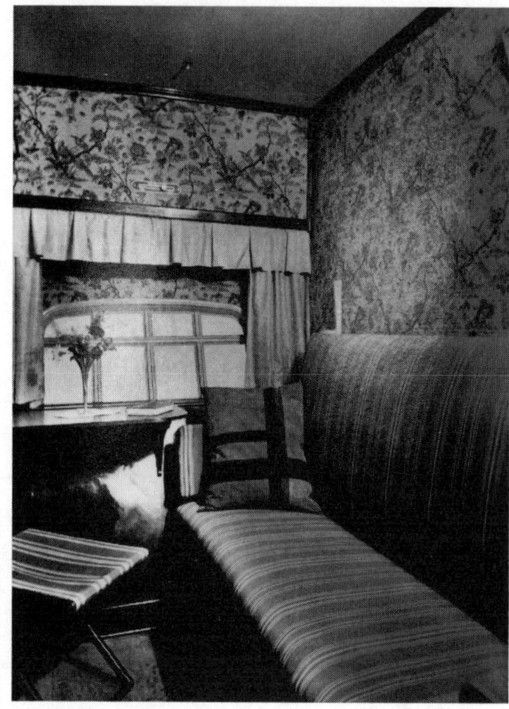

AUTHOR'S COLLECTION

One of the Graf Zeppelin*'s ten passenger cabins (left) and the dining room and lounge (opposite page).*

Germany's leaders. As soon as weather permitted, which was late March, he packed the airship's long gondola with bureaucrats and politicians and treated them to an aerial tour of Italy, Crete, Cyprus, Palestine, Egypt, and on the way home, Greece. "The weather had cleared when we reached Ulm," Eckener said of the last stretch, "and towards 8 o'clock our shed came in sight, and half an hour later we had landed, after a flight of eighty-one hours. We were sure, and heard it from our passengers in words of enthusiastic thanks, that this flight—perhaps the most splendid one could make in Europe—had created a great impression on every one of them. We were sure that henceforth they would be true friends of the Zeppelin airship."[128]

AUTHOR'S COLLECTION

Intoxicated by the potential of the *Graf*, Eckener dreamed of transpolar flights and also of taking off from Friedrichshafen to the east and, upon circumnavigating the globe, returning from the west. Unfortunately, his "true friends of the Zeppelin Airship" were not as true as he thought, and he was forced to find private donors for his ambitions. One of the donors was the newspaper publisher William Randolph Hearst, and pleased at the number of papers the reporting of Lady Drummond-Hay managed to sell, Hearst promised $100,000 if he could officially sponsor the global flight. Another $12,500 came from German publications, and the rest would come from an elite group of passengers paying up to $9,000 each per trip. Then to Eckener's surprise, a virtual gold mine was discovered in collectors eager to pay good money, and a lot of it at that, for stamps, cards, and envelopes marked as having been aboard the *Graf Zeppelin*.

Named the "Hearst-Eckener Zeppelin Flight Around the World" (with, of course, Lady Drummond-Hay aboard as a reporter), the voyage began as advertised from Lakehurst August 7, 1929, and returned on August 29 by way of the Atlantic, Europe, Russia, the Pacific, and the continental United States. Excluding the ten days taken up by diplomatic and resupply stops at Friedrichshafen, Tokyo, and Los Angeles, the 21,000-mile trip took just twelve days. By comparison, in 1924 the first round-the-world flight had taken four U.S. Army biplanes 175 days and necessitated sixty-nine stops, not to mention that two of the biplanes crashed en route. Clearly, the dirigible was the superior aerial vessel for global travel.

Looking for new worlds to conquer, so to speak, Eckener decided to fly to South America, a continent he had visited some years earlier in an effort to generate interest in airship transportation. That particular effort had not resulted in any zeppelin sales but it did establish important contacts on the continent for Eckener, and now in May of 1930 he took the *Graf* from Friedrichshafen to Rio de Janeiro, 5,317 miles away, while carrying a load of wealthy passengers and, once again, Lady Drummond-Hay with him. So as not to offend the sensibilities of the rich guests, Drummond-Hay reported, instead of being treated to riotous jest at the equator, the gentlemen were sprayed lightly with soda water and the gentlewomen with eau-de-cologne. Navigating in the southern hemisphere was a first for Eckener and his airship officers, and for each hour traveled they gained valuable knowledge for future flights.

Rio was always too far a reach and so the zeppelin landed, as planned, a thousand miles short in Recife de Pernambuco on the easternmost coast of Brazil. For the locals, Eckener said, it was "an 'epochal' event. We, too, were highly pleased that the practicability of a South American service seemed demonstrated by our experiences on this flight, and we saw it as a decisive step forward in the process of making the Zeppelin an ocean-crossing commercial vehicle. The next day we took off to carry our propaganda activity on to Rio de Janeiro."[129]

The silver zeppelin flew low over Rio Bay but could only stay in the city for an hour as Rio lacked an airship hangar, and the authorities were ambivalent about building one. Returning to Pernambuco before flying home, Eckener had better luck in convincing officials there to construct a concrete landing site with a mooring mast and hydrogen plant. This, the doctor knew, would be expensive, but it would also make Pernambuco the zeppelin capital of South America; as indeed it did become because the *Graf* was to return three times during the flying season (usually May to October) in 1931, nine times in both '32 and '33, twelve times in '34, and sixteen times in '35. By that last season, zeppelin traffic at Pernambuco had grown to 720 passengers and 30,000 pounds of mail. Ironically, having started its career as a global wanderer, and never slated for scheduled flight, the *Graf* had settled itself down to a regular job, shuttling customers to and fro across the wide ocean.

During those years of steady employment, however, the *Graf* took a few holiday excursions, the most famous being its seventy-two-hour trip to the Arctic. The original idea, hatched by the Australian adventurer Sir Hubert Wilkins, was for a submarine to navigate hundreds of miles beneath the polar ice, cut through at the Pole, and then be greeted by the zeppelin. After that, according to the plan, passengers and postal collectibles were to be exchanged between submarine and airship before both vessels going their separate ways. Skeptics may have dismissed the scheme as something out of Hollywood, but William Randolph Hearst thought it was realistic and agreed to chip in $150,000 if he were given exclusive rights to the story (which, undoubtedly, would be reported by Lady Drummond-Hay aboard the *Graf*). As an added cachet, the Norwegian explorer and Salomon Andrée's contemporary, Fridtjof Nansen, was convinced to join the expedition. Now a very old man, however,

Nansen died not long after agreeing to go. Wilkins actually managed to obtain a surplus U.S. Navy O-12 submarine, although as he neared the ice pack, and after suffering many severe setbacks along the way, had second thoughts. Hearst had also come to think the idea far too dangerous, and the expedition ended having not reached the Pole, and with one fatality (a submariner had fallen overboard). Eckener, however, still had his sights set on a northern adventure, but instead of aiming for the Pole decided upon a scientific flight to the lower Arctic regions.

As arranged, on July 27, 1931, the Soviet icebreaker *Malygin* met up with the *Graf* at Franz Josef Land. Aboard the icebreaker was none other than Umberto Nobile, helping the Russians with their plans for a separate arctic airship flight, while also scanning the icy environs for any sign of the six who went missing when part of the *Italia* floated away three years prior. Nobile found nothing of his lost men, but his spirits brightened at another sight. It was, he said, "The *Graf Zeppelin*" which "arrived towards evening . . . its great silvery bulk loomed up on the horizon, at the mouth of Britannia Channel, it was an impressive moment. At 8:45 p.m. the airship passed overhead. Half an hour later it slowly descended to settle on the waters of the bay. The surface, free of ice, was smooth as a mirror, clearly reflecting the beautiful ship."[130] The all-important postal souvenirs were quickly exchanged between the *Malygin* and the *Graf*, leaving Nobile only minutes to talk to Eckener and to briefly catch up with another man from his past, Lincoln Ellsworth, Nobile's partner along with Amundsen on the epic voyage of the *Norge* and someone, evidently, who still had a good deal of money and time on his hands. Nobile had hoped to be taken up for a brief ride, but the *Graf* was in a hurry to be off, and so he could only watch wistfully as the silver ship flew over the horizon.

In 1936 Pernambuco in Brazil lost its designation as the zeppelin capital of South America when the government of Rio de Janeiro spent

$750,000 on a modern airship station, allowing the world's newest airship, LZ 129, the *Hindenburg*, to skip Pernambuco entirely. Eckener's newest zeppelin had been long in the planning and was not, as were his other four postwar ships, an interim craft in place of the ultimate zeppelin to come. The *Hindenburg* was that ultimate zeppelin, an intercontinental cruiser built for both today and tomorrow. The *Hindenburg* could carry fifty-two passengers in luxury, travel at seventy-seven miles per hour, and fly 8,750 miles in one hop. Steering was assisted by servo motors and navigation was helped by an autopilot controlled by a gyro compass. It was the largest airship ever built, 804 feet long and 135 feet wide, and able to hold seven million cubic feet of hydrogen. Hydrogen, though, was not at all what Eckener and Dürr desired. They had wanted helium, for which the *Hindenburg* was specifically designed, but which the United States still refused to share with anybody else.

Construction of the world's largest airship became possible when the German government financed a gargantuan new shed at Friedrichshafen to house it, and the project was assisted by Germany in other ways as well. The country's rapid rearmament under Adolf Hitler, for example, led to the development of the lightweight, 1,320-horsepower, sixteen-cylinder Daimler-Benz MB 502 naval diesel engine, which when modified became ideal for LZ 129. Also of help had been Germany's master of the air, Hermann Göring, who guaranteed subsidies for the *Hindenburg* when he gave the state airline, Lufthansa, half-ownership of both it and the *Graf Zeppelin*.

The Nazis, however, held no sway when it came to getting the U.S. Navy to allow the use of Lakehurst for commercial purposes. The *Graf*'s occasional visits there had been labeled "experimental" and hence permitted, but the *Hindenburg* would need to use the air station on a regular basis for its revenue flights. Here the personal charm and diplomatic skills of Dr. Eckener came into play. Just as Count Zeppelin had sought permission from President Lincoln to observe the Union Army in 1863, so too did Eckener seek Roosevelt's approval to use Lakehurst. In the Oval Office, FDR warmly greeted him, and at the end of the interview told him that Lakehurst was his.

Roosevelt's permission, granted February 1936, came not a moment too soon because that year's flight schedule had already been printed and an initial batch of passengers booked. The *Hindenburg*'s air trials commenced on March 3, with an aim of having them completed before the start of summer flying season when the ship was due to begin service to Rio de Janeiro. Before that could happen, however, Hitler had sent his troops into the demilitarized Rhineland on March 7, and to legitimize this aggression announced it would be put to a vote of the German people. As part of a campaign to make sure the people voted "ja," Hitler's minister of propaganda, Joseph Goebbels, demanded that the *Hindenburg* and the *Graf* quickly embark on a three-day electioneering flight to broadcast slogans and drop pamphlets over Germany's largest cities and towns. "Apart from my political convictions, I considered this misuse of airships in bad taste, a sort of sacrilege, and I refused to participate," Eckener remembered. "But I could not refuse to allow the ships to be used for this purpose, for that would have been considered an open insult to the ruling Party, particularly if the Government was co-owner of the ships."[131] Word of his dissent reached Goebbels, and Eckener was removed as head of the Luftschiffbau, barred from commanding airships, and temporarily stripped of his citizenship. Henceforth the *Graf Zeppelin* and the *Hindenburg*, tail fins tattooed with the giant Nazi swastika flags, went about their political work without Eckener.

When Hitler's plebiscite passed with only one percent of voters dissenting, Germany's two zeppelins left electioneering behind and plied the Atlantic north and south, making 1936 the first and only year in history that the full potential of the passenger airship was ever realized.

The *Hindenburg*, filled to capacity, flew between Germany and New York ten times that season, and in doing so hosted 1,006 passengers and with Lufthansa's airship division, the Deutsche Zeppelin Reederei (German Zeppelin Transport Company), showing less of a loss than anticipated. The giant zeppelin also made use of Rio de Janeiro's new airship station and visited seven times, shrinking the distance from Frankfurt to Rio from two weeks by land and sea to just four days by air. In addition to ferrying people and mail, the *Hindenburg* served as an important psychological link between the Fatherland and Rio's sizable German community, while also showing the Nazi flag in distant lands. The *Graf Zeppelin* was part of this, and the dirigible supplemented the *Hindenburg*'s service to Rio by making twelve round trips there in 1936.

In the years since Lady Drummond-Hay and her flying companions had been forced to rough it, life for passengers aboard the *Graf Zeppelin* had improved markedly. There were now attendants to make the beds every morning, the supply of wine was sufficient for the duration of the flight, entertainment was provided by Captain Lehmann playing an accordion, and the cook served hot meals such as a hearty lunch of "Beef Broth with Marrow Dumplings" followed by "Rhine Salmon à la Graf Zeppelin, Roast Gosling Meunière, Mixed Salad, Pears Condé with Chocolate Sauce, Coffee, and Fresh Fruit." The dimensions of the *Graf*, though, had not changed since Drummond-Hay's time, and the well-appointed but cramped gondola could never be mistaken for the copious interior of an ocean liner. For the liner experience a flight on the *Hindenburg* was required.

Like the British imperial airships, the *Hindenburg* accommodated its guests in a two-story structure situated within the hull. The structure was both heated and well ventilated. On the first floor, B deck, was the

OVERLEAF: *From* Flight Magazine, *March 5, 1936.*

THE NEW ZEPPELIN

Germany's 5,000,000-Mark Giant : Some Remarkable Drawings Made by Max Millar at Friedrichshafen : New Facts About the Luxurious Passenger Accommodation

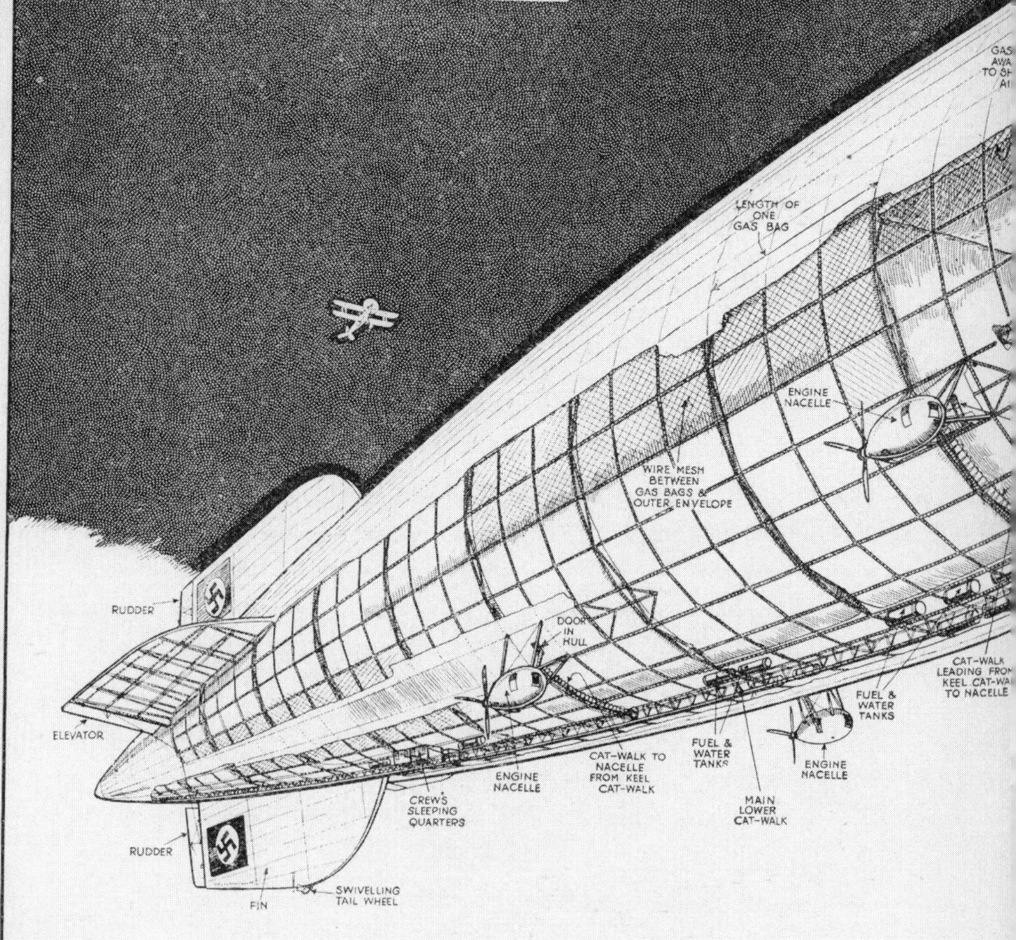

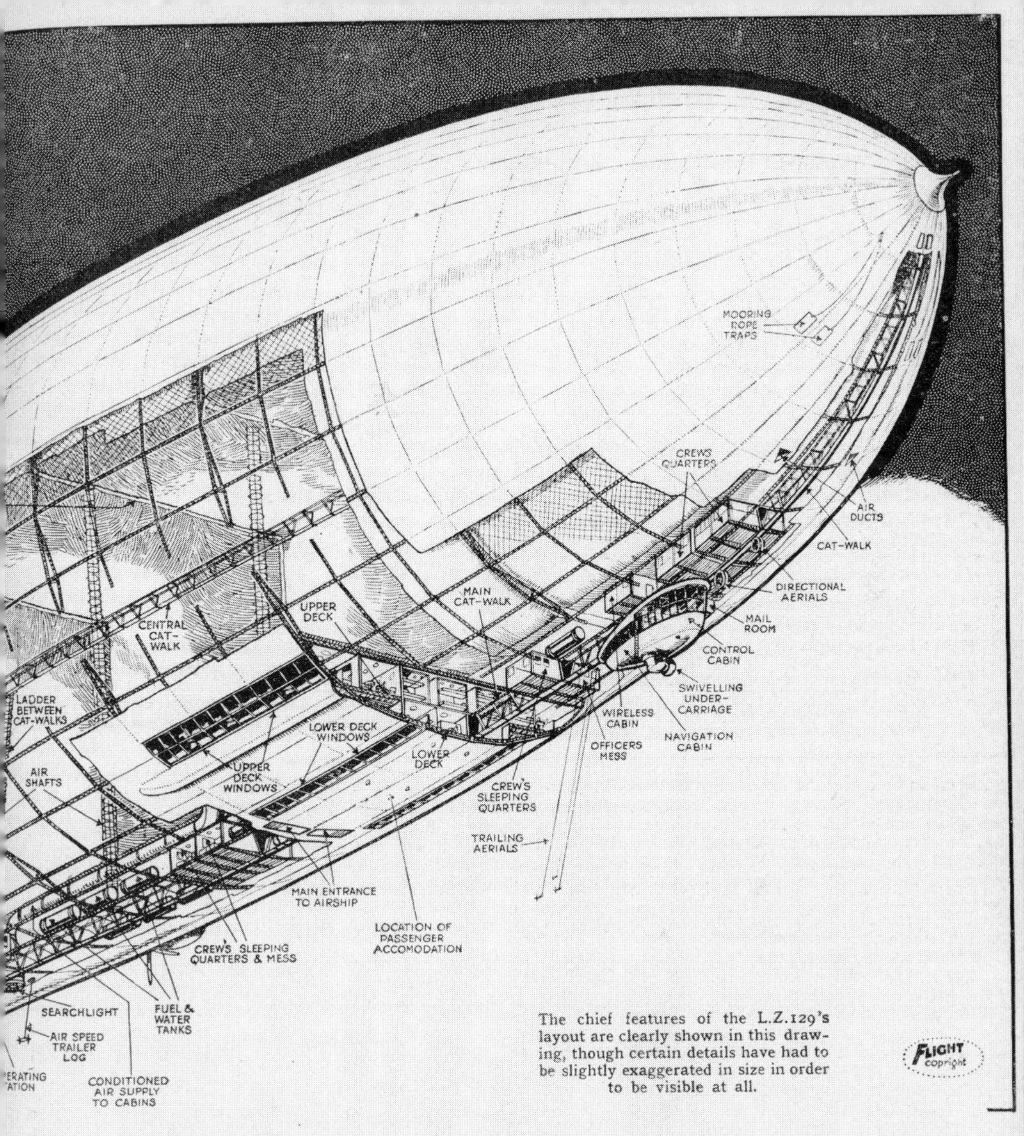

The chief features of the L.Z.129's layout are clearly shown in this drawing, though certain details have had to be slightly exaggerated in size in order to be visible at all.

THE latest Zeppelin airship, bearing the works number L.Z.129, and later to be christened the *Hindenburg*, is now all but complete in the huge shed at Friedrichshafen, on Lake Constance, and its sixteen gas bags are in process of being filled with hydrogen from the Zeppelin Company's own plant. As soon as the filling has been completed, which will probably be in a week or ten days, it is likely that the new airship will make her first flight. At the invitation of the Zeppelin Company, *Flight* visited the works at Friedrichshafen last week, and was shown the details of the airship. The sketches by Max A. Millar and the photographs used to illustrate other features of the airship are a result of this visit, and it is with considerable gratification that *Flight* is able to place before its reade the first instalment of an illustrated description of t L.Z.129. A description of certain aspects of the co structional work were given in an article in the issue October 3, 1935.

Into the design and construction of the new airsl has gone all the experience which the Zeppelin Compa has accumulated during a period of thirty-five years unbroken activity in airship work. In view of the gr success of the *Graf Zeppelin*, with a record of 13,3 flying hours during which that amazing airship l covered a distance of considerably more than 800,0 miles and has carried 12,000 passengers without a sin serious mishap during a total of 505 flights, one m

Hindenburg's spacious kitchen which, as could be expected, produced fresh fare fit for a kaiser. These were repasts titled "Fattened Duckling, Bavarian Style, with Champagne Cabbage" or "Venison Cutlets Beauval with Berny Potatoes," all of which were accompanied by a fine vintage from the zeppelin's well-stocked wine "cellar."[132] Also on B deck were toilets, a shower with automatic water shut-off (timed, it seemed, to always leave the bather covered with soap), and a cocktail bar where a favorite was a concoction called the "Maybach 12." Next to the cocktail bar, and carefully guarded by the bartender, was a smoking room. Its ceiling, walls, floor, and furnishings were fireproof, and as an added precaution, the chamber was airtight and pressurized to prevent the admittance of hydrogen.

Above B and accessible by stairs was A deck. Here guests were greeted by a bronze bust of the zeppelin's namesake, the recently deceased German field marshal and president, Paul von Hindenburg. (Eckener once wondered if he had paid a price by not naming the dirigible *Hitler*, but then realized the Führer had no affinity for zeppelins, and that the gesture would have gone unappreciated.) Also on A deck was a lounge with a piano weighing just 112 pounds, a reading and writing room, a promenade area fifty feet long on either side, a dining room that could feed all the guests in one sitting, banks of sharply angled Plexiglas windows some of which could be opened for fresh air, and twenty-five cabins. The cabins, each with two berths, a closet, a desk, and a washbasin with hot and cold water, were comfortable but windowless, and too small for day use. Instead, passengers were expected to spend the waking hours in the public spaces, whose walls depicted aviation and maritime motifs, and with furnishings designed by Fritz Bauhaus in the modernist style that bore his name.

All the *Hindenburg*'s passengers, one-quarter of whom on the North Atlantic run were usually women and children, seemed delighted with

Photographer Angelika von Braun used the Hindenburg *for a fashion shoot.*

their flights. Equally delighted were the "repeaters," those who subsequently booked their second, third, or fourth flight aboard the airship. Passengers climbed into the zeppelin via retractable stairs and once settled into their cabins could expect no disruption to daily routine. Hot breakfast, lunch, and dinner were served every day by three chefs and six stewards, requests for special diets were honored, and there were delicious snacks in-between meals. Businessmen could radio the office if they wanted to, or they could remain blissfully incommunicado. For those of adult age, eating, reading, playing, talking, napping, smoking, and drinking were all ways to enjoy the day and evening. On Sundays religious services were held.

AUTHOR'S COLLECTION

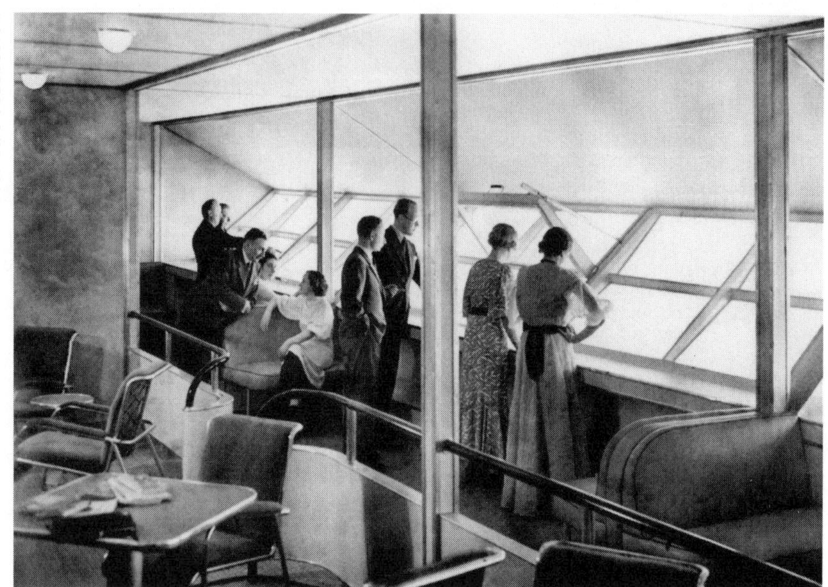

The Hindenburg*'s starboard A deck lounge and promenade (note the opened window).*

One enthusiastic witness to the *Hindenburg* experience was an engineer with the Sperry Gyroscope Company named Preston B. Bassett. Bassett noted of his voyage across the Atlantic that "At breakfast next morning after take-off" the general impression among the passengers was "It really doesn't seem possible." This was because, he explained, everything was so normal. There was no sense of acceleration, deceleration, or motion in general, nor was there any vibration. The windows were kept open yet remarkably they admitted no rain, dust, or wind. This was because, he explained, "they have been carefully installed in the neutral zone of the ship [where] there is neither positive nor negative pressure to cause air flow in or out." And above all for Bassett, life aboard the zeppelin was so quiet. According to his acoustical measurements, "The noise level in the lounge and dining-room of the *Hindenburg* was 50 decibels with the windows closed and only 61 decibels with several of the large windows open. This is actually quieter than the average New York office, or, more surprisingly yet, quieter than many of the lounges and dining salons on first-class trans-Atlantic ocean liners." He did admit that at times the ship rolled and pitched, and also that "It was possible to feel tremors in the ship's structure as the turbulent air struck local portions of the dirigible hull." However, at worst the occasional rolling was no more than one degree and the pitching no more than ten degrees, and most of the air turbulence was mitigated by the airship's 800-feet length which was, he said, "just too large to be displayed in a noticeable amount by any of the turbulent currents." Indeed, on occasion the *Hindenburg* was pushed forward by winds of up to ninety miles per hour, yet with passengers none the wiser. Concluding his scientific impressions, Bassett declared: "In my opinion, the dirigible has found a permanent position in trans ocean commercial transportation."[133]

A zeppelin flight to New York was certainly unique, as people like Bassett and Drummond-Hay discovered, but for sheer exoticism it could not be matched by an air trek down to Rio de Janeiro. At first those flights south began early in the morning at Friedrichshafen, arched over the postcard-perfect scenery of Switzerland, and then entered France. Later these flights would commence at dawn from the Reederei's new international air base at Frankfurt. Once over the French border both the *Graf Zeppelin* and *Hindenburg* were restricted to a twelve-mile-wide corridor along the Rhone valley, and French citizens were instructed to telephone authorities if the German airships were sighted anywhere else. On occasion thunderstorms blocked the corridor and zeppelin captains, knowing that overflying France was a privilege easily revoked, had to turn back and fly another day.[134]

At Sainte Maries on the Mediterranean, the zeppelins left French territory and continued along the Spanish coast from Barcelona in the north to Cabo de Gata in the south. Near the Straits of Gibraltar a turn was made toward Tangier and French Morocco. As the zeppelins hugged the African coast the lights of Casablanca appeared off their left side in the dark, and then in the morning of the second day of flight the airships struck out toward the Cape Verde Islands. It was customary for the *Graf* and *Hindenburg* to pay their respects to Porto Praia, capital of the islands, by flying low over the city and dropping mail before resuming their journeys south. By nightfall the ships' crew and passengers found themselves in the middle of the South Atlantic, they being the only humans in flight at that moment for many thousands of miles around. At daylight and into the following afternoon the sights below might include a water spout, a whale, or a relic of a time gone by, a sailing barque. The first landfall on this side of the Atlantic was the penal colony on the island of Fernando de Noronha, 475 miles from Brazil and surrounded by sharks, and then at dusk the mooring mast at Pernambuco hove into view amidst the palm trees. Seventy hours had passed since lift-off from Germany and, after refueling and topping up the gas cells with hydrogen, the *Graf* made the jaunt down to Rio, with arrival fourteen hours later. The larger *Hindenburg* with its greater fuel and hydrogen reserves could fly straight to Rio without stopping.

The two zeppelins had a duopoly on transatlantic air service and the future promised only more of the same. On the *Hindenburg*, ten cabins (each with windows) were added on B deck to accommodate twenty-two more paying guests, a stewardess joined the crew to care for women and children, the new purser was also a medical doctor, and ticket prices were increased sharply to reflect the growing demand. Knowing that demand for zeppelin travel would soon outstrip the supply of zeppelins, however, LZ 130 and LZ 131 were scheduled for delivery in 1938 and a third ship in the series, LZ 132, was ordered for 1939. But even this would be insufficient, and in the States a new company called American Zeppelin Transport was formed to build and operate two 9-million-cubic-square-feet sky ships in a joint venture with the Reederei.

It was against this backdrop of optimism that Captain Max Pruss found himself biding time over New Jersey early in the evening of May 6, 1937. His ship, the *Hindenburg*, had just arrived from Germany to inaugurate that year's North Atlantic airship season, although carrying a disappointingly small number of passengers. However, fewer guests allowed for more crew and more training, and so the normal complement of forty officers and men had been boosted to sixty-one. Among these was Captain Ernst Lehmann, now director of the Reederei and riding as a training officer.

Captain Pruss was waiting for the weather to improve at the air station and like his passengers, who included the enthralled Margaret G. Mather, he was not expecting to land anytime soon; that is until he received a radio message from Lakehurst. "Conditions now considered suitable for landing. Ground crew is ready," it read. The time was shortly after 6 p.m. and apparently there had been a break in the weather. Ten minutes later came another message confirming the first: "Recommend landing now." Evidently the Lakehurst commander, well-known dirigible man Charles Rosendahl of the U.S. Navy, thought the weather might not hold, and wanted the airship on the mast now. Making haste, therefore, Pruss headed toward the air station and upon arriving an hour later flew the *Hindenburg* in a tight circle around the mast in preparation for a quick descent. At 7:21 p.m. the zeppelin was hovering motionless at about 260 feet while water ballast was dumped and the landing lines dropped. It was four minutes later when witnesses below saw a flash of fire on the upper hull near the top fin. It was also when inside the zeppelin Margaret G. Mather said she had "heard the dull muffled sound of an explosion."

Miraculously, many emerged from the blazing ship with barely a scratch to show for it. An immaculately uniformed steward, for example, was afterwards just as immaculately uniformed as he had been an hour earlier when serving sandwiches. As another example, an elderly lady egressed from an open hatch as if it were the most normal thing in the world, and as a price for her composure suffered only minor burns. Mather with her painfully burned hands nevertheless didn't feel in need of hospital attention, and instead asked to be driven to her niece's home in Princeton. And then there was fourteen-year-old Werner Franz, soon known as "Franz the cabin boy," who tumbled onto the ground and was surrounded by fire. Providentially, just then a water ballast tank broke directly above him, and the only thing the youngster suffered in the calamity was a thorough drenching. Incredibly, several crew members stationed in the stern of the ship where the first hydrogen cells burst into flame, and where the chances of survival would seem to be nonexistent, escaped to tell their tale.

But not all, of course, were so fortunate, as Mather's descriptions of what she saw after leaving the zeppelin attests, and in the first aid station a young mechanic called alternately for his bride back in Germany and for a priest. He was one of twenty-two crew members who would perish. Thirteen passengers also died, a particularly poignant case being that of Mather's two new friends, "Mr. and Mrs. ——," who were standing next to her during the descent, and whose son had driven out from Long Island to meet them. The identity of the couple turned out to be John and Emma Pannes, he the New York director of the Hamburg–America Steamship Line, ticket agents for the Reederei. Moments before the explosion Emma had gone below to B deck to fetch her coat, and despite shouts from the ground that he jump from the open window that was right in front of him, John refused to do so without his wife and died on the ship with her.

In the *Hindenburg*'s control car the outcome among the senior officers was the same as in other parts of the zeppelin; some escaped unscathed while others, like Lehmann, were killed or, like Captain Pruss, injured. Pruss had fled the flames but then turned around to rescue his passengers, suffering severe burns. He endured a lengthy recovery and right up until his death in 1960 steadfastly maintained the incident had been sabotage.

Rosendahl as commander of the Lakehurst air station that night agreed with Pruss, suggesting that a tiny bomb placed next to a hydrogen cell had done the trick. On the other hand Eckener, who was not at the scene but heard the unbelievable news while in Austria, studied the event in tremendous detail and came to the conclusion that the explosion was a combination of human error, structural failure, and natural phenomena. According to Eckener, Pruss had been hurried to land by Rosendahl, turned the ship too fast and too sharply in the moments before the tragedy, and had over-stressed the frame. This, he theorized, caused a tension wire, one of many thousands of tension wires in the airship, to snap and fly into and rupture a hydrogen cell, releasing gas into the hull area between the cells. All it took to set things off, Eckener concluded, was for an electrostatic charge from the lingering rain and lightning in the area to ignite the deadly hydrogen-air mixture now floating freely inside the hull.

The Nazis, always willing to scapegoat innocents, uncharacteristically went out of their way to support this theory and to disprove sabotage. Not only did they not round up the usual suspects, but they re-created an entire portion of the zeppelin in Germany to demonstrate how a rip in a hydrogen cell as theorized by Eckener could fully account for the disaster. Another investigation in the United States, which like the one in Germany was heavily reliant on the testimony of Eckener, found no evidence of sabotage and concluded that his version was the most likely scenario.

AUTHOR'S COLLECTION

The second Graf Zeppelin*: in 1938 the world's newest and—as it turned out—last airship.*

Conspiracy theories regarding the cause of the crash swirled for years afterwards, yet in the immediate wake of the tragedy sentiment on both sides of the Atlantic was unanimous: for the sake of humanity Germany must be allowed helium for peaceful purposes.[135] In Washington, D.C., Congress acted quickly with Roosevelt's support, and the Helium Control Act was history. For the Luftschiffbau the ending of the export ban came at a precipitous moment, as a new ship, of the same size and basic design of the *Hindenburg*, was at an early stage of construction and could easily have been canceled. But now with helium on the horizon the old *Graf Zeppelin* was permanently retired while all awaited its replacement.

That zeppelin, LZ 130, emerged from a giant shed, even bigger than the one which spawned the *Hindenburg*, at Friedrichshafen in September 1938. Somehow, despite his disagreement with Goebbels two years earlier, Dr. Eckener found himself in the good graces of the Nazis and was given the honor of christening LZ 130 with a bottle of liquid air. Once again he chose to name his newest zeppelin after his former boss.

Because *Graf Zeppelin* II would use helium with its reduced lifting capacity, Dr. Dürr had been forced to both save weight while also finding ways to add ballast in flight so as not to valve that precious gas. The latter issue was addressed by placing gutters and spouts around the top of the hull to retain rain water, and also by capturing engine exhaust moisture just as the U.S. Navy had done with its airships. Regarding the former issue, saving weight, Dürr did the best he could, yet despite his efforts, when filled with helium the new *Graf* would be able to carry just forty passengers. This arrangement could never deliver a profit, and Eckener vowed to make his next ship, LZ 131, commensurately larger. For now, though, he was once again stuck with what he had.

In Germany, elaborate and expensive helium storage and purification facilities (helium needs to be periodically cleaned) were constructed with the expectation that the gas would arrive by sea from Galveston, Texas any day. However, that day never came thanks to the U.S. Secretary of the Interior, Harold L. Ickes. As a member of the Munitions Control Board, whose responsibility it was to approve the export of helium, his was the lone voice against transferring the gas to the Germans. At the time Commander Rosendahl was urging Congress to fund more navy blimps, and Ickes argued that this was proof that airships were of intrinsic military value. Because the Board's decision had to be unanimous, Ickes effectively vetoed the transfer. German diplomatic efforts ensued, but these became mute when Hitler shocked the American public by seizing Austria in March of 1938. That May, the first anniversary of the *Hindenburg* disaster, Eckener traveled to Washington to meet with President Roosevelt and Secretary Ickes and to argue his case in person. Ickes flatly refused, saying that Hitler wanted war and would therefore never get any of America's helium. Roosevelt in turn told Eckener that with Ickes's opposition there was nothing he could do.

Bitter at being denied by the Americans, who he had assumed were his friends, a defiant Eckener returned to Germany and had the new *Graf Zeppelin* filled with hydrogen, and on September 14, 1938, took pride at being aboard for its first flight. Although designed for oceanic service and boasting even better passenger accommodations than the *Hindenburg*, because of the growing crisis in Europe the second *Graf* never saw civilian use. Instead, the airship was employed by the Luftwaffe for electronic surveillance flights against its future adversaries. One of these missions occurred August 2–4, 1938, when the giant zeppelin approached Scotland and conducted sightings at points along the coast. Inside, Luftwaffe technicians, in an effort to detect English radar signals, were busy monitoring equipment that hung hundreds of feet below in a spy car. The mission ended when the RAF sent Spitfire fighter planes to shoo the zeppelin menace away, but not before the technicians erroneously concluded that England had no radar defenses (an error that the Luftwaffe would pay for during the upcoming Battle of Britain). At the end of the month, and having flown only thirty times and for less than a year, the new *Graf Zeppelin* was deemed of no further use to the Third Reich. Plans for LZ 131 and LZ 132 were shelved, as were plans for a revolving zeppelin hangar for the Reederei at Frankfurt.

That same year, across the Atlantic Rosendahl saw that his country had just one dirigible, the *Los Angeles*, which was grounded but flyable, and no intentions of acquiring more. "What about the airship?" he asked. Excluding the unfortunate *Hindenburg*, which if inflated with helium, he noted, would never have exploded, German passenger zeppelins since 1912 had transported 48,778 people over 20,877 hours and 1,193,501 miles of flight with not a single fatality or even serious injury. "Are there any basic reasons why airships—and particularly American airships—cannot succeed?" Rosendahl implored. "Are American brains such as those which designed and built the Douglas airplane, the Martin and Sikorsky flying boats, the Holland Tunnel, the Washington Bridge, and Boulder Dam, stumped by the problems of airships when others in the world have solved them?"[136] The question was rhetorical. The Goodyear Company, builders of the *Akron* and *Macon* just a few years before, had the people and technology to fulfill any contract for any airship the United States might want, and of course America had the helium to ensure it would fly safely. Indeed, Rosendahl stated there were no "basic reasons" why the airship could not succeed, but his advocacy was soon sidelined by the urgent needs of a nation at war.

Promoted to admiral, Rosendahl led America's blimp campaign against the German U-boat, and while his humble "gas-bags" may not have been the glorious zeppelins that Captain Peter Strasser had flown during the last war, they were a far more practical weapon. Between 1942 and 1944 over a hundred U.S. Navy blimps flying from airbases stretching from Massachusetts to Texas escorted an estimated 89,000 surface vessels and assisted in the damage or sinking of several U-boats. Similar patrol duty was also undertaken in the Caribbean and Brazil, and additionally in the Pacific against the Japanese. Unfortunately, air and ground accidents destroyed dozens of blimps and killed eighty-three officers and sailors, but only one blimp and one airshipman were lost due to enemy action. As importantly, with one possible exception, no allied ship was sunk while under the watchful eye of a U.S. Navy blimp.

By the end of the war a new blimp, the M-types of 647,468 cubic feet, had been introduced to supplement the smaller K-types then in service, and armed with eight antisubmarine bombs they represented the most

COURTESY GOODYEAR TIRE AND RUBBER COMPANY

A day on board an Airship

ON some not too distant day you may make a voyage like this, a magic-carpet flight to overseas lands by airship. It will be air travel as you have never imagined it before, surrounded by every comfort and convenience — in the spacious luxury of a giant sky hotel soaring serenely through space at three to four times the speed of surface lines.

Who will travel on these queens of the air? All that vast legion who demand comfort, pleasure and privacy in their journeyings—the same people who patronize crack limiteds, blue ribbon liners and famed hotels the world over.

What make the prospect of such postwar travel a practical reality are facts like these:

Airships have low enough fuel consumption per ton of cargo to make these aerial leviathans economically attractive.

America has an unlimited supply of noninflammable helium to give their operation maximum safety.

America has, in Goodyear Aircraft Corporation, a company ready today with complete plans and production facilities for building de luxe passenger and express cargo airships of 10,000,000-cubic-foot capacity — airships that will excel any other aircraft now visualized both in passenger comfort and payload revenue.

It is the one field of air transport where America can have no real competition.

GOODYEAR AIRCRAFT CORPORATION
Akron, Ohio Litchfield Park, Arizona

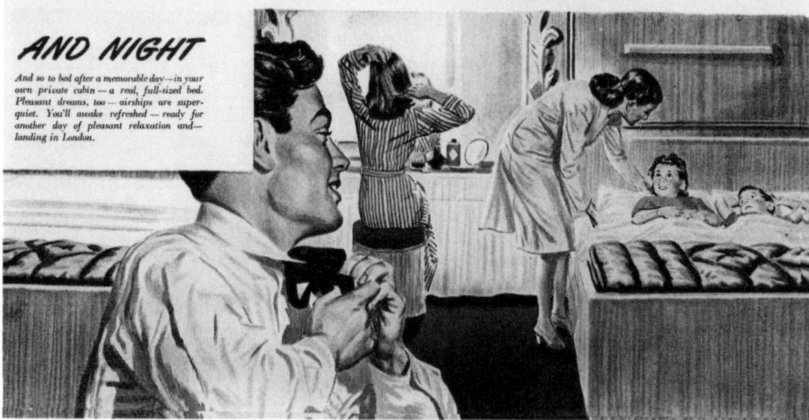

AND NIGHT
And so to bed after a memorable day—in your own private cabin — a real, full-sized bed. Pleasant dreams, too — airships are super-quiet. You'll awake refreshed — ready for another day of pleasant relaxation and—landing in London.

After the war, Goodyear Aircraft made its case for a new American airship program in advertisements like this one from the Saturday Evening Post.

advanced blimp design to date. However, for Rosendahl the M-types were still "nonrigids," and although able to reach airship-like speeds of over seventy miles per hour, they had a range of just 2,400 miles, an endurance capability of only forty-eight hours, and could carry only fourteen men. The admiral, who had served on all four of America's dirigibles from the *Shenandoah* to the *Macon*, and had also been a frequent observer aboard both the *Graf* and *Hindenburg*, had an incurable case of dirigible fever and after the war in 1946 sent a young lieutenant, J. Gordon Vaeth, to Germany to find Hugo Eckener.

Eckener had not been heard of since the outbreak of war in 1939, but if he were still alive Rosendahl was keen to know details regarding the water recovery apparatus on the second *Graf Zeppelin*, and also about electric heaters purportedly developed by the Luftschiffbau to increase hydrogen lift. He also wanted to ask whether Eckener and his colleagues might be interested in continuing their careers in the United States.

During the war the Luftschiffbau had designed and produced radar, jet fighters, and V-2 rocket components, and its sheds and factories had been bombed by the Allies accordingly. What was once the charming town of Friedrichshafen had been reduced to "collateral" rubble, and it was feared that Eckener had not survived. Vaeth, though, located him in the nearby community of Konstanz, looking older, understandably, than he had appeared in prewar photographs, but in good health nevertheless and willing to talk. Eckener, who spoke fine English, quickly discounted Allied rumors that the two *Graf Zeppelins* had become aerial aircraft carriers but instead, he said, had been shamefully broken up for their duralumin on orders from Göring. "From the past we turned to the future," Vaeth recounted of the conversation, "He talked of starting again, of building new airships, and of reweaving a web of commercial Zeppelin passenger and cargo routes."[137]

A few months later Eckener was persuaded to come to America, and in April of 1947 the former zeppelin commander flew, via intermediate refueling stops, from Frankfurt to the States in an army airplane. Strapped in his seat and deafened by the roar of the engines, how he must have missed the romanticism of zeppelin flight, but there was still hope; it all depended upon the Americans. In Akron, Ohio, he worked with the Goodyear Aircraft Corporation on plans for a new rigid airship. It would be nearly 1,000 feet long and 140 feet wide, hold 10 million cubic feet of helium, and carry 232 passengers from London to New York for prices starting at just $200 per person. Alternatively, as a floating hospital, it would be able to accommodate 248 beds, or as an aerial freighter its 20,000 cubic feet of storage space could loft ninety tons of cargo. After spending seven months in America, Eckener returned home to Germany and left the final details to the Americans. Sadly, though, these "final details" turned out to be the decision to cancel the project, and some years later, in 1952, Eckener died in Friedrichshafen at age eighty-six.

At the time of his death the first truly reliable transoceanic airliner, the DC-7C of 1956, had yet to fly, steamships still accounted for the vast majority of travel across the seas, and were it not for Hitler's rise to power, the airship would yet have had a place in global transportation. But while that place vanished forever on the eve of World War II, in the decades since then many have held fast to their dirigible dreams. For example, there was this: a 1957 plan for an atomic-powered airship of unlimited range with a helicopter deck and hangar along with retractable pontoons for water landings. And this: a 1974 concept which would also be atomic-powered but able to continuously circle the globe, picking up and dropping off passengers by jet airplane housed in an internal bay. And this: a 1996 proposal for a cargo airship that, crawling along the sky at a mere five miles per hour, could lift outsized loads of over 160 tons. And this: a 2011 call for a "bacterial dirigible" serving humanity as a flying pharmaceutical factory and able to deliver its life-saving cargo anywhere in the world. And this . . .

NOTES

INTRODUCTION

1 All quotes from Margaret G. Mather, "I Was on the Hindenburg," *Harper's*, November 1937.

CHAPTER ONE

2 All quotes from Alberto Santos-Dumont, *My Airships: The Story of My Life* (1904), New York: Dover Publications, 1973, unless otherwise noted.

3 Santos-Dumont, "How I Became an Aëronaut and My Experience with Airships [Part II]," *McClure's*, September 1902, 456.

4 Santos-Dumont, "How I Became an Aëronaut and My Experience with Airships [Part I]," *McClure's*, August 1902, 309.

5 Ibid., 310.

6 Ibid., 312.

7 Ibid., 313.

8 Ibid., 312.

9 Santos-Dumont, "How I Became an Aëronaut: Part II," 461.

10 Ibid., 457.

11 Ibid., 462.

12 Sterling Heilig,"The Over-Sea Experiments of Santos-Dumont: The Story of His Mishap at Monte Carlo," *McClure's*, July 1902, 196–97.

13 Paul Hoffman, *Wings of Madness: Alberto Santos-Dumont and the Invention of Flight*, New York: Theia, 2003, 1–2.

14 Ibid., 59–60.

15 Peter Wykeham, *Santos-Dumont: A Study in Obsession*, New York; Harcourt, Brace and World, 1962, 176.

16 Ibid., 176.

17 All remaining quotes from the Swedish Anthropological and Geographic Society's account of the expedition, published under Andrée's name in 1930 as *Andrée's Story*. Salomon August Andrée, Nils Strindberg, and Edward Adams-Ray, *Svenska sällskapet för antropologi och geografi* [*Andrée's Story; The Complete Record of His Polar Flight, 1897, from the Diaries and Journals of S. A. Andrée, Nils Strindberg, and K. Frænkel, Found on White Island in the Summer of 1930*], New

York: Viking Press, 1930. For three other perspectives of the expedition see P. J. Capelotti's *By Airship to the North Pole: An Archaeology of Human Exploration* (Rutgers University Press, 1999), David Hempleman-Adams's *At the Mercy of the Winds: Two Remarkable Journeys to the North Pole: A Modern Hero and a Victorian Romance* (Bantam, 2001), and Jan Troell's feature film *Ingenjör Andrées luftfärd* (1982).

18 The Pole-buoy washed ashore on King Charles Land two years later, leading some to believe that Andrée had dropped it over the Pole and it had later drifted south.

CHAPTER TWO

19 All quotes from Wellman, *The Aerial Age*, unless otherwise noted. Walter Wellman, *The Aerial Age; A Thousand Miles by Airship over the Atlantic Ocean; Airship Voyages over the Polar Sea; The Past, the Present and the Future of Aerial Navigation*, New York: A. R. Keller, 1911.

20 Walter Wellman, "Walter Wellman's Expedition to the North Pole," *National Geographic*, April 1906, 206.

21 Edward Mabley, *The Motor Balloon "America,"* Brattleboro, VT: Stephen Greene Press, 1969, 64–65.

22 Ibid., 79.

CHAPTER THREE

23 Hugo Eckener and H. Leigh Farnell, *Count Zeppelin, the Man and His Work*, London: Massie Publishing Company, 1938, 32.

24 Margaret Goldsmith, *Zeppelin: A Biography*, New York: William Morrow, 1931, 41.

25 Ibid., 81.

26 Ibid., 91.

27 Ibid., 103.

28 Ibid., 104.

29 Peter W. Brooks, *Zeppelin: Rigid Airships 1893–1940*, Washington, DC: Smithsonian Institution Press, 1992, 30.

30 Goldsmith, *Zeppelin: A Biography*, 115.

31 Guillaume de Syon, *Zeppelin! Germany and the Airship, 1900–1939*, Baltimore, MD: Johns Hopkins University Press, 2002, 41.

32 Goldsmith, *Zeppelin: A Biography*, 122.

33 Ibid., 124.

34 Ibid., 138.

35 Henry Cord Meyer, *Airshipmen, Businessmen, and Politics, 1890–1940*, Washington, DC: Smithsonian Institution Press, 1991, 36.

36 Goldsmith, *Zeppelin: A Biography*, 145.

37 Ibid., 196.

38 Douglas H. Robinson, *The Zeppelin in Combat: A History of the German Naval Airship Division 1912–1918*, Atglen, PA: Schiffer, 1994, 81.

39 Ian Castle, *London 1914–17: The Zeppelin Menace*, Oxford, UK: Osprey Publishing, 2008, 30.

40 Robinson, *The Zeppelin in Combat*, 198, 201.

41 Peter J. C. Smith, *Zeppelins over Lancashire: The Story of the Air Raids on the County of Lancashire in 1916 and 1918*, Neil Richardson, 1991, 20.

42 Treusch von Buttlar-Brandenfels, *Zeppelins over England*, London: George G. Harrap and Co., 1931, 139.

43 Ibid., 149.

44 Robinson, *The Zeppelin in Combat*, 374.

45 Rolf Marben, *Zeppelin Adventures* (1931), London: Greenhill Aeolus, 1986, 216–17.

46 Robinson, *The Zeppelin in Combat*, appendix B, and Marben, *Zeppelin Adventures*, 215–20.

47 Buttlar-Brandenfels, *Zeppelins over England*, 167.

48 Ibid., 166.

49 Ibid., 202.

50 Peter W. Brooks, *Zeppelin: Rigid Airships 1893–1940*, Washington, DC: Smithsonian Institution Press, 1992, 100.

51 Buttlar-Brandenfels, *Zeppelins over England*, 214.

52 Meyer, *Airshipmen, Businessmen, and Politics, 1890–1940*, 44.

CHAPTER FOUR

53 Unless otherwise noted, all quotes from E. M. Maitland and Rudyard Kipling, *The Log of H.M.A. R 34: Journey to America and Back: With a Letter from Rudyard Kipling*, London: Hodder and Stoughton, 1920.

54 Upon returning to England, the stowaway Ballantyne received no punishment other than temporary removal from the airship service.

55 Patrick Abbott, *Airship: The Story of R.34 and the First East-West Crossing of the Atlantic by Air*, New York: Charles Scribner's Sons, 1973, 129.

CHAPTER FIVE

56 William F. Trimble, *Admiral William A. Moffett: Architect of Naval Aviation*, Annapolis: Naval Institute Press, 2007, 47.

57 Edward Arpee, *From Frigates to Flat-Tops: The Story of the Life and Achievements of Rear Admiral William Adger Moffett, U.S.N. "The Father of Naval Aviation,"* Edward Arpee, 1953, 68.

58 Ibid., 61–62.

59 Ibid., 86.

60 Ibid., 125.

61 Thom Hook, *Shenandoah Saga*, Baltimore: Airshow Publishers, 1973, 59–61.

62 Junius B. Wood, "Seeing America from the 'Shenandoah'," *National Geographic*, January 1925, 2–6.

63 Hook, *Shenandoah Saga*, 172.

64 Charles E. Rosendahl, *Up Ship!*, New York: Dodd, Mead and Company, 1931, 73.

65 Arpee, *From Frigates to Flat-Tops*, 200.

66 Richard K. Smith, *The Airships Akron & Macon: Flying Aircraft Carriers of the United States Navy*, Annapolis, MD: United States Naval Institute, 1965, 69.

67 Arpee, *From Frigates to Flat-Tops*, 235.

68 Ibid., 245.

69 Rosendahl, *What about the Airship? The Challenge to the United States*, New York: Charles Scribner's Sons, 1938, 118.

CHAPTER SIX

70 Roald Amundsen and Lincoln Ellsworth, *Our Polar Flight: The Amundsen-Ellsworth Polar Flight*, New York: Dodd, Meade and Company, 1925, 14.

71 General Umberto Nobile, *My Polar Flights: An Account of the Voyages of the Airships Italia and Norge*. London: Frederick Muller, 1961, 15.

72 Ibid., 30.

73 General Umberto Nobile, "Navigating the 'Norge' from Rome to the North Pole and Beyond," *National Geographic*, August 1927, 185.

74 Nobile, *My Polar Flights*, 31.

75 Ibid., 39.

76 Ibid., 43–44.

77 Ibid., 44.

78 Careful analysis of the flying characteristics of Byrd's airplane, a notoriously slow model, suggest he could not have made the flight to the Pole and back

between the time he departed Kings Bay to the time he returned. In this respect his claim of improbable speed mirrored the earlier one made by Peary.

79 Ibid., 56.

80 Ibid., 62–63.

81 Ibid., 67.

82 Roald Amundsen, *My Life as an Explorer*, New York: Doubleday, Page and Company, 1927, 176.

83 Nobile, *My Polar Flights*, 68–69.

84 Amundsen, *My Life as an Explorer*, 150.

85 Nobile, "Navigating the 'Norge' from Rome to the North Pole and Beyond," 215. Neither Amundsen nor Ellsworth had read their *New York Times* contract before reaching Teller, and were shocked to learn that it called for them to write a series of articles totaling 75,000 words, or the length of a book. They protested, but the *Times* would not relent. After three weeks of steady composing, however, the two had the job done.

86 Amundsen, *My Life as an Explorer*, 134.

87 Ibid., 138–39.

88 Ibid., 164.

89 Ibid., 166.

90 Ibid., 184. In his memoir *Beyond Horizons*, Ellsworth contradicts Amundsen by describing how all the flags were affixed to poles designed to stick into the ice and then dropped in an orderly fashion during the time that the *Norge*, engines off and propellers stopped, loitered over the Pole.

91 Odd Arnesen, *The Polar Adventure: The "Italia" Tragedy Seen at Close Quarters*, London: Victor Gollancz, 1929, 11–12.

92 Ibid., 25.

93 Ibid., 50.

94 Ibid., 28.

95 Ibid., 61.

96 Ibid., 76.

97 General Umberto Nobile, *With the "Italia" to the North Pole*, New York: Dodd, Mead and Company, 1931, 154.

98 Ibid., 155.

99 This is also the title of an otherworldly depiction of the dirigible tragedy. A joint Italian-Soviet film made in 1969, *The Red Tent* was directed by Mikhail Kalatozov and starred Sean Connery as Amundsen and Peter Finch as Nobile.

100 Nobile, *With the "Italia" to the North Pole*, 237–38.

101 Davide Giudici, *The Tragedy of the Italia: With the Rescuers to the Red Tent*, London: Ernest Benn, 1928, 68.

102 Ibid., 100.

CHAPTER SEVEN

103 Nevil Shute, *Slide Rule: An Autobiography of an Engineer* (1954), Cornwall, UK: House of Stratus, 2000, 43.

104 Ibid., 45.

105 Ibid., 48.

106 Ibid.

107 Ibid., 55–56.

108 Ibid., 40.

109 Ibid.

110 Ibid., 73.

111 Ibid., 85.

112 Peter G. Mansfield and William Kimber, *To Ride the Storm: The Story of the Airship R.101*, London: William Kimber and Co., 1982, 207–9.

113 Ibid., 20.

114 Ibid., 323–24.

115 Ibid., 42.

116 Nick Le Neve Walmsley, *R101: A Pictorial History*, Gloucestershire, UK: The History Press, 2010, 122.

CHAPTER EIGHT

117 Hugo Eckener, *My Zeppelins*, London: Putnam, 1958, 11.

118 Ibid., 12.

119 Ibid., 13.

120 Ibid.

121 Ibid., 15.

122 Ibid., 16.

123 Ibid., 18.

124 Ibid., 32.

125 Ibid., 29.

126 Meyer, *Airshipmen, Businessmen, and Politics, 1890–1940*, 132.

127 All quotations, unless otherwise noted, are from Drummond-Hay's narrative

of the *Graf*'s flight that appeared (under the name "Lady Drummond Hay") in Hearst's *Boston Evening American*, October 11–16, 1928.

128 Eckener, *My Zeppelins*, 65–66.

129 Ibid., 105.

130 General Umberto Nobile, *My Five Years with Soviet Airships*, Akron, OH: The Lighter-Than-Air Society, 1987, 25.

131 Eckener, *My Zeppelins*, 150.

132 Rick Archbold, *Hindenburg: An Illustrated History*, New York: Madison Press, 1994, 152.

133 Rosendahl, *What about the Airship?*, 203–7.

134 Suspicions that the Nazis might be using the zeppelins for spying were, it transpired, hardly misplaced. After World War II the British found aerial photos of militarily sensitive sites in England, photos obviously taken from the *Graf Zeppelin* during a prewar fly-over.

135 Despite the fact that no person or group ever claimed responsibility for the destruction of the *Hindenburg*, the critical problem with all sabotage theories is that the explosion occurred when the zeppelin was flying low and minutes away from a safe landing and not dangerously high in the air, as it had been for the previous four days. In regards to a time bomb, at the moment of ignition, 7:25 p.m., the weather-delayed *Hindenburg* was scheduled to be on the mast preparing for the return flight to Germany and empty of passengers.

136 Rosendahl, *What about the Airship?*, 40.

137 J. Gordon Vaeth, *Graf Zeppelin: The Adventures of an Aerial Globetrotter*, New York: Harper and Brothers, 1958, 223.

BIBLIOGRAPHY

Abbott, Patrick. *Airship: The Story of R.34 and the First East-West Crossing of the Atlantic by Air*. New York: Charles Scribner's Sons, 1973.

———. *Sky Ships: A History of the Airship in the United States Navy*. Pacifica, CA: Pacifica Press, 1990.

Althoff, William F. *USS Los Angeles: The Navy's Venerable Airship and Aviation Technology*. Washington, DC: Potomac Books, 2004.

Amundsen, Roald. *My Life as an Explorer*. New York: Doubleday, Page and Company, 1927.

Amundsen, Roald, and Lincoln Ellsworth. *The First Flight across the Polar Sea*. London: Hutchinson and Co., ca. 1927.

———. *Our Polar Flight: The Amundsen-Ellsworth Polar Flight*. New York: Dodd, Meade and Company, 1925.

Andrée, Salomon August, Nils Strindberg, and Edward Adams-Ray. *Svenska sällskapet för antropologi och geografi* [*Andrée's Story; The Complete Record of His Polar Flight, 1897, from the Diaries and Journals of S. A. Andrée, Nils Strindberg, and K. Frænkel, Found on White Island in the Summer of 1930*]. New York: Viking Press, 1930.

Archbold, Rick. *Hindenburg: An Illustrated History*. New York: Madison Press, 1994.

Arnesen, Odd. *The Polar Adventure: The "Italia" Tragedy Seen at Close Quarters*. London: Victor Gollancz, 1929.

Arpee, Edward. *From Frigates to Flat-Tops: The Story of the Life and Achievements of Rear Admiral William Adger Moffett, U.S.N. "The Father of Naval Aviation."* Edward Arpee, 1953.

Beaty, David. *The Story of Transatlantic Flight*. Shrewsbury, UK: Airlife Publishing, 2003.

Beith, Margaret. *The Story of the WWI Zeppelin Raid on Eldon (The Dene Valley), 5th/6th April, 1916*. Chester, UK: Richard Beith Associates, 1999.

Bentele, Eugen. *The Story of a Zeppelin Mechanic. My Flights 1931–1938*. Friedrichshafen, DE: Zeppelin-Museum, 1992.

Bottling, Douglas. *Dr. Eckener's Dream Machine. The Great Zeppelin and the Dawn of Air Travel*. New York: Henry Holt and Company, 2001.

Bomann-Larsen, Tor. *Roald Amundsen*. Gloucestershire, UK: The History Press, 2011.

Brooks, Peter W. *Zeppelin: Rigid Airships 1893–1940*. Washington, DC: Smithsonian Institution Press, 1992.

Buttlar-Brandenfels, Treusch von. *Zeppelins over England*. London: George G. Harrap and Co., 1931.

Castle, Ian. *British Airships 1905–1930*. Oxford, UK: Osprey Publishing, 2009.

———. *London 1914–17: The Zeppelin Menace*. Oxford, UK: Osprey Publishing, 2008.

Countryman, Barry. *R100 in Canada*. Erin, ON: The Boston Mills Press, 1982.

Cross, Wilbur. *Zeppelins of World War I*. New York: Paragon House, 1991.

de Syon, Guillaume. *Zeppelin! Germany and the Airship, 1900–1939*. Baltimore: Johns Hopkins University Press, 2002.

Dick, Harold G., and Douglas H. Robinson. *The Golden Age of the Great Passenger Airships Graf Zeppelin & Hindenburg*. Washington, DC: Smithsonian Institution Press, 1985.

Drummond-Hay, Lady Grace. "I Love the Zepp, It Has a Soul—Lady Drummond Hay" and other dispatches published in the *Boston Evening American*, October 11–16, 1928.

Eckener, Hugo. *My Zeppelins*. London: Putnam, 1958.

Eckener, Hugo, and H. Leigh Farnell. *Count Zeppelin, the Man and His Work*. London: Massie Publishing Company, 1938.

Ellsworth, Lincoln. *Beyond Horizons*. New York: Doubleday, Doran, and Company, 1937.

Giudici, Davide. *The Tragedy of the Italia: With the Rescuers to the Red Tent*. London: Ernest Benn, 1928.

Goldsmith, Margaret. *Zeppelin: A Biography*. New York: William Morrow and Company, 1931.

Goodyear Aviation advertisement, *Saturday Evening Post*, November 24, 1945.

Haddow, G. W., and Peter M. Grosz. *The German Giants: The Story of the R-planes 1914–1919*. New York: Funk and Wagnalls, 1969.

Heilig, Sterling. "The Over-Sea Experiments of Santos-Dumont: The Story of His Mishap at Monte Carlo." *McClure's*, July 1902.

Hoffman, Paul. *Wings of Madness: Alberto Santos-Dumont and the Invention of Flight*. New York: Theia, 2003.

Hook, Thom. *Shenandoah Saga*. Baltimore: Airshow Publishers, 1973.

Keirns, Aaron J. *Ohio's Airship Disaster: The Story of the Crash of the USS Shenandoah*. Howard, OH: Little River Publishing, 2006.

Keller, C. L. *USS Shenandoah*. West Roxbury, MA: World War I Aero Publishers, 1965.

Kirschner, Edwin J. *The Zeppelin in the Atomic Age: The Past, Present, and Future of the Rigid Lighter-Than-Air Aircraft*. Urbana, IL: University of Illinois Press, 1957.

Leasor, James. *The Millionth Chance: The Story of the R.101* (1957). Cornwall, UK: House of Stratus, 2001.

Lehmann, Captain Ernst A. *Zeppelin: The Story of Lighter-Than-Air Craft*. London: Longmans, Green and Co., 1937.

Litchfield, P. W., and Hugh Allen. *Why? Why has America No Rigid Airships?* (1945). Riverside, CT: 7 C's Press, 1976.

Mabley, Edward. *The Motor Balloon "America."* Brattleboro, VT: Stephen Greene Press, 1969.

Maitland, E. M., and Rudyard Kipling. *The Log of H.M.A. R 34: Journey to America and Back: With a Letter from Rudyard Kipling*. London: Hodder and Stoughton, 1920.

Mansfield, Peter G., and William Kimber. *To Ride the Storm: The Story of the Airship R.101*. London: William Kimber and Co., 1982.

Marben, Rolf. *Zeppelin Adventures* (1931). London: Greenhill Aeolus, 1986.

Mather, Margaret G. "I Was on the Hindenburg." *Harper's*, November 1937.

Meager, A. F. C., Captain George. *My Airship Flights 1915–1930*. London: William Kimber, 1970.

Meyer, Henry Cord. *Airshipmen, Businessmen, and Politics, 1890–1940*. Washington, DC: Smithsonian Institution Press, 1991.

Mower, Mark. *Zeppelin over Suffolk: The Final Raid of the L48*. South Yorkshire, UK: Pen and Sword Books, 2008.

Niderost, Eric. "Germany's Deceitful Dirigible." *World War II*, April, 2004.

Nielsen, Thor. *The Zeppelin Story*. London: Allan Wingate, 1955.

Nobile, General Umberto. "Navigating the 'Norge' from Rome to the North Pole and Beyond," *National Geographic*, August 1927.

———. *My Polar Flights: An Account of the Voyages of the Airships Italia and Norge*. London: Frederick Muller, 1961.

———. *My Five Years with Soviet Airships*. Akron, OH: The Lighter-Than-Air Society, 1987.

———. *With the "Italia" to the North Pole*. New York: Dodd, Mead and Company, 1931.

Pearson, John F. "Don't Sell the Airship Short." *Popular Mechanics*, September 1974.

R.101: The Airship Disaster, 1930. London: The Stationery Office, 1999.

Robinson, Douglas H. *Giants in the Sky: A History of the Rigid Airship*. Seattle: University of Washington Press, 1973.

———. *LZ 129 "Hindenburg."* Fallbrook, CA: Aero Publishers, n.d.

———*The Zeppelin in Combat: A History of the German Naval Airship Division 1912–1918*. Atglen, PA: Schiffer, 1994.

Rosendahl, Charles E. *Up Ship!* New York: Dodd, Mead and Company, 1931.

———. *What about the Airship? The Challenge to the United States*. New York: Charles Scribner's Sons, 1938.

Santos-Dumont, Alberto. *My Airships: The Story of My Life* (1904). New York: Dover Publications, 1973.

———. "How I Became an Aëronaut and my Experience with Air-Ships [Part I]." *McClure's*, August 1902.

———. "How I Became an Aëronaut and my Experience with Air-Ships: Part II." *McClure's*, September 1902.

Shute, Nevil. *Slide Rule: An Autobiography of an Engineer* (1954). Cornwall, UK: House of Stratus, 2000.

Smith, Peter J. C. *Zeppelins over Lancaster: The Story of the Air Raids on the County of Lancashire in 1916 and 1918*. Neil Richardson, 1991.

Smith, Richard K. *The Airships Akron & Macon: Flying Aircraft Carriers of the United States Navy*. Annapolis, MD: United States Naval Institute, 1965.

"The Fate of Vaniman." *Scientific American*, 20 July 1912.

"The First Airship Flight around the World." *National Geographic*, June 1930.

"The French Airship Catastrophe: The 'Dixmude' Now Assumed Lost." *Flight*, 3 January 1924.

"The New Zeppelin," *Flight*, March 5, 1936.

Trimble, William F. *Admiral William A. Moffett: Architect of Naval Aviation*. Annapolis: Naval Institute Press, 2007.

Vaeth, J. Gordon. *Graf Zeppelin: The Adventures of an Aerial Globetrotter*. New York: Harper and Brothers, 1958.

Walmsley, Nick Le Neve. *R101: A Pictorial History*. Gloucestershire, UK: The History Press, 2010.

"Walter Wellman's Expedition to the North Pole." *National Geographic*, April 1906.

Wellman, Walter. "By Airship to the North Pole." *McClure's*, June 1907.

———. *The Aerial Age; A Thousand Miles by Airship over the Atlantic Ocean; Airship Voyages over the Polar Sea; The Past, the Present and the Future of Aerial Navigation*. New York: A. R. Keller, 1911.

———. “Will the ‘America’ Fly to the Pole?” *McClure’s*, July 1907.

Wood, Junius B. “Seeing America from the ‘Shenandoah’.” *National Geographic*, January 1925.

Wykeham, Peter. *Santos-Dumont: A Study in Obsession*. New York; Harcourt, Brace and World, 1962.

INDEX

Page numbers in italics refer to illustrations.